LEFT BEHIND IN A MEGACHURC
TUCKER, RUTH   0710 1 MIN
13.75
OUR PRICE
List 16.99
9780801012693 2006   221p

Left Behind in a
Megachurch World

Left Behind in a
Megachurch World

*How God Works
through Ordinary Churches*

Ruth A. Tucker

BakerBooks
Grand Rapids, Michigan

© 2006 by Ruth A. Tucker

Published by Baker Books
a division of Baker Publishing Group
P.O. Box 6287, Grand Rapids, MI 49516-6287
www.bakerbooks.com

Printed in the United States of America

Library of Congress Cataloging-in-Publication Data
Tucker, Ruth, 1945–
    Left behind in a megachurch world : how God works through ordinary churches / Ruth A. Tucker.
        p.   cm.
    Includes bibliographical references and index.
    ISBN 10: 0-8010-1269-4 (cloth)
    ISBN 978-0-8010-1269-3 (cloth)
    1. Small churches. I. Title.
    BV637.8.T83 2006
    250.973—dc22   2005030614

To
Rik and Denise Stevenson
by the grace of God
serving faithfully and seeing growth
in an
interracial,
intergenerational,
inner-city,
and
flourishing
left-behind church

Contents

Introduction

Left Behind with Purpose

Go into a book shop, browse the shelves and it won't take long to find books about being a success. We have to go to workshops and conferences on Church growth, the emerging Church and a new paradigm for Church because we're afraid we'll be left behind.

Neil Sims

If my great-granddaughter—yet to be born—were to follow in my footsteps as a church historian and look back in the year 2100 on the landscape of North American Christianity as it proudly pampers and grooms itself today, she would surely see a lot of glitz. She would recognize it as a multi-billion-dollar enterprise—part of the world's largest and most well-financed religion. She would discover large, suburban campuses that are home to churches the size of some denominations, and she would find literature, music, and videos—too plentiful to scan—that tell the story of this gospel of prosperity.

Such a landscape was unimaginable a hundred years ago in the world of my grandmother. There was very little glamour—at least in religion. This was an era before Billy Sunday and Aimee Semple McPherson and the fictional Elmer Gantry. The biggest event that a 1907 version of *Christianity Today* might have featured would have been the strange goings-on in a little left-behind church in Los Angeles. There William Seymour, a largely self-educated Black preacher, was praying with his head under a shoebox, and lots of folks, white and black alike, were finding God. There was no pretention—no posturing. This Azusa Street Revival marked the beginning of the twentieth-century Pentecostal-charismatic movement—a movement that is a leader today in the competitive corporate Christian world of prosperity and glitter.

During much of the twentieth century, evangelicals were backwater Christians with clapboard churches and badly tuned pianos. The big churches of stone and brick with stained glass windows and bell towers were the ones, we were convinced, had gone the way of modernism (following the fundamentalist-modernist controversy of the 1920s). And with the passage of decades they became more and more liberal—sometimes, we suspected, going to great lengths to water down the gospel. The *liberal* churches had the gimmicks and glamour. They were—some of them—like the People's Liberal Church of Peter De Vries's novel, *The Mackerel Plaza*. Here the church is described by Reverend Mackerel as only De Vries in his witty cynicism can do.

> Our church is, I believe, the first split-level church in America. It has five rooms and two baths downstairs—dining area, kitchen and three parlors for committee and groups meetings. . . . Upstairs is one huge all purpose interior, divisible into different-sized components by means of sliding walls and convertible into an auditorium for putting on plays, a gymnasium for athletics, and a ballroom for dances. There is a small worship area at one end. This has a platform, with a free-form pulpit designed by Noguchi. It consists of a slab of marble set on four legs of four delicately differing fruitwoods, to symbolize the four Gospels, and their failure to harmonize. Behind it dangles a large multicolored mobile, its interdenominational parts swaying, as one might fancy, in perpetual reminder of the Pauline stricture against those "blown by every wind of doctrine."[1]

The church of De Vries's description also included "a newly erected clinic, with medical and neuropsychiatric wings . . . a church designed to meet the needs of today, and to serve the whole man." And, most important to Reverend Mackerel, the

People's Liberal Church includes "worship of a God free of outmoded theological definitions" that deaden the atmosphere. "It is," as the Reverend had preached, "the final proof of God's omnipotence that he need not exist in order to save us."[2]

Mainline Decline

Today the tables are turned. The change has come slowly, but in the 1990s in the midst of much congressional debate over welfare, many conservative policy makers were insisting that churches step up to the plate and become more involved in helping the needy. "Mainline Protestant leaders, however," writes Thomas Reeves, "were among the first to remind Americans that their churches were in no condition to assume new and potentially awesome responsibilities." They knew well the trends that studies and statistics were showing. "Indeed, an abundance of literature," continues Reeves, "revealed that these once prominent and affluent denominations were declining and in disarray—ironically, at a time when religious belief in America seemed to be extraordinarily high." The "seven sisters" are getting old. These seven churches (not of Revelation 2 and 3, but of North America) are the Episcopal Church, the Evangelical Lutheran Church, the United Methodists, the Presbyterian Church (USA), American Baptists, the United Church of Christ, and the Christian Church or Disciples of Christ. "Today, these one-time pillars of the religious establishment are frequently ignored, their power to bestow social prestige has greatly dissipated, and their defining theological doctrines have been largely forgotten. . . . Some observers have predicted their eventual demise."[3]

Many observers have argued that mainline denominations long ago ceased being a conscience for America—that they did not even enlist or put on a uniform to fight as the culture wars erupted or, worse yet, they fought the battles but were on the wrong side. The criticism is well placed. The seven sisters have failed to stand as a moral and ethical challenge to the deterioration of Western culture. They have not claimed their countercultural role; rather they have caved into cultural trends. Their theological foundations have crumbled even as their voices have been muted in the arena of modern life. Moreover, they do not "retain their own children once they have reached the age of decision," writes Reeves. "Presbyterians, Methodists, and Episcopalians lose nearly half their young people for good. . . . The mainline membership is graying rapidly. . . . Morale throughout the mainline ranks is low. . . . Missionary zeal has been almost lost."[4] Simply stated, they are weak and spineless. They do not represent the moral high ground.

The moral high ground is now held by the evangelicals.

Or is it?

Evangelical Expansion

There is little doubt that the *liberals* in the mainline denominations are now left behind. At the same time, evangelicals—at least those in the megachurch world—are riding high, wielding power that their predecessors could not have imagined. But have evangelicals assumed the high ground in taking a stand against cultural decline? Do evangelicals represent what the Christian faith stands for? Or are they ignoring the critical battles of our day? Have they claimed conscientious-objector status in fighting the biggest war of all? Have they gone AWOL at a time when they are most needed? An insidious ethos of materialistic individualism permeates American culture—a worldview far removed from the ideals of the nation's founders. When this erosion began is debatable, but it is safe to say that it has not slowed down in recent decades. "Beginning with the post–World War II United States, personal identifications came to be linked more to lifestyles and consumption, and less to an economic ethic that had long been undergirded by religious values," writes Wade Clark Roof. "This reversal in historic influences, giving greater autonomy to the culture sphere, set in motion a proliferation of popular cultural forms . . . and gave rise to a whole new set of industries—the 'cultural industries.'"[5]

The dangers associated with this ethos of materialistic individualism were identified in a widely discussed book of the 1980s, but the message seemed to fall on deaf ears while the erosion of dominant culture continued. This book, *Habits of the Heart,* by sociologist Robert Bellah and his associates,[6] stirred debate not only among scholars and politicians but also among religious leaders. "From the very first pages of the book, the authors expressed alarm that individualism was becoming increasingly 'cancerous to American society.' They worried not just about organized religion but about family, political participation, community involvement, and public life."[7]

Where are biblically based evangelicals in this cancerous culture war? Have the "seven sisters"—the septuplets—been replaced by a new set of siblings, ones that are not so easily recognized? Are these triplets of evangelicalism coming of age in the guise of corporate capitalism, political conservatism, and megachurch religion? Is evangelicalism so infected with the disease that it can neither recognize nor fight against it? As the denominational sisters age and die, these *postmodern* sisters mix the boundaries of business, politics, and church in such a way that it makes a countercultural stance virtually impossible. Evangelicals have been swept away by culture—and megachurches are leading the way.

In this mother of all battles, evangelicals have surrendered without a shot being fired. True, some are speaking out against rich Christians in a hungry world, but no draft has been activated, no battalions have been trained, no rounds have been fired, and no prisoners have been taken in a culture war against materialistic individualism.

When Jim Wallis asked, "Who speaks for God?" (in a book by that title), he discovered that when random people on the street were asked what words best described evangelical Christians, the responses were primarily in the *anti* category, such as *anti-gay, anti-abortion, anti-big government* (although not *anti-big business* and *anti-racism*). But when asked what words best described Jesus, they responded with words like *love, compassion,* and *helping the poor.*[8] Is there a disconnect here? Have evangelicals forfeited the high ground before they even waged a battle for it? Or did evangelicals once hold the higher ground only to relinquish it as they have become successful in megarealms?

Left-Behind Spirituality

Can authentic spiritual leadership emerge from positions of power—from the *inside* so to speak? I wonder if we are now

13

seeing another reversal—a reversal in spiritual leadership. Is it possible that amid the dying denominations there are voices that are more authentic than the powerful, purpose-driven voices of evangelicalism? There are, of course, still voices of power and beating of drums rising up from the seven sisters. But there are other voices that challenge us from a position of weakness.

In the decades before the church growth movement of the 1970s and 80s and beyond, some of the most thought-provoking devotional literature was being written by evangelicals. Those were the days of A. W. Tozer, G. Campbell Morgan, Oswald Chambers, D. M. Lloyd-Jones, Andrew Murray, Robert Murray McCheyne, and many others whose works are all but forgotten in this megachurch world. But today, with mainline churches being left behind in the midst of the mushrooming evangelicals and charismatics of all stripes, the most profound literature of spiritual formation is coming, to a large degree, from those in the more *liberal* camp. From Kathleen Norris, Frederick Buechner, and Barbara Brown Taylor to Fleming Rutledge and Martin Marty, the widely read writers of spiritual formation hail from denominations that evangelicals have pronounced as sick and dying. The literature being produced by evangelicals, on the other hand, has the decided triumphalist slant of the purpose-driven prayer of Jabez.

These liberal writers have surely not *saved* the mainline denominations—and most of their readers are evangelicals—but they do represent a large segment of Christians left behind in a megachurch world. In his book lamenting the mainline decline, Thomas Reeves maintains that among many mainline Christians "there is a profound need for dignity, reverence, beauty, learning, traditions, and a sense of the numinous." He speaks of his own mainline identity and of the Episcopal Church where he worships in Milwaukee—where "many of the most faithful and deeply Anglican members have virtually no status at all in the eyes of the world." They are not the kind of people we think of when we imagine the high liturgical churches. Yet this is the atmosphere in which they feel at home. "Few evangelical and fundamentalist churches," he continues, "are designed to satisfy the needs of such people. Warehouselike buildings, sobbing pop gospel soloists, garish theatrics, shouting preachers, and boisterous worshippers cannot appeal to many of us."[9]

To be sure, there is no great divide between mainline and left-behind on the one side and evangelical and megachurch on the other. Vast numbers of evangelicals are left behind today, and some mainline (though rarely liberal) congregations are megachurches. Should it surprise us that some of the most authentic spirituality arises most naturally out of weakness and failure? That is not to say that Bill Hybels and Rick Warren cannot write books on spiritual formation, but their names are associated with success and power. It is difficult to combine wealth, success, and expansionism with spirituality. We know that from the teachings of Jesus and Paul, and we know that from church history. The monks who founded monastic orders surely knew that. Indeed, there is a long and influential tradition in Catholicism that combines spirituality with self-denial and weakness. When Martin of Tours, a fourth-century military officer, gave his coat to a poor beggar in whose face Martin saw Jesus, he gave up his wealth and founded a monastic community committed to personal self-denial and service to others. So also with Francis of Assisi and many other Catholics who were primarily searching for God in a way that cannot be done in a fast-paced world that is all-consumed with growth. My most recent leisure reading has focused on the lives of Thomas Merton, Dorothy Day, and Father Joe; they all did their deepest searching in a setting that was entirely apart from the glitz and glamour that was everywhere in the wider world.

Challenges for Today

In this book I will combine three themes that relate to spiritual formation, church revitalization, and the gospel and culture. With graduate degrees in American studies and history, I have branched out considerably in my teaching over the last three decades. Among the seminary courses that I teach are Christian Biography and Spiritual Formation, Revitalization of the Local Church, and The Gospel and Western Culture. In this book I bring these rather diverse fields of study together to show that any church revitalization that does not tackle the question of how Christians should relate to culture and that does not address issues of spiritual formation is of little value. I urge ministers and laypeople to take a fresh look at their left-behind circumstances and view them as unique—and pleasantly surprising—settings for spiritual growth and engagement with culture.

Here I would particularly challenge the young pastor or the older pastor to look upon the left-behind church not necessarily as one that will double in size in less than a decade or one that is a stepping stone to success or a place to wind down in retirement but rather as one that will offer a *monastic* space for spiritual development—whether out in the country at the end of a dirt road or in the midst of a bustling city. Such a church can be viewed as a sacred space such as Thomas Merton's hermitage in the remote Kentucky hills of Gethsemani or a spiritual retreat in a bustling city such as Dorothy Day's two-room flat amidst the traffic and horns and garbage collections on busy, noisy New York streets. Here the administrative hassles of running a megachurch are absent, and what administrative hassles there are can be—or ought to be—set aside. There is time to just be a pastor—a shepherd who often does nothing but survey the flock and muse about the One who holds the whole world in his hands. There is time to write a journal or poetry. There is time to read—beyond sermon-preparation material. There is time to meditate, contemplate, reminisce, and reflect. And there is time to encourage the congregation to slow down and "Be still and know that I am God."

The pastor and congregation of the left-behind church have a unique opportunity to form a spiritual community bound together in its search for God. Sometimes we become so tied up with religion and church that we fail to comprehend our Creator and the world around us. Rooney Vail, a childless, agnostic, religious seeker in Frederick Buechner's *The Final Beast*, is frustrated that ministers and churches are focused on the wrong things. She fumes at her pastor's complacency: "If I were God, I'm damned if I'd be so interested in religion and churches. I'd be interested in making things. I'd always be making marvelous new worlds, and marvelous new kinds of people to put in them . . . babies."[10]

Left-behind churches are in a unique position to reach out in community service with the love of Christ and to be countercultural—particularly in the area of materialism and self-centeredness. Left-behind churches can reach out in their neighborhoods more effectively in many ways than can the megachurch. They are part of the community themselves, and it is out of their poverty that they most effectively serve others. That is not to say that megachurches are not concerned with caring ministries. Indeed, to suggest that megachurches do not give money to help tsunami victims would be mean-spirited and false. They sponsor mission projects and have access to volunteers and funds that no left-behind church could ever match. But in matters of lifestyle, the megachurch mentality promotes an outlook that embraces materialism far more than it repels it. In that realm, the megachurch world has abdicated its responsibility. And, considering its very nature of being defined by size and success, can it ever be a credible advocate for a Christianity of sacrifice and self-denial?

By default, is not the left-behind church the most credible and convincing representative of such faith and service? The examples in real life as well as fiction are infinite. Father Hobbs, who serves in the Church of St. Aidan in Toronto, is an example. In *The Cunning Man*, Robertson Davies introduces this fictional character as "a very good old man" who, despite his shortcomings, was the most beloved priest in this neighborhood Anglican parish. When a reporter came to write a piece on the village that surrounded the church, she was looking particularly for something picturesque. She had heard about the "saint" of the parish and asked a longtime parishioner to elucidate. His response explains one way a left-behind parish and pastor confronts culture:

> "Didn't heat the rectory properly. Didn't dress himself in anything but ancient clothes. . . . Ate awful food. . . . Gave every penny he had to the poor. . . . He used to roam around the parish on winter nights, up and down all the alleys, looking for bums who might have dropped down drunk, and who might freeze. Time and again he brought one of them home and put him in his own bed, while he slept on a sofa. . . . He was very generous to whores who were down on their luck. He made their more prosperous sisters stump up to help them in bad times. Got the whores to come to Confession and be scrubbed up, spiritually. . . . You should have seen the whores at his funeral. Got into trouble because he let the church fabric run down, giving away money that should have gone for heating. . . ."

Of course with an example like that, money rolled in. St. Aidan's wasn't a rich parish by any means, but people stumped up astonishingly to help Father Hobbs, because he never spared himself. . . . There was an extraordinary atmosphere about the place.[11]

Stories and Inspiration

This book in many ways traces my own pilgrimage from a childhood nurtured in a left-behind country church, to a young adult who served as pastor's wife in two tiny churches, and to my current membership in a relatively large church, though one that is purposely and self-consciously left behind by the megachurch movement. In these pages I refer to the "messy spirituality" that is found in left-behind churches (and often more hidden and disguised in megachurches), as well as the desire to find God in the midst of our fallenness and proclivity to sin. There are no *secret sins* in the left-behind church.

These pages will serve as a forum for the pain, the disillusionment and doubts, and the burnout of ministers caught in the rat race of the church growth movement in all its contemporary guises. It will also focus on that very success syndrome, with its emphasis on pastoral *leadership* and *healthy* churches and its infinite number of publications, seminars, PowerPoint presentations, and principles. All of this supposedly is drawn from the Gospels and Epistles—those inspired writings that more accurately set forth a theology of failure and suffering: a theology of the cross.

But this book is not stuck in failure, at least as we contemplate the truly negative aspects of that term. The left-behind church is—for good and for ill—left behind in community. To its good fortune, it is sometimes left behind with a woman's touch—a woman minister whose only call comes from a left-behind church. And if this church does not take itself too seriously and has been so gifted by God, it is left behind with a sense of humor.

There are many positive aspects of the left-behind church—in the memories that spur many of us on during tough times. And there are examples of left-behind churches that have served and sacrificed far beyond their size—these *Little Churches That Could*. There are other left-behind churches that are in the valley of the shadow of death, and the life supports are shut down, perhaps with good reason.

These are the opportunities of the left-behind church—a church that not only *is* a community but also one that exists in the midst of a larger community. By its very nature it ministers to those both inside and outside its doors. It is not on the cutting edge. Indeed, it is probably very old-fashioned. All the good deeds and kind words have been done and said before—beginning in biblical times and continuing down through the centuries. There is truly *nothing new under the sun*. But sometimes our candles are hid under a bushel. The lights of the left-behind church must burn brightly again.

This then is not a sentimental book about the joys of a little church. I've been part of little left-behind churches, and I know all too well that the devil is just as active there—maybe more so—than in the largest megachurch.

The stories in this book—drawn from travels, personal interviews, biographies, fiction, and how-to volumes of all stripes—do not present new ideas or new trends. Rather, they are little stories that are carried along in the streams and tributaries that began as a trickle in a Garden only to one day join together as one mighty river flowing into New Jerusalem. It is true that *small* has gotten a bad press in religious journalism in recent years and that left-behind churches have a reputation for drowning in low self-esteem. But vast numbers of them are healthy and happy and are effectively carrying out the work of the Lord. So in these pages I offer a challenge to those who are feeling the sting of being left behind even as I celebrate the ministry going on in these one-of-a-kind places of worship and ministry.

It is important to recognize that the left-behind church is not an entity unto itself that is unrelated to our own individual perspectives and ways of thinking. Such a church is not made up of people living in plush mansions on three-acre spreads in suburbia whose lifestyle has no relationship to the gospel. Rather, these are folks who take lifestyle seriously—lifestyle formed by the gospel.

The Bible and the Newspaper

As I contemplate the gospel on the one hand and culture on the other, I'm reminded of the challenge that is often made to ministers to preach with the Bible in one hand and the newspaper in the other. For this Sunday morning's sermon, I might choose from one of a number of texts, or I might string a bunch of them together. *Take up your cross and follow me. . . . Come unto me all you who labor and are heavy burdened. . . . The first shall be last. . . .* From this Sunday morning's newspaper (May 22, 2005), just like biblical texts, there are too many stories from which to choose. The lead story is President George W. Bush's graduation speech at Calvin College yesterday. This is proof positive how far evangelicals have advanced—that they would have one of their own as President speak at commencement—though yesterday's paper carried ads and editorials opposing the president's record on the biblical concerns for peace, for the poor, and for the environment.

Besides President Bush, the only other person featured on the front page was Sidney Jansma Jr., who happens to be the president of the board of Calvin Theological Seminary (where I have taught for the past six years). But the two-part story was not about his board leadership; rather it featured his recent discovery of what is believed to be the largest oil well in the contiguous United States, located in Utah. The title of this article is "New Oil Tycoon Has Altruistic Plans." Here is a man who heads Wolverine Gas and Oil Corporation with some twenty-five employees, by any standard *left-behind* among the big boys of gas and oil, who is not focused on accumulating more for himself. "This is God's money, not mine," Jansma says. "My dad used to say, 'there are no pockets in a shroud.'"[12] This sudden wealth, he vows, will not change his lifestyle. He lives in a city neighborhood and is active in what might be termed a left-behind church.

The other story in today's business section that caught my eye was entitled, "Is Wal-Mart Losing Its Competitive Edge?" With megachurches patterned after Wal-Mart, this question has analogies too numerous to mention.

Still another headline that captured my attention on the front page of the Home and Garden section was entitled "New Urbanism." Here John Hogan reports that "America's love affair with oversized homes on oversized lots is losing luster. . . . Yes, bungalows are back." This is part of the growing desire for community.[13]

This book is a sermon of sorts, with the Bible in one hand and the newspaper in the other. It is sometimes tempting, with both hands full, to put down the Bible and let the newspaper guide us through the maze of our culture. We use the newspaper as a tool to *contextualize* the gospel with our culture, often without even considering how profoundly the Bible *confronts* culture.

The challenge of this volume is one of *confrontation*—confronting the materialistic individualism of our culture head-on. This is done most effectively by living out the gospel in community, and that community often includes the left-behind church.

1

Personal Reflections on Left-Behind Churches

I was born into a left-behind church. From infancy until high school graduation I rarely missed Sunday services. I was not, however, a child of the covenant. No baptism. No dedication. No confirmation. I was a stepchild of the faith. My parents attended regularly but remained all their lives on the fringe. They had never gotten properly saved—and that made all the difference. I did get saved. It is a story I have told in various settings, including my book *Walking Away from Faith*.[1]

I went back to that little country church a year ago. Grass was growing through the cracks in the sidewalk, and the weeds sprouting everywhere were telltale signs of abandonment. The church is now closed. Many seasons had passed since I walked through those weathered wooden doors. I expected it to be locked. But the door creaked open—barred only by spider webs and boxes partially blocking the inner hallway leading to the sanctuary. I call it a sanctuary, but that's a fancy word that was never used when I was growing up. This once-filled rectangular room had been shorn of its pews and pulpit. Around the walls were assorted pieces of furniture, boxes, and bags that had been left by generous neighbors following a devastating tornado.

I have fond memories of that little church—a church that never amounted to much at all, certainly not by megachurch standards. A church growth expert would have taken its pulse and pronounced it dead long before it actually expired. By all standards, it was a loser. The numbers just didn't add up, and every pastor we ever had was forced to get work on the side to make a living. But it would be difficult for me to exaggerate the formative influence that church has had on my life—not only my spiritual pilgrimage but also on my vocational ministry.

The setting for the "home mission" work that became known as Green Grove Alliance Church is where Lewis Road intersects County Road H. There is very little traffic except for farmers and fishermen. The Green Grove School, now used for community activities, is situated across the road, and in every direction there are dairy farms, several within easy walking distance.

As I was growing up, the church was a center of activity— whether scheduled or not. On a Saturday morning I would sometimes ride my bike the three miles from home, and from there our gang of four—Janice, Jane, Judy, and I—would decide how to best kill a few hours. We were all active in youth group, and though separated by as much as seven miles in distance and three years in age, we bonded through our faith and our rural heritage. Judy and I have rekindled friendship through email, and we dream of having a little reunion with Janice and Jane. But besides bringing a group of girls together, the little church offered youth activities that would be difficult to match in a twenty-first-century megachurch. I will carry memories of those spirited times to the grave, whether the free-for-all softball games with the pastor as pitcher or the sultry days of summer Bible camp or the rollicking harvest hayrides or the frigid sledding parties with a bonfire at the top of the hill. These times linger vividly in my memory with all their colors, sounds, and smells. In college, attending a much larger church, I'm sure I must have participated in social events, but I have forgotten every one of them. But not the hastily organized youth events of my childhood.

Youth ministry (though we didn't have any such term in those days), however, was only one aspect of outreach. The church served as a social center on a much broader scale. Neighborhood funerals, weddings, and anniversaries depended on church support, especially that of the ladies' aid society.

Before Miss Salthammer and Miss Cowan arrived, there was no church for miles around. The town of Spooner, ten miles to the east, was home to several churches, and some neighbors drove the distance. But for most families in our rural community, church did not seem an option until these two "lady-preachers" entered the picture. Their work began in the 1930s, long before I was born. They were what we would today call *church planters*. Without books, seminars, and special training, they simply went about doing the work of starting a new church. They lived in the community and spent their days and nights in neighborhood visitation, teaching Sunday school, conducting Sunday services, and organizing lay ministries and leadership.

When the church was established and on its own legs, they moved on to do home mission work elsewhere. As women, they were officially regarded as *missionaries*. After them came a succession of male *preachers*—Douglas, Bronko, Kovnesky, Bradford—who carried on with the work for some four decades. Those years included the bad along with the good. In the spring of 1961, a beloved pastor was forced to leave. It was a traumatic time, especially for those of us in the youth group who were not only losing our youth leader and pastor but also his kids, who were our friends. Sorrow and anger clashed in our adolescent emotions as the church was rocked with turmoil and rancor. June 4 was his last Sunday. I wept through the whole service. Looking back, knowing what I now know, the church leaders had no other choice but to do what they did. Indeed, they demonstrated sensitivity and Christian maturity in their handling of a situation that might easily have blown the church to bits. The church survived and so did our youth group. For a half century—for better or for worse—the little church served a community that had no other church options for those who might have been inclined to go church shopping.

As I think back of Miss Salthammer and Miss Cowan (I'm not sure if they had first names), I sometimes wonder what their hopes and dreams were as they entered that rural neighborhood. Did they imagine that by the turn of the next century the church would be only a memory? Did they imagine that their little ripple effect—their humble and often awkward efforts—would nurture sons and daughters whose ministries, vocations, and influence have spanned the globe? For me, there is much more than nostalgia connected with that little white church with peeling paint that now stands empty on the corner of Lewis Road and County Road H. I often wonder where I would be today if these two self-sacrificing women had not devoted themselves to our community.

A Left-Behind Pastor's Wife

These memories of a left-behind church, however, are very personal—and perhaps are much more nostalgic than they are useful in a practical way for folks who are enduring left-behind struggles in the here-and-now. But my experiences as a child and youth are not the only memories that come to mind when I consider my familiarity with left-behind churches. I was reminded of that today as I was walking out of the campus library with a dozen books that related to ministers and church life. One of the theological librarians asked about my research. When I told him that I was looking for biographies and autobiographies that focused on ministers of left-behind churches, he suggested that what I really needed was a book written not by the pastor but by the pastor's wife. It was not until hours later that it occurred to me that I am that pastor's wife—and indeed, I have already written the book, *Private Lives of Pastors' Wives*.[2] It is a book about pastors (of mostly left-behind churches) as much as about their wives, from Katie Luther to Jill Briscoe. Years ago when I wrote the book I found myself in those pages as I resonated in varying degrees with the fourteen featured women and their struggles and joys.

I have mixed emotions when I think of my years as a pastor's wife. The first little left-behind church was landlocked on a busy five-street intersection—a good place to hang a banner but not good for parking or for expansion beyond the sanctuary that during our years of ministry began to fill up with more than a hundred people. Despite its lack of appeal as churches go, there were five candidates who had preached and interviewed before my husband, a brand-new seminary graduate, was chosen for the job. For me, location was critical—not the intersection, but that the town was within driving distance of the university where I was completing my graduate work. That my husband barely received a majority vote seemed insignificant in light of my future studies. Despite my distractions with graduate work, I accepted my new position with eagerness and optimism. I was a dutiful pastor's wife—though I quickly learned that the expectations were far greater at this little church than those of a minister's wife of a large, multistaff church. It was simply assumed that I would become a leader of the Awana Clubs, and when I did not, there were hard feelings. Serving as a substitute leader, teaching Sunday school, organizing a Bible study, coordinating Vacation Bible School, participating in the ladies' missionary society, and attending all regular church meetings was just not good enough. But the expectations did not end with my church involvement. I was observed and scrutinized as first lady of that parish. What I was wearing, how my hair was done up, what I brought to the potluck dinner, how I cuddled my baby, how I presented myself at every public moment was fodder for talk and speculation. There was no place to hide, especially in that tiny sanctuary.

I sometimes felt like Sarah Edwards, wife of Jonathan, who for twenty-three years served as pastor of the Northampton church in the Bay Colony. On Sunday mornings all eyes were on her—what she and her daughters were wearing, including jewelry, how enthusiastically she sang, and how her face responded to every word her husband was saying. The only one more scrutinized than she was her husband, a matter that often troubled her deeply. Like Sarah, my own perceived deficiencies distressed me far less than did my husband's.

Kicked Out of a Left-Behind Church

Sometimes left-behind churches almost seem to outdo one another in doctrinal extremism, especially if they fall into any of the various categories of fundamentalism. The pastors would not have their positions if they were not sufficiently extreme themselves, and when the pastor gets out of sync with the congregation, explosions easily occur. As my husband moved more and more into *hyperdispensationalism*—so hyper that the validity of baptism and even the Lord's Supper was questioned—voices of protest arose.

And then when he preached—and ranted—against all holiday celebrations the week before Christmas, members threatened to leave the church.

For Jonathan Edwards, the issues were not altogether different. His aloof personality and his poor judgment combined with doctrinal differences set the stage for his dismissal after twenty-three years of ministry. He was determined to tighten up membership requirements by dispensing with the Halfway Covenant, initiated by his beloved predecessor and grandfather, Solomon Stoddard. As the pastor's wife, Sarah was caught between her husband and the congregation. So was I. I spoke my mind behind closed doors, but in public I was a loyal pastor's wife. For Sarah, the ongoing ordeal was painful, though the record indicates that she and her husband maintained a close relationship through it all.

Unlike Jonathan Edwards, my husband was relieved of his duties after only three years of ministry. In his case it was a betrayal of trust—petty theft and an arrest. It was a disgrace for this little church situated on five corners in small-town America, and it was a double disgrace for me, both parishioner and pastor's wife. Through my insistence, the pastor preached a properly penitential sermon, but I knew instinctively our days were numbered—and rightly so.

I thought at the time, and I still think thirty years later, that he was probably the only one of all of us who did not feel the sting of shame. But whatever shame the congregation felt, I have no doubt I felt it tenfold. I learned, as the congregation must have suspected, that this incident was only one of many. There were folks who treated us—and me, in particular—with kindness. But there were others who viewed his sins as my own and shunned me like a Hester Prynne with a scarlet letter. How I wished I might have been able to hide out at home, as I fantasized a minister's wife in a multistaff church might have done in a similar situation. But I thought I had no choice but to continue to attend every church meeting, adorned with my toothy smile, until we had finished loading the U-Haul truck almost three months later.

Independent churches are just that—independent. There is often very little cross-pollination. So when a minister is forced to leave one church, he can often find work at another church, especially if this other church is left behind on its last legs. No one wants to ask too many questions of an intelligent, good-looking, well-dressed, charming ministerial candidate and his smiling, supportive wife. So we moved from one left-behind church to another that was so left behind that we did not have a church building. All forty of us met in the basement of a Farm Bureau Insurance building, the way this little group had been meeting for years. We tried hard to grow and often had some good prospects who came two or three Sundays in a row. But once the visitors realized how dysfunctional and needy we were, they created kind excuses as to why they could no longer come.

We had our own excuses as to why we did not grow. Our best one aimed our arrows straight at Jack Hyles and his First Baptist Church of Hammond. His buses from twenty miles away came through our neighborhoods and picked up children—some of our own Sunday school kids—offering them treats, programs, and facilities, enticing them away with things we could not provide. Our best joke in those years was to catch someone off guard with a tragic news story: *Did you hear about the terrible accident? Two church buses collided. Dozens of children injured on their way home from Sunday school.* The punch line: *One of Jack Hyles's buses crashed head-on with one of Jerry Falwell's buses on a narrow mountain pass in Pennsylvania.*

During my years as a pastor's wife, I was frequently asked if I would rather be the preacher than the preacher's wife. I never hesitated saying *no.* Though I had sensed a profound *call* at age thirteen to be a missionary, it never occurred to me that a woman could be a preacher. In the early 1970s, when on the verge of entering the ministry as a pastor's wife, I learned of a nearby church that had called a woman as its pastor. I remember commenting to a friend that I could never sit under the preaching of a woman. But a lot of water has gone over the dam in the decades since. Not only could I sit under a woman pastor, but I've dreamed of being a pastor myself—a dream that has been spurred by fiction, poetry, art, music, and film, and especially the call to discipleship.

A Left-Behind Dream

One of my favorite Hollywood films is *The Apostle.* Sonny, played by Robert Duvall, is a preacher with feet of clay and a heart for God. Having committed a crime of passion, he's on the run from the law. But he can't run away from God and his call to preach the gospel. With the help of a retired and frail black preacher, Sonny opens a closed church, working on the side to make money for the ministry. He is as self-sacrificing as he is tempted by sin, and the little church serves the community. Indeed, it reaches out more effectively than most churches many times its size do. As I am pulled into the film, I rejoice with the Apostle Paul that "whether from false motives or true, Christ is preached" (Phil. 1:18). In the end, Sonny is arrested, and as the credits roll we see him amid a Black chain gang singing gospel songs.

Every time I show this film to my students, I am reminded of my own long-held fantasy of opening a closed-down country church—even the shut-down Green Grove Alliance Church in northern Wisconsin where I grew up—and reaching out with the love of Jesus to the surrounding community. I have imagined getting a phone call on a late spring Sunday morning as I'm walking out the door, sermon in hand, heading over to the church to open windows for some fresh air. But the call stops me dead in my tracks. A little boy has slipped out of a farmhouse overnight, and the frantic parents cannot find him. I do not know the family, but that's beside the point. The sermon is set aside as I make the first call for our round-robin phoning system. Worship service is canceled. I throw my sweater and skirt on the bed and pull on my jeans and boots. The church becomes grand central station for child-care, bag lunches, and search-team strategy. Adults and youth volunteer to get out in the woods or to man the base operations. In the end, I imagine the little boy is found and brought back home safe and sound before sunset. There is no grand finale or great revival in the community. The church doesn't double in size overnight. But there is joy over one little lost boy who has been found.

I have retold the story of this dream in various classroom settings. But there is a long road between a dream drawn from the country church of one's childhood to a book on church revitalization. How does a left-behind background lead to a left-behind book?

From Left-Behind Background to Left-Behind Book

Teachers at small colleges and seminaries often find themselves teaching courses for which they were not academically prepared. Such has been the case with many of the courses I have taught—including a seminary course titled Revitalization of the Local Church. That I had served as a pastor's wife in two small churches was hardly sufficient preparation for such a teaching assignment, but my interest in the topic and my willingness to do hard research made up for other deficiencies. My teaching style also served me well. I seek to draw out the best in students, and in this particular class there were several whose insights and years of experience greatly enhanced the discussion. But there was one component that we all found lacking—the texts. As hard as I searched for the right book, nothing fit the bill. In the end, I chose four texts and dozens of short articles, primarily from *Leadership Journal*.

I am picky about a text and in several courses have written a text when I could find nothing else suitable. But entering this *men-only* field seemed daunting. It is a well-known fact that most seminary texts are written by men, and men as a general rule write differently than do women. In the area of church revitalization, all of the books are authored by men. Not surprisingly, most of those books tend to focus either on statistics, facts, and figures or on lists of rules, principles, and strategies. My writing style is more narrative. Like many women, I learn best and teach best through stories, whether drawn from history, biography, fiction, case studies, or my own experiences.

But my problem in finding a text related to more than writing style and substance. It was also a matter of perspective. Most of the material written in the area of church revitalization comes from a church growth viewpoint. If a church is not growing in numbers, it must be revitalized or turned around—or shut down. Numerical growth is the goal, though it is often disguised in less stark terms such as church health, spiritual vitality, or dynamic ministry. In these books there is rarely any mention of the possibility of God working amid declining numbers. Yet historical and biographical studies as well as fictional accounts are full of stories of spiritual vitality in little congregations and left-behind churches.

31

The texts were also written primarily for ministers. But matters relating to church revitalization belong to the congregation as much as to the clergy. Churches, as entities, may be left behind in a megachurch world, but so are people and whole communities.

A Left-Behind Church Tour

It was the *textbook* problem—and encouragement from students—that prompted the research and writing of this book. I have followed the usual paths in conducting my research—through books and articles, exploring libraries and Internet sites. But I have also interviewed pastors and parishioners and have traveled through back roads and bustling cities, visiting churches, looking for left-behind stories and case studies. In the past year alone, my husband, John (always with camera in tow), and I have visited churches in Canada, England, and Scotland, as well as ones in twenty states from southern Florida to northern Wisconsin, Colorado, California, and Texas. The size of the churches we visited has ranged from a tiny storefront of a few dozen people to a church housed in a mall that hosts 10,000 every Sunday. My travels have also taken me to historic churches—churches as diverse as the historic Baptist church of Roger Williams in Providence, Rhode Island; the Cane Ridge church east of Lexington, Kentucky (where the frontier revival movement was born); the Brooklyn Tabernacle in New York City, world-famous for its choir; Angeles Temple (founded by Aimee Semple McPherson) in Los Angeles; and the Anglican church in Epworth, England, where Samuel Wesley served as parish priest, Susanna presided over the rectory, and John, Charles, and many more Wesley children grew up.

One of our church tours took us from our home in Grand Rapids, Michigan, through the Midwest as far as Nebraska and Colorado for the purpose of visiting churches in our own denomination, the Christian Reformed Church. We had deadlines to meet and interviews to conduct and services to visit. All in all, we discovered healthier churches in the heartland than we had anticipated. What they lacked in size, they often compensated for in a community spirit and a concern for the needy.

One of the common elements we found in many of the churches we visited—whether in the U.K. or the U.S.—was programs for vitality and growth. Alpha and Purpose-Driven and Healthy Congregation materials were regularly displayed. In most cases the prepackaged promotional literature promised far more than the congregations were experiencing, but nobody blamed the promises—only themselves.

There were many surprises in our travels, not the least of which was how this research affected our own spiritual lives. Some of our stops along the way were not churches *per se* but ministries. In northwest Iowa we visited Hope Haven, founded by John Van Zanten. Here in the little town of Rock Valley is a ministry known around the world for providing wheelchairs for those in poor countries who most need them. Close by are other humanitarian ministries as well as a state-of-the-art factory *manned* by workers who might not be hired elsewhere due to mental and physical handicaps. Here in this left-behind town in the middle of nowhere—whether churches are growing numerically or not—many Christian folks are behaving like Christian folks are supposed to behave.

Thousands of miles away from Rock Valley in the Lake District of the English countryside was another icon of the Christian faith that was for centuries and is still today left behind. Here, with the help of maps and guidebooks, we found the old mansion house at Swarthmore, the home of Margaret Fell and the headquarters for the early Quakers or Society of Friends. As we explored this three-hundred-year-old house with our guide, we could almost feel the lingering spirit of this dear woman, tireless and self-sacrificing as she was. And as I walked behind the house out into the lush, damp meadows on that sunny September morning, dew sparkling like diamonds, I thought of how left-behind and persecuted those early Quakers were and how influential they have been in the centuries since—these ordinary folks never amounting to anything more than a left-behind community of Christians.

While the media, the political pollsters, and the denominational bean counters focus on megachurches, there is another whole world outside the glare of cameras—a world in which the Spirit is still at work. It is this world of my heritage and this world of my research that I seek to share with my readers. It is a world that continues to challenge me, a world that since childhood has captured my heart. Indeed, in the process of research, we formed our own little secret ministry. Slipping into unlocked churches—often when no one is around—we pause for a few minutes of worship and thanksgiving. John finds his way to the piano and plays an old hymn with a touch of rhythm and blues, and then I raise my hands and pray a blessing—a blessing not only on the ongoing ministry of the church but a blessing on the past, often represented by the adjoining graveyard, and a blessing on the future of this little congregation. It is our very own little calling—a calling we aim to continue as we travel in the years to come, a little ministry that we hope to one day identify by our calling card, a left-behind copy of this book.

2

The Wal-Mart Gospel Blues

W is for Wal-Mart effect—the economic impact of the retail chain, from forcing smaller competitors out of business and driving down wages to keeping goods cheap, inflation low, and productivity high.

Tom Kuntz

In an annual guide to new "dictionary" definitions, Tom Kuntz (New York Times News Service) offered this definition in his "A-to-Z Guide to the Language that defined 2003." Proper nouns often become part of our everyday usage, and Wal-Mart is one of many that has found its place in common speech and understanding.[1]

Some years ago I spent a week in a small town in Indiana teaching a one-week, intensive course in church history. When the school had confirmed the housing arrangement with me, I was pleased to hear that it was a hotel less than a block from the town square. I love small-town squares, and this would be, as I had imagined it, an experience of déjà vu. I had lived within close walking distance of two small-town squares in Woodstock, Illinois, and Crown Point, Indiana. These were lively centers of activity where merchants mingled freely with their neighbors, giving detailed how-to explanations with every purchase of a seven-dollar shut-off valve. This was where we walked to the pizza joint during the first snowfall of the year—pizza with fresh toppings and all the irregularities of homemade dough. This was where the volunteer band played on Friday evenings in the summer and where politicians came to give speeches and be photographed with an opera-house backdrop.

But that was not what I found on the town square in this Indiana town. I was exhausted after my first day of teaching. As soon as I shut the door to my hotel room, I kicked off my shoes and threw my dress clothes on the bed, and within minutes I was in shorts and sneakers headed for the town square. I was hoping to find a funky little restaurant where I could order a meatloaf sandwich or a bowl of homemade chili—then maybe stroll further around the square for an ice-cream cone. But the first thing I noticed as I was approaching the square was that there were no cars competing for parking spaces. Indeed, there were no cars at all—and no people. It seemed like I was walking into a Nevada ghost town. Many of the storefronts were boarded up or soaped over, and "For Rent" signs were everywhere. What had happened, I wondered. What kind of disaster had struck this little town?

When I returned with no supper, I inquired at the hotel desk, thinking that perhaps some local industries had closed, resulting in a population drop. But such was not the case. In fact, the town was growing. People were moving into the community. Among the newcomers was Wal-Mart. For some people, this had been a positive turn of events. The stores downtown offered far fewer selections than did a superstore, and the closest Wal-Mart had previously been almost fifty miles away. Convenience and cost, so they reasoned, was more important than community. Wal-Mart is a symbol of progress, and if these proprietors on the square had business instincts like Sam Walton, they would not falter in the face of competition. If they were like Sam Walton, they would build a corporate giant like he did and not worry about their cramped space on the town square. If they were like Sam Walton. . . . If they were like Bill Hybels. . . . If they were like Rick Warren. . . .

When a town square dies, a community suffers. The loss touches every aspect of hometown life. So also when town churches die.

What conclusion can we draw from this? *Wal-Mart is bad. Megachurches are bad.* That might be the knee-jerk reaction, but it is too simplistic. Not all that comes with a superstore is negative, and some of us who are most critical sometimes shop there ourselves. The story of Sam Walton is inspiring. He started out as a small-town merchant himself. With hard work and ingenuity he became a billionaire who was never too sophisticated to drive around in his beat-up old pickup truck. He rose to the top through good old-fashioned competition. Any one of the merchants in that boarded-up town square could have done the same thing he did. That they failed when confronted with competition says more about their own lack of resourcefulness than it says about the new store in town—thus the reasoning goes.

So also with neighborhood churches when the megachurch comes to town. The competition can seem overwhelming, and sometimes the churches, like the drugstore and the jeweler, go out of business. The story of the megachurch-founding pastor may be as inspirational as that of Sam Walton—far more inspiring than the no-name pastor of the little neighborhood church. North Americans are impressed with size, and that mentality, like other aspects of American culture, has spread throughout the world.

The Changing American Landscape

In an article in the *Austin Chronicle* entitled "The Wal-Marts of Religion," Erica Barnett writes how superchurches have changed the landscape of American religious life in recent years. "Once upon a time in America, before the days of six-lane freeways, super-Kmarts, and SUVs," she muses, "the massive megachurch was unusual enough to raise eyebrows among members of nearly every Christian denomination. In the days when walking to a small neighborhood church on Sunday morning was the gold standard of religious expression, giant, 2,000-plus-member churches were an impressive anomaly, attended by a narrow cross section of aging baby boomers and crowded into the suburban hinterlands." But that is no longer the case. On Sunday mornings, shopping-mall-size parking lots in suburbs across the country are filled with pricy cars and vans as casually dressed middle-class and affluent consumers engage in designer worship.[2]

As I was contemplating "The Wal-Mart Gospel Blues," it had not occurred to me that some church leaders might see Wal-Mart as the ultimate model for a small-town church. But that is exactly what Tom Nebel suggests in his book *Big Dreams in Small Places*. Here he offers Sam Walton as an example—a retailer who went into small towns because of the growth potential: "the operational expenses were significantly less, and the opportunity to build without competition was incredible." For Sam Walton there was very little competition when he started building his big chain stores in suburbs and small towns. Local retailers, he reasoned, could never match his low prices.[3]

Wal-Mart sucks the very lifeblood out of many small shops, even as the company's counterpart in churches sometimes sucks the lifeblood out of the left-behind churches. But it is fair play, the church growth experts would say, and if the numbers are there, if the books balance, and if there is a profit at the end of the day, we can call it a success and maybe even a megachurch.

There are others who promote the Wal-Mart church as well. In *A Church for the 21st Century*, Leith Anderson offers that model as one that "may be the most promising prospect for rural America in the twenty-first century." He is convinced that the Wal-Mart model offers hope for small towns and rural areas in North America—those that are seeing a decreasing population and a shut-down of small businesses. This same model, he argues, can be used for churches in small-town America. "Recently our family drove through a rural Kansas town early on Sunday morning," he writes. "On the right side of the road sat a lovely church building with red brick walls and stained-glass windows. . . . My guess is that the church went out of business because the town didn't have enough people and money to support it."

What is the solution for such shut-down churches?

Wal-Marts are huge stores with lots of employees. . . . Wal-Mart gives us lots of choices—more than any of the little stores around. Wal-Mart offers excellence. Wal-Mart is user friendly and consumer sensitive. . . . We need Wal-Mart churches: churches that will serve regional rural markets; churches that are friendly, carry lots of programs, are customer-driven rather than institution-driven; churches that transcend the deep traditions of small communities and give permission to worship without alienating family histories and relationships.[4]

The Megachurch Image

Megachurch theorists are not unaware of an image problem—the Wal-Mart brand where steeples used to be. For all their programs and professionalism, these large churches are often accused of lacking community and treating people as numbers. How can people feel part of such a large church? One way is to create a down-home atmosphere. Like Wal-Mart that moves into small-town America and becomes part of the community, so also megachurches can be just regular places where plain folks worship. "*Authenticity* is the watchword of a generation that is suspicious of squeaky-clean, franchise Christianity," writes Andy Crouch, who recently spoke at a thriving new church with the motto, "real church for real people." Some churches seem to try way too hard to be *real*, however. He tells of visiting a megachurch in which everyone was "invited to turn to the stranger" seated alongside and "share a deep personal need in the next two minutes." This stretch for authenticity, he points out, is all too reminiscent of what is going on in consumer culture. Joe's Crab Shack, for example, "a ramshackle dive that you might think would fall down any minute," was actually constructed by "a speedy professional crew that travels around the country building Joe's Crab Shacks." Authenticity is also the appeal for the Cracker Barrel Old Country Store restaurant chain. Such chain stores and such churches "only reinforce consumer culture's latest trend: the good life, the 'authentic' life, is available for purchase, and all the hard work has already been done."[5]

Crouch challenges Christians to be wary of their own instincts as they are pulled into church as consumers—consumers who buy stonewashed jeans with an authentic, well-worn look. "So we connoisseurs of the authentic," he writes, "go shopping for a church, and our senses are well-tuned." But many will ask, isn't a chain crab shack as good as the real thing? Perhaps. And what is real? Is there anything left today that is authentic? Crouch insists that there is:

Down the road is a sanctuary where the stained glass is a bit tacky, the prayers are formal, and an uncomfortable number of the people are old. They've been singing the same songs for decades now, hymns that sound stiff and unyielding at first. Downstairs is a food pantry that opened for business when faded denim was a sign of need rather than ease [or style].
We walk in, uncertain of where we should sit. The regulars make room and hand us a hymnbook. We hold it—heavy, thick, and unfamiliar—in our hands. Its cover is threadbare at the edges. We open it and try to sing along.[6]

The picture Crouch is painting may not be sleek, stylish, and pretty, but it has an air of authenticity that is so lacking in many churches today.

Marketing strategy is very clever and subtle—whether in business or in church—and notwithstanding the glowing assessments of Leith Anderson and Tom Nebel, Wal-Mart is not as innocent and wonderful as its publicity suggests. A recent editorial in the *Detroit Free Press* offers a very different picture that ought to be a warning to church growth gurus. Here John Sweeney begins by reminding us of the advertisements—a store where a college graduate can furnish her first apartment for a reasonable price, where "a mentally-challenged man" has "found a job he loves," where senior citizens "come to shop and socialize." This "feel-good image" is "part of a calculated and cynical effort to cover up some of the lowest, most heartless practices in business—practices that Wal-Mart has helped to become industry standards." Sweeney tells the story of Dolly, who worked for a year and a half at a Wal-Mart in Ohio. She never earned more than $5.85 an hour, was punished when she asked to take off work when her daughter was hospitalized, and could not afford the health-care plan that cost $250 a month. "Dolly's story isn't unusual or extreme." Wal-Mart's own statistics show that its average employee earns, according to Sweeney, "well below the federal poverty level for a family of four." The standard response is: *If you don't like Wal-Mart, just get another job!* But Wal-Mart's demand for low-priced merchandise is forcing factory jobs overseas, and Wal-Mart's power easily shuts down local competition. In some communities, the only jobs available are at Wal-Mart.[7]

The Corporate Bottom Line

Considering the nature of the church, it would be difficult to make the above charges in parallel fashion. But there is something very tragic about a Wal-Mart church in God's kingdom shutting down a left-behind church—even if the bottom line of marketing strategy tells us it deserves to be shut down. Wal-Mart churches, like the stores, are not first and foremost concerned with people. They are concerned with numbers. The publicity tells us otherwise—that this is where folks come to worship and socialize and where everyone is happy with all the services and programs they receive at a discount price. But services and programs and discounts come with a price.

I recently visited a large, beautifully designed, twelve-year-old church located in an upscale neighborhood in Lexington, Kentucky. Some fifteen hundred people attend one of three Sunday morning services in its sanctuary with a seating capacity of around a thousand. On the surface, it would appear as though the church could double in size before needing more space. But the church has an option on land on the outskirts of the city—with plans to build a whole new campus with plenty of room for parking. The present location is short of parking space—thus the rationale for the planned move.

Frequently, decisions to move a congregation to a new location are propelled by a professional staff. The fact that time and fuel are wasted in traveling to the more distant location is typically ignored by those who are focused on church growth and numbers—as is the fact that the new land and construction is a massive amount of the Lord's money to be expended on the congregation itself. A more efficient use of funds would be to help support a sister church in the new location—if there is no church in the area—and to use the money for ministry outreach.

Size and efficiency, however, are often what shape the Western Christian worldview. But this is not what church is supposed to be about. Church is not the place where I get the best deal. It is not a health club or spa where I check out the facilities, programs, and monthly fees—though I recently learned of a Florida megachurch that now offers upscale health-club facilities. "Presently, some . . . churches seem to be growing numerically by riding the current wave of user-friendliness," writes

41

Philip Kenneson, "but some wonder whether the majority of people attracted by these methods will be interested in making the difficult transition from 'self-interested seeker' to 'other-interested disciple.'"[8] Many church programs are self-serving endeavors that could be eliminated without doing a disservice to the kingdom of God. Church represents many things, but every church ought to be a community of believers seeking God and sometimes finding God in *the least of these* among the poor and needy—people who may be in the congregation or out in the neighborhood.

Yet because of corporate megachurch marketing strategies, many Christians in America today are singing the Wal-Mart Gospel Blues. They are involved in left-behind churches while watching the media advertisements that make them long for a better product—one that will offer them a better deal.

Today this kind of megachurch marketing has spread around the world. But a century ago that perspective was thought by some to be uniquely American. Asia, on the other hand, especially in matters of religion, had been spared such a materialist, numbers-oriented religious mentality. That was the view of Kanzo Uchimura, a brilliant Japanese church leader and social critic of Western culture:

> Americans themselves know all too well that their genius is not in religion. . . . Americans are great people; there is no doubt about that. They are great in building cities and railroads. . . . Americans too are great inventors. They invented or perfected telegraphs, telephones, talking and hearing machines, automobiles . . . poison gasses. . . . They are great in democracy. . . . Needless to say, they are great in money. . . . They first make money before they undertake any serious work. . . . Americans are great in all these things and much else; but *not in Religion.* . . . Americans must *count religion* in order to see or show its value. . . . To them big churches are successful churches. . . . To win the greatest number of converts with the least expense is their constant endeavour. . . . Numbers, numbers, oh, how they value numbers! . . . Mankind goes down to America to learn how to live the earthly life; but to live the heavenly life, they go to some other people.[9]

The title of Kanzo's article, "Can Americans Teach Japanese in Religion?" in many respects has been answered by the very slow growth of the Japanese church. Japan has embraced much of Western culture, but not its religion. Yet where Kanzo seemed to get it right with Japan, he failed to anticipate what would happen elsewhere—as in the case of Korea. Today his critique applies to Korean Christians. They "must *count religion* in order to see or show its value. . . . To them big churches are successful churches. . . . Numbers, numbers, oh, how they value numbers!"[10]

The focus on numbers in America today is fueled to a large degree by church corporate executives. Every denomination, even little denominations like my own, has CEOs and middle managers who are very conscious of growth charts. Decreasing numbers mean cutbacks at headquarters, and one of the most tempting ways to bring those numbers up is to plant new churches hoping that one or more may become a megachurch and make up for all the other losses.

The Left-Behind Profile

The left-behind church has a mentality that is unmistakably different from the megachurch mentality. The theoretical differences that separate them are what denominational differences were a generation ago—perhaps as different as Catholics and Protestants were in a bygone era. Steve Bierly captures the profile of a left-behind church that has no denominational uniqueness. The profile would be essentially the same were it a Baptist, Methodist, Reformed, or Lutheran church—perhaps even a Catholic church:

> You're in a congregation that concentrates on preserving the traditions of the past. They see no need to make five-and-ten-year plans for the church or to "cast a vision" for the church's future. They know exactly what the church's future is going to look like. Every September, Rally Day will kick off the Sunday school year. In October, there will be the annual Harvest Dinner. . . . Woe betide anyone who attempts to change the sacred schedule![11]

"Members of this church feel a strong sense of ownership," writes Jane Newstead of her left-behind church in Iowa. "Every month or so I'll find someone I didn't expect in or around the building taking care of a squeaking door, a messy cupboard, a singing toilet, and the like. New plants miraculously appear in the flower beds." But all the positive features have negative counterparts. "It is wonderful in the church to know that year after year, through thick and thin, Marge will still be teaching kindergarten on Sunday morning." But, "how do you ask the faithful treasurer of the last twenty-five years, who has turned in only one written report per year, incomplete and inaccurate at that, to resign, when she is mother, sister, aunt in six other families in the congregation?"[12]

The left-behind church is often associated with negative terminology: decay, decline, deterioration, death—and failure. It may be a lovely chapel in the vale or it may be a crumbling stone edifice in a decaying city neighborhood or it may be a stark, corrugated-metal, prefab worship center just outside town. By whatever description, it is declining in numbers—and in self-confidence. The enthusiasm and optimism of younger years has evaporated long ago. The shrubs and grass cry for attention; a stained-glass pane pokes out of the soil; the untuned upright piano offends our auditory senses. Shingles are missing, and rainwater drips into buckets. But leaky roof or not, the Sunday service is as parched as a sun-scorched desert—almost as dry as the brittle pages of the dusty hymnbooks.

The reasons are as predictable as they are unique to their own circumstances—debt-ridden farmers in the final stages of bankruptcy, young families moving to the suburbs, a new highway bypassing town, a smoke-billowing factory shutting down, an upstart megachurch moving in, or a pastor leaving town under the cloud of scandal.

Such setbacks, however, are not lacking ready solutions. Ideas for church revitalization emerge in unlimited supplies—like mushrooms popping up after a spring rain. Books and seminars abound: twelve steps, ten rules, six simple strategies, or five fundamental principles. They're all purpose-driven, and any pastor and congregation with willpower and prayer can restore this ailing patient's health. Committees offer suggestions from glitzy youth outings to old-fashioned food pantries, from friendship evangelism to evangelism explosion, from remodeling the sanctuary to recycling the pastor.

Many people "have a gnawing feeling that the small church is somehow second-rate," write William Willimon and Robert Wilson, "particularly the clergy and denominational leaders [who] view the small church as an anachronism, kept alive by stubborn people who are holding on to an institution that should be allowed or even encouraged to die. They see such churches as impediments to the development of the kind of congregation needed today."[13]

The Left-Behind Vicious Cycle

In many ways the left-behind church is caught in a vicious cycle as it seeks to stay alive in a cutthroat, competitive world. Ministers in virtually all denominations are in short supply. Vacant pulpits abound. Statistics show that the turnover rate in recent years has grown significantly. One report tells of a minister forced out of his church in June 2003, thus becoming "one of an estimated 1,500 to 1,700 clergy nationwide who left or were forced out of their congregations in that month alone." Today the total length of time a minister remains in pastoral work is an average of seventeen years.[14] So the left-behind church often considers itself lucky to have a resident pastor—knowing that if he or she performs well, the call to move on to greener pastures will be an ever-present temptation.

I encountered this sentiment some months ago as I was traveling west from Michigan through the Dakotas and on to Colorado and California, visiting Christian Reformed churches and former students now in pastoral ministry. In one particular church the overwhelming consensus was an expression of love for the pastor and his family. But almost everyone added a qualifier to their attachment—a concern that they would lose him to a bigger church. And he himself confided that he would like a church with more challenge, though he insisted he would stay for at least five years.

Willimon and Wilson tell the story of a recent seminary graduate, Donald Sheldon, who serves two tiny churches in the Midwest. "My friends tell me I'm wasting my talents by staying with these small churches," he confessed, reflecting on another opportunity that had come his way. "I would prefer to remain, but I am concerned about the effect on my career if I turn down this invitation." So the left-behind church is left even further behind when it loses its pastor. "These congregations need pastors but can afford only modest salaries. The success of a minister is determined by his or her ability to move to larger congregations. In a society that values growth and size, the small church remains the same; it does not grow and it refuses to die."[15]

A Left-Behind Church Parable

The church growth movement of the 1980s, with its more recent versions coming out of Willow Creek and Saddleback, sets a high standard and pushes some left-behind churches over the edge. The *purpose*-driven easily becomes the *precipice*-driven church. Seminars, programs, and workbooks abound. Even though much of the literature would say otherwise, *driven* is the key word. Pastors are expected to serve as CEOs, and numbers fill the ledgers. The pastor, like the CEO, is watching the bottom—and top—line.

Sometimes it is good to consider the left-behind church in the form of a parable. *The left-behind church is like a shop on the town square after Wal-Mart has moved in. . . .* Or, *the left-behind church is like the Lady Chaparrals of ChristWay Academy.* I take this parable from Martin Marty, a Lutheran minister and professor emeritus at the University of Chicago. He offers practical and philosophical advice for the left-behind rural church in a speech that he gave in 1999. But before a left-behind church can contemplate how it should move forward, it needs to see itself in light of the gospel message. Here Marty offers an illustration from an article in *Sports Illustrated* (March 1999).

The setting is in Texas, at a tiny high school, the ChristWay Academy. The girls' basketball team, the Lady Chaparrals, were playing against Arlington Oakridge. The contest was hopelessly lopsided. Throughout the game, Coach Jennifer Marks thought, *If only we could score. Or, If only we could get the ball to midcourt.* No luck. The final score was 103–0. Marks's husband, Scott, who was training for pastoral ministry, tried to comfort her in her misery—long days and sleepless nights of self-doubt and second-guessing her coaching calls. "He did the best thing he could do, which was to just hold me and listen."

The team lost the next two games, 86–7 and 76–15. But John Walters writes in *Sports Illustrated*, "a funny thing happened to the ChristWay girls: nothing. Nobody quit. Nobody whined. Nobody, including Marks, blamed anyone else." Seven of her nine players had never bounced a ball until that season. They'd like to win, "but most of them are just learning how to play," she said. No doubt they held on to hope when they played Gospel Lighthouse of Dallas, a team that came with a 1–19 record. Still, they stood a chance of retaining their reputation of being Christian martyrs ready to be eaten by Christian lions.

It happened, however, that Lighthouse had only five girls to suit up. And in their straits, they played sufficiently un-Christianly that one after another fouled out. With 17 seconds left to play, Lighthouse was down to one player. She had no one left to whom to throw the ball, even though her team still led 43–40. "Game over!" shouted the referee. "Officially the Lady Chaparrals had a 2–0 win—their first and, as it would turn out, only victory of the season," writes Marks. "It wasn't pretty, but who deserved to win more?"[16]

Here is the parable: *The left-behind church is like the Lady Chaparrals of ChristWay Academy*. It is a parable that sets the stage for something better—though not necessarily of "one telling of a turnaround the next year," writes Marty, "when the Lady Chaparrals would have won, say, 17 games." No, the left-behind parable only sets the stage as Jesus set the stage in his parables—stories in which "there must first be upsetting, overturning: the first shall be last and the last first. The smallest seed, the mustard, grows into a great tree. The grain of wheat that dies, lives. The lost gets found. The uninvited get invited to the banquet." The left-behind church must see itself as Jesus sees it—the last that will be first, with hope of an eschatological future that can only be imagined here and now.[17]

The best lesson we can draw from the Lady Chaparrals for the left-behind church is that it nurtured a faithful and steady spirit. What happened to these losers? Nothing. They persevered. They were not like the boy's basketball team in Mike Lupica's *Travel Team*. This is a "rousing tale," as the front fold tells us, "of the underdog that will leave you cheering through the final page."[18] Yes, those stories happen, and they make the news. And left-behind churches sometimes defy odds and turn into mega-churches. But most do not. For them, the Lady Chaparrels serve as profound inspiration.

3

The Precipice-Driven Pastor

Ministers today face far greater expectations and pressures than did their counterparts in previous generations. Today ministers are compared to the superstars in their ranks. Victorian England had its Charles Haddon Spurgeon, and New York City had its Henry Ward Beecher. But they did not represent a superchurch phenomenon. Today every city has at least one luminary or, if not that, a celebrity in the making. Among "The 25 Most Influential Evangelicals in America" featured in a cover story of a 2005 issue of *Time* were megachurch ministers: Rick Warren "who pastors the 22,000-member Saddleback megachurch in Lake Forest, Calif."; T. D. Jakes, pastor of "the Potter's House, his 35,000-member suburban Dallas church"; and the minister some think of as the *father* of the megachurch, Bill Hybels, whose church in Barrington Hills, Illinois, "attracts 17,500 worshippers each week."[1]

But the proliferation of megaministers is far less threatening to the average, no-name, run-of-the-mill pastor than are the intimidating *networks*. Hybels, for example, "leads a network of 10,500 churches and trains more than 100,000 pastors each year."[2] Every pastor has a network choice—to join or not to join. Either way, the pressure is on.

Never before have there been so many seminars, workshops, conferences, books, journals, and magazines to tell ministers how to perform well. Follow the rules. Employ the principles. The church will be a winner. Coaches offer tried and true strategies. Athletic analogies are appropriate in this high-stakes game. Church is a competitive sport. The professional teams are in the megachurch big leagues. Below them are farm teams, college teams, hometown teams, little league teams, and sand-lot ball. Church competition, like that of sports, can be addictive for player and spectator alike. The drive to win—and crush the opponent—is often all-consuming. And this drive, often fueled by testosterone, spans all levels of competition from the pros to the peewee players.

Church Growth Addiction

Some ministers openly testify to their church growth addiction. "I personally experienced the misery of megachurch mania when I fell under its intoxicating influence during the late 1980s while serving as a church planter in southern California," writes Samuel Rima, a Baptist minister. "In all honesty, I began my church planting effort with nothing but the most spiritually altruistic of intentions. I did not set out intending to build the next Crystal Cathedral or Willow Creek. My sole desire was, by God's grace, to establish a foothold for the kingdom amid the rapidly growing area of southern California to which I had been assigned." His goal was spiritual health, not simply numbers.[3]

But without even realizing it, Rima's focus began to change. "Almost imperceptibly, my motives and desires began to subtly shift." He tasted success. "As our little church began to grow, even beyond my expectations, my initial standards for ministry success were no longer sufficient." Soon growth became an obsession: "I began to believe that if only I did the right things, applied the proper techniques, and raised enough money I could simply manufacture church growth, just like a mortgage banker increases his or her market share." Finally, it turned into an addiction: "I was experiencing the onset of full-blown mega-church mania and I was growing increasingly miserable in ministry. . . . I have personally experienced the frantic, manic ministry life produced by my own dark side and fragile personal ego needs."[4]

Rima's words are disquieting. He speaks as an insider, a minister whose church had reached one thousand in attendance. His concerns are worth pondering. Warnings are everywhere. The church building is not a sports stadium. Ministers are not sports stars. People who show up at Sunday worship are not stats. This is not a game we're playing.

Yet the competition continues. "It would be safe to say that in the last 20 years many ministers have become mega-church maniacs," writes Rima. "For these pastors size and growth have become the all-consuming objects of their excitement and enthusiasm." But when the numbers don't add up, the joy in ministry vanishes and pastoral burnout follows.[5]

The preacher in the left-behind church is continually compared to the preacher in the megachurch. It may be a self-inflicted comparison, or it may come from people in the congregation, but whatever its source, the lowly preacher never quite makes the cut. He is a second-string preacher on the B team. He will never be a star. But the *stars* are larger than life and as close to home as the TV screen in the living room. Garrison Keillor humorously portrays this struggle for a small-town preacher in Lake Wobegon:

> Church was half full and restless. Pastor Ingqvist's Lenten sermons have gotten longer. Val Tollefson has been after him to liven up his preaching. Sunday morning before church, Val tunes into "Power for Tomorrow" on TV from the Turquoise Temple in Anaheim, and there is a gleam in Reverend La Coste's eye that Val wishes Pastor Ingqvist would emulate and also use more dramatic inflection, rising, falling inflection, cry out sometimes, use long pauses to give solemnity to the sermon.[6]

Leadership and the Career Ladder

Today the hottest topic in continuing education for pastors is *leadership*. It is presumed that there has been an absence of effective leadership in the church for two thousand years. But thanks to corporate management models, we can now move forward. Conferences are designed around the theme of pastoral leadership. Seminars, books, and tapes promise success. Pastors are suddenly discovering the missing element in their ministry. Like the CEOs and middle managers in the local Rotary Club, they can chart their leadership abilities through the same bottom-line assessments and five-year plans that corporations use. The problem with such models is that church and corporation are very different. Standards for success in the business world are not the same as the standards for faithfully following Jesus. Pastors are particularly vulnerable. Everything in today's culture screams for success, size, fame, and prestige—and upward mobility.

"I had been inducted into the pastoral career system," writes Eugene Peterson; "get career counseling, work out career patterns, work yourself up the career ladder. . . . Somehow, without us noticing it, the pastoral vocation was redefined in terms of American careerism. We quit thinking of the parish as a location for spirituality and started thinking of it as an opportunity for advancement."[7]

Peterson maintains that the career ladder and the temptations associated with it are more sinister for the pastor than for those in the corporate world—more sinister in the "world of religion, where I can manipulate people and acquire godlike attributes to myself. The moment I entertain the possibility of glory for myself, I want to blot out the face of the Lord and seek a place where I can develop my power." The lust for power is not unique to pastors, "but pastors have the temptation compounded because we have a constituency with which to act godlike. Unlike other temptations, this one easily escapes detection, passing itself off as a virtue."[8]

One way to become a megachurch pastor is to *plant* a church in a fast-growing, upscale development. It's simple. Just do what Rick did in California or what Bill did in Illinois. That model of church growth is the one we most often associate with the megachurch. But some ministers work their way into a large church even as managers work their way up the corporate ladder and as corporate executives work their way into bigger companies. Peterson challenges the pastor today to stay put. He tells how St. Benedict struggled with the problem of his monks being restless. "It was not unusual for monks to seek another monastery, supposing themselves to be responding to a great challenge, attempting a more austere holiness." But was this actually a quest for holiness or *God's* will? Or was "this restlessness disguised as spiritual questing"? Benedict saw through the disguise. He "put a stop to it. He introduced the vow of stability: stay where you are."[9]

But the Benedictine vow is not for everyone. Some pastors do move on to "greener pastures"—those who, in hindsight, made the right choice when we consider the larger scheme of things. Indeed, for every critical—and not so critical—decision we make in life, there is always the question, *What if* I'd done things differently? *What if* a young pastor, fresh from doctoral studies in Europe, had stayed put in Paterson, New Jersey? Surely the life and legacy of Lewis Smedes—writer, theologian, professor—would have been very different. He tells of his short years as pastor of a left-behind church in his memoir, *My God and I*. "When Doris and I came home from Europe," he writes, "I was called to be the pastor of a small congregation in Paterson, New Jersey, located in a rundown section of that rundown town, doing nobody in the needy neighborhood much good." But the feelings among those in the neighborhood were mutual. They "returned the compliment by paying no notice at all to our cozy little brick church hibernating on Madison Avenue near Tenth." Smedes had been called to this church for a specific purpose: "to lead this faithful group of Sunday visitors into a new identity as a 'live-in' servant *of* the community." He was, however, ill-prepared. "I had been spending my time in Europe thinking deep thoughts about God and did not have a single practical notion of how a church of commuters could be transformed into a neighborhood ministry of grace." The result, by his own account: "I failed." But Smedes's failure is not the end of the story:

> I dreamt the dream . . . and others more savvy and gifted than I was, eventually made the dream come true. The little church that nobody noticed back then is now the control center of a ministry for all the needs of all the people in the area who need help of whatever kind. And the small group of white worshippers that I once served has become a many-colored community that every day does more—in proportion to its size—for needy people than any other church I know.[10]

Besetting Sins

For many ministers, the emphasis on numbers equates with constant stress—especially when the numbers do not add up. There is often intense pressure on pastors of smaller churches to produce, to submit a growth chart that mirrors megachurch statistics. Not long ago I was talking to one of my students, a recent seminary graduate. His complaint was that he could never do well enough in the numbers game to satisfy those at headquarters. He felt constant stress on matters of numerical growth and confessed that he secretly hoped his colleagues (or competitors) in the denomination who were also receiving funds were doing worse than he was. His continuation in the program was dependent on the charts. If the numbers did not add up, he was out of a job.

This is a dog-eat-dog world, and it is no secret that the left-behind church is no utopia, nor is the pastor a canonized saint. Indeed, there are peculiar struggles and sins that seem to beset the pastor of a small church. It is easy, for example, to enter the blame game, taking on a defensive posture to explain why the church is not as big as the one down the street. Resentment and envy are part of this mind-set. The pastor easily points the finger at the "successful" pastor with accusations of arrogance, hypocrisy, and duplicity while secretly wanting to trade places. Christianity, unlike witchcraft and animism, offers no outlets through curses. If it did, many big churches and their pastors might be cursed into oblivion by the struggling pastor on the wrong side of the railroad tracks. But Christians have no *spiritual* tactics for revenge, apart from calling forth the imprecatory psalms, which are anything but politically correct in this era of tolerance. So the most natural response is to wallow in self-pity, low self-esteem, and low-grade depression—an outlook that only makes matters worse. Depression leads to decrease of energy and decrease of energy to indolence and lethargy. Unlike a small business, where the boss is working overtime and the employees are forced to pull their weight, pastors have no such personal investment and oversight. Indeed, the very atmosphere of the left-behind church often favors the pastor who lacks self-discipline.

"The tendency to slough off and put my brain on hold isn't helped by the fact that small churches may not hold me to very exacting professional standards," writes Steve Bierly. They consider themselves fortunate to have anyone fill the pulpit whether the individual sees the church as a stepping stone to something better or a last stop before retirement. They almost expect that the pastor will give less than the pastor of a megachurch. "I remember," Bierly continues, "one small congregation constantly praising me for doing above and beyond what previous pastors had done, while all I thought I was doing was just my minimum job requirements."[11]

But there are other issues as well. When ministers are focused on numbers, it easily draws their attention away from God. What is the real purpose of church? Is it numbers and size? What is the calling of a minister? To preside over numbers and size? "In the course of organizing a new congregation in the suburbs," Peterson writes, "I felt pressure to get a lot of people together as quickly as possible in such a way that they would provide the financial resources to build an adequate sanctuary for the worship of God." For some ministers, such an assignment is as stressful as it is difficult. For Peterson, the task was invigorating and challenging, and he was supported by his church. But there were matters that were of graver consequence: "I found that gathering a religious crowd was pretty easy, provided I didn't get too involved with God. My ecclesiastical superiors sent me to workshops that showed me how to do it. I observed the success of other pastors who did it." The know-how for new church development, as Peterson observed, was not rocket science. "Religious consumers, like all other consumers, respond to packaging and bargains." This was not, however, what he identified as the calling of a pastor. "To follow this route I would have to abandon the very thing that gave the life of a pastor its worth: a passion for God."[12]

Necessity of Pastoral Renewal

Losing one's passion for God arises out of many circumstances. George MacDonald, a nineteenth-century preacher and writer (who had a profound influence on C. S. Lewis), wrote novels that frequently featured an Anglican minister who carried on with his routine responsibilities without any enthusiasm or compassion.

In *The Curate's Awakening* it is the gatekeeper, a dwarf named Polwarth, who reaches out with "a pastor's heart" to minister to others. The story, however, has a happy ending. Through Polwarth's loving service, the minister himself is *awakened* to a radiant passion and compassion in his calling.[13]

In *The Prodigal Apprentice* MacDonald spins another story of a minister in a left-behind church. Here whatever natural gifts and abilities the minister may have lacked was more than compensated by his profound *belief*. Belief in God may seem like the most obvious requisite for pastoral ministry. That ministers make such a profession is to be expected, but that their belief is truly genuine and is sincerely transmitted to those in their congregation is not necessarily a given. What is the one reason more than any other that accounts for church vitality? It surprised me when I read what seemed like something too apparent to even mention. In a study entitled "Mainline Churches: The Real Reason for Decline," researchers concluded that "The single best predictor of church participation turned out to be *belief*."[14]

Belief is transmitted from pastor to parishioner. Such *believing* ministers should be as ordinary as is the left-behind minister MacDonald captures in his fiction:

> Some people considered Mr. Fuller very silly for believing that he might do good in a church like this, and with a congregation like this, by speaking that which he knew, and testifying to that which he had seen. But he did actually believe it. Because he was so much in the habit of looking up to the Father, the prayers took hold of him every time he read them and he so delighted in the truths he saw that he rejoiced to set them forth—was actually glad to *talk* about them to anyone who would listen.[15]

Of course, not all left-behind ministers are like Mr. Fuller. The constant stress of competition and comparison, however, are not the only anxieties that kill the pastoral spirit. Sometimes a minister becomes so discouraged with routine duties that he abandons his calling—and in worst-case scenarios, runs away and leaves the left-behind church behind. So it was with the widower "Bluebeard" (so named because he always looked like he needed a shave). This fictitious minister in Frederick Buechner's *The Final Beast* got up one morning and walked out, leaving his children with his housekeeper. He was convinced he could not keep yet another deathwatch for an aged parishioner:

> His church was old ladies, and another [minister] could do for them as well. He must know that. She [his housekeeper] had seen him come back haggard from their dying, his stomach in knots. The doctor told him that there was nothing wrong with him but just that he had sat out too many terminal cancers. . . . There was God, of course, but God . . . asked so much of His servants and rendered so little: marry and bury, christen and counsel, joke with, solicit from, try somehow to live by Him, live with Him. It emptied a man. Yet skinny and bright-eyed in his black robe, he still had to stand up in the pulpit Sunday after Sunday and speak to Him and about Him to that big, white, half-filled meeting-house of a church with the turkey-red carpet. . . . Why should Bluebeard stay for the sake of God?[16]

The left-behind pastor's wife struggles no less with her role, and in many instances she has no sense of calling and has made no choice about being in the circumstances in which she finds herself. Klara, in Olov Hartman's *Holy Masquerade*, bemoans her role that requires far more than the wife of a teacher or carpenter or sales manager. She is regarded as an extension of the pastor and his ministry. And worse yet, she sees her husband, Albert, behind the scenes. Behind closed doors, he is very different from what he pretends in public: "He mirrors himself to the pious opinion of good people and conforms himself to their ideal of a minister." But not only him; she has been infected also. This "hypocritical spirit," she laments, "has gripped me as well." In ministry, she points out, there are higher expectations than in other professions. "I saw the formulary for ordination not so long ago," but "this does not concern me"—at least not directly. There is a larger concern. What is her role as a minister's wife? It is this matter that troubles her most:

> What does concern me, on the other hand, is my own ordination to the call of a pastor's wife. Why isn't there a special kind of marriage ceremony for clerical brides? . . . For we wives of pastors are bound by the whole apparatus of piety. Perhaps we are bound even more than our husbands, for a minister receives some indulgences. But for a minister's wife, nothing is forgiven either in this world or in the world to come.[17]

The temptations and struggles that pastors and their spouses face are in many ways unique to the ministerial profession. There are, however, exceptions to the rule. The pastoral managers and CEOs of corporate megachurches are largely immune to the problems of the more community-oriented, smaller churches. Here the pastor must understand the issues involved and seek camaraderie and counsel with others.

Counsel and Guidance

How can the pastor avoid the stress and pressure that comes with competition and the numbers game? The pastor must feed the inner life—and that occurs in part through being in touch with others who have *been there, done that*, so to speak. For Gordon MacDonald, that translates into a conscious effort to "fly in formation"—to fly "with a select collection of authors." For each pastor, that collection might be different. For MacDonald, they are writers who challenged him in his own spiritual formation—all of them sharing their insights during the last half of the twentieth century:

> Paul Tournier taught me about people. Elton Trueblood gave me a love for ideas and the life of the mind. A. W. Tozer elevated my concept of God and worship; Stanley Jones became my inspiration for evangelism and the Kingdom. John Stott taught me the power and dignity of preaching and a hunger for biblical scholarship that had the "streets" of the real world in mind. And dear Henri Nouwen revealed to me the disciplines of the interior life. In the books of these authors, I found a point of stability that protected me from running too quickly to the claims of instant success that came from other quarters.[18]

The pastor is the leader of the church. Few would question the obvious. But Donald Morgan insists that denying that truism was the first step in turning around the First Church of Christ in Weathersfield, Connecticut. Soon after he began his pastoral ministry at the church, a tourist asked him if the old, historic building was "a church or a museum." It had been declining in membership for most of a decade, with grim predictions for the future due to population shifts in the area. Today this same church is the largest in the denomination in New England, with the attendance five times what it was when Morgan began his work. He dates the beginning of the revitalization to one meeting:

> I then told my leaders I was resigning from my role as leader of the church. They were stunned. *What was this all about?* they wondered. I quickly explained I was not leaving and that I would still fulfill my responsibilities. I would preach on Sunday mornings and do the other pastoral things. But in a profound sense, I was stepping aside. From that moment on, I told them, Jesus would be in charge. Jesus would be at the helm. He would make any growth happen! I invited them to join me in following his leading.
>
> You have no idea how liberating this conviction became to me. I was a new man, with a new style. I was a better leader.[19]

Morgan's testimony is one that all ministers should take to heart—though with humility and an awareness of their own vulnerability to self-deception. Such a commitment can truly change a life, but it can also be a means of manipulation. A pastor must take very great care not to claim Jesus is the leader when in actuality the pastor is pulling the strings.

The matter of spiritual guidance is a knotty conundrum for Christians in all walks of life, but it is particularly challenging for those whose very career is inexorably tied to the *leading of the Lord*. We so easily speak for God—as I write in my most recent book *God Talk: Cautions for Those Who Hear the Voice of God* (InterVarsity, 2005). We so easily claim guidance and confirmation and sometimes explicit instructions when we're involved in *the work of the Lord*. But when are the words we hear the words of God, and when are they our own imaginings? When is the good result of our leadership a unique blessing from God, and when is it a result of our own innate leadership skills—and when is the opposite true when things go awry? Do we hold God hostage through prayer as we storm heaven in the race to win the numbers game? As the competition continues to heat up and the stakes grow higher and the expectations proliferate, these questions will loom larger.

Although megachurches capture media attention, they are clearly the exception to the rule. Yet the megachurch mentality runs rampant in American Christianity, even though there are warnings against false expectations by a growing number of church growth experts. For example, Larry Gilbert, who serves with the Church Growth Institute, cautions his readers to be realistic. "Taking the 102-member church and turning it into a 5,000-member church requires extraordinary leadership. That cannot be our definition of success. . . . We need to help pastors turn a 102-member church into a 112-member church."[20]

Ministers often try to copy programs and principles that simply will not work in their own situations. Steve Bierly offers straightforward advice in plain language: [If you still don't understand,] "let me turn up the juice a little more so that you can really feel it. Many of those ideas in your church-growth conference notebook? They won't work for you! Let me hit the button again. They won't work for you! Why not? Well, look in the mirror. . . . *You're not Bill Hybels or John Maxwell or James Kennedy or Chuck Swindoll!* Stop driving yourself crazy trying to be."[21]

The problem of a pastor being left behind in a megachurch world is the problem that we all face in the rat race of life. The definition of success in Western culture is one that is equated with *bigger and better*. And ministers—especially left-behind ministers—are particularly vulnerable. They stand alone in the pulpit every Sunday facing down their employer, the congregation. The pressure to produce is often enormous. If that minister can relax and serve God with passion, there is hope for that left-behind church.

"I don't know what I expected to find at the end of that narrow road through the bare trees in Marion County, Indiana," writes Paul Harvey Jr., "but what I found was a little red-brick church. A 'meetinghouse,' the Quakers call it." The tiny congregation was seated around on folding chairs. Behind the wooden pulpit sat a lean-faced man with his head bowed and hands folded. "When the youthful pastor stood, the appearance of piety vanished," continues Harvey. "It was clear, in a quiet sort of way, that he loved these people in the folding chairs. And that they loved him." His was not a "speaker's voice." Rather it was a voice that "measured the words it spoke the way a journeyman carpenter measures wood. And so, one rafter, one casement at a time, did Philip Gulley craft for us in the folding chairs a house, of sorts, in which we dwelled for the next twenty minutes." Here Harvey found a church that he had believed was "inaccessible in these turbulent high-tech times."[22]

Who is this pastor who has since gone on to serve in another left-behind church in Indiana? How does he challenge the left-behind pastor today?

As I've grown older, my understanding of happiness has changed. It used to take a new piece of furniture to make me happy; now if the boys are healthy and Joan and I go to bed cuddled like spoons, that's about as good as it gets. . . .

In high school, I worked at a grocery store. Every Monday we took inventory to find out what we had and what we lacked. So, too, in the Christian life, should we take regular inventory of all we are and all Christ summons us to be. This I'm learning in my middle years, in my small pulpit in a big city, among all my many friends.[23]

4

A Left-Behind Theology

In terms of the prevailing cultural climate where success is power and prestige, wealth and status, the mission of the church is clear: to be a failure.

Leonard L. Sweet

"I pastor the slowest growing church in America." These are the words of the late Michael Yaconelli. Most ministers would leave the ministry before they would make such an admission—especially in print. However, it becomes clear in reading his book *Messy Spirituality* that for him the church is much more than numbers. The message of the gospel is often upside down and backwards. The greatest is the least and vice versa. So also with the church. "We started twelve years ago with ninety members and have un-grown to thirty," writes Yaconelli. "We are about as far as you can get from a user-friendly church—not because our congregation is unfriendly but because our services are unpredictable, unpolished, and inconsistent. We are an 'odd friendly' church, attracting unique and different followers of Christ who make every service a surprise." For many people, such worship is disgraceful—and it represents everything that was wrong with the evangelical wing of the church in generations past. But in a very strange sense, it is easier to imagine Jesus in a church like this than in a megachurch with a contemporary praise band or in a cathedral with a perfectly choreographed liturgy. Here in this miserable, left-behind setting, raw emotions and sincere worship often intersect:

> One Sunday morning, during the time for prayer requests, a member began describing her father's critical illness. Because she was close to her father, her request for prayer was frequently interrupted by tears. Those around her reached out a hand or nodded with sadness. Some found their eyes filling with tears. The woman finished her request as best as she could. Seated in the front row was Sadie. Sadie stood and walked up the aisle until she saw the woman in the middle of her row. Stepping over the feet of other people in the aisle, Sadie reached the woman, bent down on her knees, laid her head on the woman's lap, and cried with her. Sadie inconvenienced an entire row of people, stepped on their shoes, and forced them to make room for her, but none of us will ever forget that moment. Sadie is *still* teaching the rest of us what the odd compassion of Christ's church looks like.[1]

The Left-Behindness of Jesus

There is a *left-behind* ideal—the picturesque white-steepled church or the little brown church in the vale—that should not be confused with a left-behind church that consciously embraces its role as servant. This servant role is the New Testament model that was carried on into the early church—a model that is all but forgotten in a world that identifies worth with power, numbers, size, and money. Yet there are individuals and churches and even whole denominations that take seriously the call to simplicity, sacrifice, and discipleship. When I think of churches that embrace this standard, I'm reminded of Canadian Mennonites. Mennonites all over the world maintain these principles, but my encounters have been primarily in Canada. I call to mind a Mennonite community near Winnipeg, defined less by its plainness in dress and lifestyle than by its generosity with neighbors close by and around the world. That tradition is still alive among Mennonite communities today—Christians intentionally left behind. These are ones who take seriously Jesus's words of blessing to the poor in spirit, the meek, the merciful, the pure in heart, the peacemakers. This was a radical message for Jews of the first century, even as it is for Christians today.

There is a profound *left-behindness* in Jesus's call to discipleship. Those who take up the cross and follow Jesus are themselves left behind even as they leave others behind—mother, father, brother, sister. And their call to service is ministry to those left furthest behind, the least of these brothers and sisters who represent the incarnate Son, the definitive left-behind God. When we contemplate his lowly life and death on the cross, Jesus does not easily fit into the fashionable megachurch mentality of the twenty-first century. Jesus asks us today, "Who do you say that I am?" Our answer to that question ought to reflect an image of who we are as followers of Jesus—even as we recognize more fully the face of Jesus in the oppressed and the marginalized among us.

Indeed, is it possible that a genuine left-behind church in its humble authenticity points to Jesus in a way that no megachurch with all its user-friendliness could? Jesus said, "The first shall be last." Do we ever even remotely comprehend the meaning of those words in relation to how we do church? Is it possible that the successful churches accorded with great honor based on the world's standards might just end up with the least honor *when the roll is called up yonder*?

How then does a pastor or an ordinary layperson function in a megachurch world? One way is to *Become A Loser*. This was the slogan headlining posters on buses and elsewhere in New York City. The posters promoted a campaign sponsored by the Fifth Avenue Episcopal Church. Smaller print offered further details: "If you're looking for the courage to give up the things in this world that keep you from being the best you can be, give us a call. We'll help you lose your life and build a new one. After all, Jesus Christ lost everything, and he gained the whole world."[2]

Become A Winner is the message the church is offering today. The left-behind church is a loser by megachurch standards. And that's okay. But can this left-behind congregation, with pastoral care and leadership, lose its life and build a new one? That is the only question worth asking.

The emphasis on church growth and success that pastors face in the ministry derives little authority from Scripture. There certainly are examples of large numbers coming to see Jesus and large numbers that were added to the infant church. But when Jesus sent out his disciples, he warned of failure and setbacks. Failure—particularly in the image of the cross—is a dominant theme of discipleship. In calling his disciples, Jesus gave clear warnings—truth in advertising: "Anyone who does not take his cross and follow me is not worthy of me. Whoever finds his life will lose it, and whoever loses his life for my sake will find it" (Matt. 10:38–39). In reflecting on this passage, Leonard Sweet writes:

> How desperately we need to redefine what it means to have a successful church. Is success to be tallied on the tote-board of baptisms, budgets, buses, and buildings? Or is success to be measured instead, as Matthew 10 measures it, in terms of how much nerve we can muster to fail: to fail to become rich, as the church "Gets Poor" (vv. 9–10) in terms of what it keeps to itself, giving itself away in sacrificial self-surrender; to fail to become respectable, as the church "Gets into Trouble" (vv. 17–19; 34–35) in the world on behalf of the weak, the weary, the forlorn, and forgotten; to fail to become particularized, as the church "Gets Lost" (vv. 38–39) in a world of darkness and despair by concerning itself, not with how to get people *into* church, but with how to send people *out of* church; to fail to become relevant, as the church "Gets Obstinate" (vv. 27–28) in its resistance to trendy, half-baked theologies which are constantly being dished out by short-order theologians who stand ready to cook up some "special" in response to the social problem of the month, specials which end up littering the theological landscape in our "throw-away culture."[3]

"When Christians talk about what the church has to offer the world," writes Barbara Brown Taylor, "one thing we do not often mention is an adequate theology of failure." The primary reason for this is the success-focus of our culture. Everywhere we look, whether in business or academia or television commercials, the most important thing in life is being successful. The high-stakes competition means that many people will fail. But the very culture that "creates these conditions for failure is not equipped to deal with it." The only place where we will discover how to deal with failure is where the gospel is preached in an authentic way. "At church," Taylor continues, "the loser shows up right above the altar."

I go to church to remember this—not to hear about the victory of the cross but to be reminded that there is no shame in failure at the foot of the cross. . . . This is such good news that I cannot hear it often enough. Sometimes I have to listen really hard, especially when the hymns are full of triumph, the preacher is flawless and the bulletin offers me a dozen ways to become a better Christian, but as long as there is a cross in view I can usually resist these enticements to spiritual success.

Jesus was not pretending while he was hanging there. He really did lose everything. . . . When I am feeling my most hurt and futile, my most abandoned by God, I am not far from him but as close as I can get, poised to fail—spectacularly—in my own bid for true and lasting life.[4]

Paul's Theology of Failure

Where would the Christian faith be today if Saul (aka Paul) had not been converted on the road to Damascus? Imagine the past two thousand years without him. At the beginning of the term I challenge my church history students with a series of counterfactuals. What if, for example, Martin Luther had backed down when threatened by Pope Leo X? But I always start with the New Testament era. What if Paul had refused to acknowledge the voice of Jesus and had continued to persecute the church? Can any of us even conceive of how different civilization would be today? Paul's influence on the infant church was enormous, and the legacy of this first-century Jew, whether transmitted correctly or not, casts its beam not just on Christianity as a world religion but on American Christianity and American foreign policy and thus the whole planet. The extraordinary accomplishments of Paul—especially as a missionary and evangelist—have prompted missiologists to argue that his methods should be closely, if not precisely, emulated today. Roland Allen in his book *Missionary Methods: St. Paul's or Ours?* makes a strong case for this—if for no other reason than the fact that Paul's methods worked:

In little more than ten years St. Paul established the Church in four provinces of the Empire, Galatia, Macedonia, Achaia and Asia. Before AD 47 there were no Churches in these provinces; in AD 57 St. Paul could speak as if his work there was done. . . . This

is truly an astonishing fact. That Churches should be founded
so rapidly, so securely, seems to us today, accustomed to the difficulties, the uncertainties, the failures, the disastrous relapses of
our own missionary work, almost incredible. . . . Today if a man
ventures to suggest that there may be something in the methods
by which St. Paul attained such wonderful results worthy of our
careful attention, and perhaps of our imitation, he is in danger
of being accused of revolutionary tendencies.[5]

If Paul could realize such success in church growth, so also
should we—whether in a cross-cultural mission context or in
our own culture, so the reasoning goes. Paul is our model, and
we should follow his example as pastors and missionaries. For
some, however, Paul and his ministry are intimidating. He is
an impossible act to follow. But are we seeing Paul for who he
was? Michael Duncan, in an article entitled "The Other Side of
Paul," emphasizes the failures in ministry that Paul endured: "It
would almost seem as though Paul's early years produced little
fruit. . . . He had an incredible ministry, yes: but we must not
read the current heresy of triumphalism back into his life."[6]

This heresy includes the triumphalism sometimes associated
with church growth—that which emphasizes size and numbers.
But this was not the focus of Paul, who confided his hardships
and struggles as much as his successes. Paul acknowledged weakness and failure and proclaims the ultimate understated reversal:
"When I am weak then I am strong" (2 Cor. 12:10).

In his commentary on 2 Corinthians 10–13 entitled *From
Triumphalism to Maturity*, D. A. Carson asks, what if Paul had
written a letter to those supporting him that summarized his
successes:

I have established more churches; I have preached the Gospel
in more lands and to more ethnic groups; I have traveled more
miles; I have won more converts; I have written more books;
I have raised more money; I have dominated more councils; I
have walked with God more frequently and seen more visions; I
have commanded the greatest crowds and performed the most
spectacular miracles.[7]

"Many folks might have thought Paul more than a bit self-
absorbed and pompous, but they would have most likely con-

67

cluded that their money was well spent in supporting him financially."[8] But that is not what Paul wrote. Consider his personal testimony in 2 Corinthians 11:

> I have worked much harder, been in prison more frequently, been flogged more severely, and been exposed to death again and again. Five times I received from the Jews the forty lashes minus one. Three times I was beaten with rods, once I was stoned, three times I was shipwrecked, I spent a night and a day in the open sea, I have been constantly on the move. I have been in danger from rivers, in danger from bandits, in danger from my own country-men, in danger from Gentiles; in danger in the city, in danger in the country, in danger at sea; and in danger from false brothers. I have labored and toiled and have often gone without sleep; I have known hunger and thirst and have often gone without food; I have been cold and naked. Besides everything else, I face daily the pressure of my concern for all the churches.
>
> 2 Corinthians 11:23–28

From that passage Carson concludes that "it is almost as if the primary (if not the only) incontestable criterion of true apostle-ship is massive suffering in the service of Christ."[9]

In Paul's life and ministry, Duncan has derived a theology of failure: "Paul's ministry grew out of the soil of wilderness years, painful theological debate, ruptured friendships, spoiled church growth, numerous hardships and dubious project success." But despite the setbacks, "Paul could look back on all the failure, pain and hardships and still conclude that he had been running in the grandest run of all."[10]

Drawing from Paul, Martin Luther speaks of the theology of the cross, which he contrasts with the theology of glory. Today it is easy to fall into a spirit of triumphalism and glory. Some years ago I was talking with some students from a Methodist seminary who were commenting on a Methodist megachurch in Grand Rapids that was filling its pews with people who had come from Reformed churches. There was a triumphalistic air about what they were saying. I could imagine how some students from the seminary where I teach might speak in the same way if a Christian Reformed megachurch was growing at the expense of left-behind Methodist churches. But there is no room for such self-glory. "Where the Church recognizes her hopelessness and helplessness she finds the key to her continued existence as the Church of God in the World," Luther reminds us. "In her weakness lies her greatest strength. . . . The theology of the cross is thus a theology of hope for those who despair, then as now, of the seeming weakness and foolishness of the Christian Church."[11]

The most powerful Christian symbol of suffering and weakness is, of course, the cross. But the suffering of the cross does not surely exclude joy. Indeed, when Jesus was eating his last meal with his disciples, he seemed to offer an oxymoron by telling them that "these things I have spoken to you, that my joy may be in you" (John 15:11 RSV). The church that rises out of a theology of the cross—a theology of suffering and failure—should be a church of joy. But too often the church is left behind because it has lost its joy. "Could anyone guess by looking at us that joy is at the heart of what goes on in church Sunday after Sunday?" asks Frederick Buechner.

> Maybe in the freshness and fragrance of the flowers on the altar we catch some flicker of it, and in the candles' burning. Maybe we can feel some reverberation of it in just all of us being together as human beings longing for and reaching out for we are not quite sure what. Maybe every once in a great while something joyful stirs in us as the taste of wine touches our tongues or some phrase of a hymn or prayer or sermon comes alive for a second and touches our hearts. The crimson and peacock blue of a stained glass window with the sun shining through it can sometimes speak of it the way jewels do. But in all honesty I have to confess that I for one have found little joy like that in the churches we go to year after year.[12]

Same Old, Same Old

Part of what we perceive as failure in the church today relates to a change in society. No longer does the church wield power as it once did. And without *power* the church cannot be successful—except, of course, the megachurches. They wield power by virtue of their very size.

The old world of church power, often referred to as Christendom, began with Emperor Constantine in AD 313 and ended on a Sunday evening in 1963. The setting was Greenville, South

Carolina. That was the night that "in defiance of the state's time-honored blue laws, the Fox Theater opened on Sunday," and seven Methodist adolescents slipped out the back door of their nearby church and substituted a John Wayne movie for their regular youth group.

> That evening has come to represent a watershed in the history of Christendom, South Carolina style. On that night, Greenville, South Carolina—the last pocket of resistance to secularity in the Western world—served notice that it would no longer be a prop for the church. There would be no more free passes for the church, no more free rides. The Fox Theater went head to head with the church over who would provide the world view for the young. That night in 1963, the Fox Theater won the opening skirmish.[13]

Instead of recognizing that this was a positive turning point, many people lament the status of the church today—a church that has no more free passes and is not propped up by culture. What they fail to realize is that this is the way it is supposed to be, the way it was for the first generations of Christians.

While some churchmen seem to argue that increased size and influence is the answer to the left-behind church, others insist the issue is *relevance*. New ideas that speak to the present generation are the only way to turn around the church. This is the perspective Brian McLaren offers in *A New Kind of Christian: A Tale of Two Friends on a Spiritual Journey*. "Doesn't the religious community . . . have anything fresh and incisive to say?" he asks. "Isn't it even asking any new questions? Has it nothing to offer than the stock formulas that it has been offering? Is there not a Saint Francis . . . or C. S. Lewis in the house with some fresh ideas and energy?"[14]

In a *Christianity Today* editorial Mark Galli responds to McLaren's questions, pointing out that Lewis, by his own testimony, made no effort to be "original" and that whether he was dealing with "the problem of pain" or "mere Christianity," anything that was new or "novel" was "a result of my ignorance." So also with Saint Francis. "He so patterned his life on Jesus' teachings that many refer to him as 'the second Christ.'" McLaren challenges his readers with what he appears to think is a slam-dunk question: "Has the 'good news' been reduced to the 'good same-old same-old'?" Galli again responds: "In fact, it needs to be *expanded* to the same-old same-old. Otherwise, it will never be good news but only postmodern news. Our culture needs more than that."[15]

The left-behind church is a place where authentic spirituality has potential to flourish. In many ways it is much easier for a pastor and people to display a pretense of spirituality in a megachurch where seminars, conferences, and growth groups are polished and professional. But in the church where growth charts are as flat as a Midwestern prairie, people are real people. Phony spirituality is spotted in an instant.

In most people's minds, the left-behind church is the last place to *get spiritual*. Yet the occasions for spiritual growth are only an optical illusion away, as Steve Bierly suggests. He tells of going to the Schenectady Children's Museum and enjoying the *eye tricks* with his kids. One of the common ones we have all seen is a drawing of either a young woman with a fancy hat or an old crone, depending on one's optical perspective. As he tried to focus his eyes, he realized the picture was an analogy of his ministry. "If I looked at it one way, it was a drag, a trial, a frustration, even a curse. But if I looked at it another way it was exciting, a chance for spiritual growth, a joy, and a blessing." An important aspect of spiritual growth is humility, and one of the *blessings* to which Bierly testifies is that ministry in a small church serves to keep him humble, and that such circumstances may be God's very means of bestowing humility. Being "stranded in a forgotten part of God's kingdom," he confesses has potential benefits.[16]

The megachurch movement does not reflect the theological underpinnings of the cross and of failure. The mall churches exude success and greatness. *The last shall be first. When I am weak, then I am strong.* Here the left-behind church has an opportunity to stand out as an authentic countercultural model in the world of Christendom today.

Burnout in the Parsonage and Parish

Despite the mesmerizing fiction set in the small-town church, those who play the main characters in the real-life stories often find their days enveloped in boredom. "These were gray months for my wife and me," writes Richard Lischer, a pastor of a rural Lutheran church in southern Illinois. "We seemed to be shriveling into people who haunted an old house and an older church." They had been graduate students who browsed bookstores, sipped wine, and discussed high culture and philosophy. "In the space of a few months we had become creatures of the sanctuary, the parish hall, the drafty parsonage, my office, and the cemetery. . . . Everything in our lives was occurring within a one-hundred-foot radius of our new washer and dryer."[1]

Many left-behind churches still have a parsonage. Whether this dwelling is actually called a *parsonage* or a *rectory* or a *manse*, the residence of the pastor and family has a different aura than does an ordinary dwelling. That was true in times past and is still true in situations where the minister and family actually live in a home adjacent to the church or where the pastor's home doubles as a center for hospitality. But more significant than the house itself is the behind-the-scenes family goings-on of the parsonage.

This house is supposed to be a holy space where pious people dwell. But ministers and their families are regular folks. Their sins and foibles are of special interest and thus are the topic of biography and fiction in every era and in every denomination. What goes on behind the closed door of the parsonage? The structure is sometimes referred to as a glass house. It's difficult to keep secrets—especially if the manse is close to the church. Screen doors and windows are open in the summer, and even in the winter a deacon standing on the porch hears things he's not supposed to hear. The minister's wife often suffers the consequences. (The minister's *husband* does not typically feel as much pressure as does the wife.) The book titles speak for themselves: Denise Turner's *Home Sweet Fishbowl: Confessions of a Minister's Wife* and Frances Nordland, *The Unprivate Life of a Pastor's Wife.*[2]

The minister is not like other professionals, whose spouse and children are often so far in the background that they would not be recognized by fellow workers. Nor is this minister like the megachurch minister who is one of several—or dozens—on the pastoral staff where there is typically no single prominent pastor's wife. (Aren't all megachurch ministers' spouses *wives?*) But in the left-behind church, the family and personal life of the pastor are in plain view for all to see. Such a ministry and life can be delightful—a beloved, small-town minister and family finding baskets of fruit and bottles of maple syrup on their doorstep and volunteers offering everything from free babysitting to engine overhauls. *It's a wonderful life.*

Personal Reflections

My own knowledge of this behind-the-scenes activity comes from personal experience and from researching and writing *Private Lives of Pastors' Wives.* Here I studied marriages and family dynamics of fourteen women, from Katie (and Martin) Luther residing in a medieval manse in Wittenberg to Jill (and Stuart) Briscoe living in suburban Milwaukee. Analyzing their lives was in many ways easier than analyzing my own, but I discovered that the pain and dysfunction—and fulfillment and pleasure—of one era is little different from that of another. Looking back over my years as a pastor's wife during my first marriage, I tend to remember the goodwill, the community spirit, and the happy times. But during those years there were painful episodes—some so painful that, even with decades in between, I still cannot come to terms with them.

At twenty-seven, I embraced my new role as minister's wife. I knew before our life in the parsonage began (though we had purchased our own home) that I was different. This left-behind church was part of the IFCA (Independent Fundamentalist Churches of America), and though there were some women ministers in the embryonic stages of that movement, by the early 1970s women's roles had been vastly diminished. Not that I was a raving feminist. Indeed, at that time in my life, I had not even contemplated the idea of women ministers, and the emerging feminist movement completely passed me by. But by personality and aspirations, I was anything but a subdued, submissive lady. I was finishing my doctoral work in history at a nearby university, where socialist (and Marxist) teachings had profoundly altered my thinking. I was a fundamentalist, to be sure, but a fundamentalist who voted for every Socialist candidate on the ballot and a fundamentalist who carried in her purse a little red book containing the sayings of Mao. I kept my philosophical views in the shadows and behind closed doors, but at the same time I saw no conflict with my college background in theology and biblical studies (including two years of Greek) and my new political and social perspective. Nor did I see conflict with my role as first lady of the parish.

What conflict there may have been about me (in the minds of the parishioners) related more to lifestyle, a matter that I confess in the introduction to my book on pastors' wives: "I sought too much to identify with teenagers (and am horrified as I look back at the photos of my stylish short skirts of the early 1970s)."[3] As I look back now, I imagine there must have been a lot of whispering about my immodesty, but at the time I was oblivious to any such gossip. Rather, I was very conscious of their support. If they were rolling their eyes behind my back at my short skirts, to my face they expressed appreciation for my reaching out to the young people and bonding with them. I charmed the visitors—as did my husband—and the church grew.

But in the parsonage there was tension that sometimes exploded in anger. Ministers and their wives are just as vulnerable—or more so—to marriage problems as are couples outside the profession. Their *fallenness* is no less part of their human natures than is that of their parishioners. In my husband's case, there were deep, unresolved problems that had troubled him since childhood, which subsequently would lead to his dismissal as pastor and follow him into the next pastorate and beyond. But in the meantime we fought those demons behind closed doors. At home, with the door locked, I was often angry and bitter. I yelled and screamed and wept—sometimes shouting in rage. "But you told me these problems were behind you! You told me the previous arrests and counseling had changed things!" But in church and at social functions, I was the smiling, encouraging wife—always at his side for support.

Where does a pastor's wife go for help in the 1970s or even today? If her story gets out, it will end her husband's profession. It will result in public embarrassment. And most dreaded of all, it will bring disgrace to the cause of Christ.

It will disgrace the cause of Christ. How often those words rang in my subconscious as I sobbed in secret. Is there any way to resolve this terrible mess I'm in? Is there anyone I can trust with my story? Fear gripped me. My story remained secret for several years until my teenage son, who often witnessed domestic violence, insisted otherwise. We escaped and reached out for help.

Leaving Ruin

Sometimes the secrets behind the parsonage doors are very different. In fact, there is sometimes a siege mentality with pastor and family holed up in the house with the big, bad world on the outside—a world represented by the enemies in the congregation. One of the best books detailing this scenario is a novel, *Leaving Ruin*.[4] I learned of the book through Dick Staub, whose radio program is heard by millions. His words whet my appetite: "This weekend I finally read Jeff Berryman's *Leaving Ruin*, and I am urging everybody to read it. In my dark distant past I pastored a church straight out of seminary. It was the most enriching, rewarding and life-threatening experience of my life. Berryman captures all that and more in this tale of a pastor with a rich inner life and a tad too much honesty, who is about to be voted out of his church. Read it and weep."[5]

The story is about the Reverend Cyrus Manning, his wife, Sara, and their two sons, who have been living in the parsonage in Ruin, Texas, for eleven years and are on the verge of being kicked out. The process of going through this ordeal spans from August 17 to November 23, though there are many flashbacks to fill in the gaps of time gone by. This is not the first time that Cyrus has been in this predicament: "Once back in my former congregation in East Texas, I stood up on a Sunday morning and tried to preach on the comedy of the cross," he confesses, "because . . . Frederick Buechner does it beautifully, but he's Presbyterian, and I'm not. That afternoon, the elders called me into their office and said there was nothing funny about it. I lost my job then and there."[6]

Now Cyrus is in Ruin, pastor of First Church, with a respectable size of some three hundred people in the pews on any given Sunday. The church sign carries a subtitle, "A Church of the Bible"—one added long before Cyrus came because there had been "a series of inquiries wondering if the church of Ruin might be a satanic cult." But even the subtitle did not fully define the congregation. "As a Bible church, its beliefs are non-descript, not easily defined," he explains, "one of those amorphous flavors that pop up when people get tired of creeds and traditions, and decide to split, and divide, and innovate—all to the glory of . . . well, you get the picture. The initial founders—the first eighteen—were a mixed bunch; a couple of Baptists, two Church of Christ couples, and at least five Presbyterians. . . . They wanted to get closer to the Bible, they said."[7]

But Cyrus is not helping the people get closer to the Bible. In fact, he has more questions than he has answers. And they want answers. Whether the matter is homosexuality or non-Christian religions or some other hot-button issue, they want answers in black and white. There are no gray areas. Sara senses things have gone wrong even before Cyrus does.

> Sara turned back to the kitchen without a word. I stood rock still, knowing it was coming, and soon she was back, angry, but trying to rein it in as best she could.
> "They don't want us, Cyrus."

She said she saw Francis at the drug store on Tuesday, and said hi, and Francis didn't speak. Literally. And that she was in the bathroom at church Wednesday night, and heard Tina Cooser say Sam met with Jack and Roland, and that Sam said if we weren't gone by Christmas, he knew 30 families that would leave and start a new church, where they taught the truth, instead of this damn junk. She said she came out of the stall, and Tina looked at her, and didn't even stop to take a breath, but just kept going on and on about Sam and Jack and Roland, and how they told Sam it was all going to be okay *that things were in the works.* It's getting old, Cyrus, Sara threw at me, and I didn't sign up for this. Wayne didn't get invited to Carl's birthday party, and he cried about it, and I don't know why you won't do something, Cyrus, and I said I know you didn't sign up for this, you didn't sign up for being alive, either—none of us did.[8]

The following week Cyrus met the church's biggest contributor, Harry Johns, at his country club for lunch. "I'm a wuss," Cyrus confesses. "He has oil wells." Harry accused Cyrus of preaching on compassion, which was really "a piece of rhetoric, a fancy synonym for liberal, a good word kidnapped and used in a way God would hate, and that true compassion was in telling the truth . . . that it was time for this church to get serious, get new elders, get new programs, and when was I going to stop mealy-mouthing the gospel."[9]

The Diary of a Country Priest

The parsonage—or rectory—for the Catholic priest is very different from the home of the Protestant minister. The distractions of family difficulties are absent—no marital stress or little ones crying in the night with earaches. But the struggle of trying to keep a parish of people excited about spiritual matters comes in every denominational stripe. "Mine is a parish like all the rest. They're all alike," the country priest pens in his diary. "My parish is bored stiff; no other word for it. Like so many others! We can see them being eaten up by boredom, and we can't do anything about it. Some day perhaps we shall catch it ourselves." His is a little village parish in France, the fictional author of *The Diary of a Country Priest.* But if he is down on his parish and toys with doubts about himself, the older priest whom he visits confirms his self-deprecation. "I'm wondering what you've got in your veins these days, you young priests! When I was your age we had *men* in the church . . . heads of parish, masters, my boy, *rulers*. They could hold a whole country together. . . . Nowadays the seminaries turn out little choirboys. . . . They go snivelling around instead of giving orders. They read stacks of books . . . whining that the priesthood isn't quite what they imagined."[10]

For the young priest, however, the parish is much more than a place to rule. He has high ideals and he longs for his life to have meaning. His prayers are his longings—for himself as much as for his parish:

> This morning I prayed hard for my parish, my poor parish, my first and perhaps my last, since I ask no better than to die here. My parish! The words can't even be spoken without a kind of soaring love. . . . I know that my parish is a reality, that we belong to each other for all eternity; it is not a mere administrative fiction, but a living cell of everlasting Church. But if only the good God would open my eyes and unseal my ears, so that I might behold the face of my parish and hear its voice. . . . What does it want of me? Does it even want anything of me? . . . Whatever I were to do, were I to pour out my last drop of blood (and indeed sometimes I fancy the village has nailed me up here on a cross and is at least watching me die) I could never possess it. . . . I can never forget it has been there for centuries. . . . I am merely a passer-by. . . . A terrible night. No sooner had I shut my eyes than desolation came upon me. . . . How little we know what a human life really is—even our own.[11]

The lament of the country priest makes us wonder why he stays. He's not appreciated, and both he and the church might be better off if he left. But a theology of the cross and of failure recognizes that suffering has it purposes. His own desolation allows him to reach out more effectively to others in their desolation. The pastor must be able to identify with those who hurt.

Identifying with Those Who Hurt

When things go wrong—badly wrong in the left-behind church—who is to blame, the pastor or the congregation? Robert Moeller tells of his experience in two different churches. One was an inner-city ministry. It consisted of "a group of people who once had been ready to disband and give their building to a parachurch organization." But after he had served as their pastor for five years, the church was alive and well. "It was feeding local street people and attracting Native Americans to worship services. It distributed hundreds of pounds of clothes to the destitute." Reflecting back on the experience, he writes, "My wife and I were overwhelmed with the love we received in that small, urban church." Their farewell dinner was on a Sunday afternoon that could only be termed *sweet sorrow*. But less than three years later on another Sunday afternoon in another church, the setting and atmosphere were very different. "The . . . afternoon began with an awkward lunch. The atmosphere reminded me of the meal following a funeral. . . . What had begun sixteen months earlier as minor skirmishes was now full-blown conflict. . . . I had hoped that with the help of . . . men from the outside, we could confront the issues directly and resolve the conflict. . . . My wife and I were exhausted from the hit-and-run warfare. We had nothing left to give."[12]

Moeller and his wife and children left that church amid pain and sorrow, but as he considers the two pastoral experiences, his thoughts seem surprising: "I would gladly serve a thousand churches like the first, but I wouldn't trade all of them for my years in the church that I struggled so deeply." He confesses that when things were going well in his church, he enjoyed spending time with people he viewed as winners. "I had little time for someone who seemed headed nowhere. If colleagues were in trouble, it was their fault. . . . I'm afraid I walked past many a wounded pastor on the road to Jericho." He saw that same attitude in others. When he was sharing his struggles with a fellow pastor, the response seemed arrogant: "I've never experienced anything like that. . . . I can't remember anyone leaving my churches in anger." Moeller says that his initial hurt and anger turned to pity. "He couldn't help me at that moment because he was handicapped."[13] The humiliation that comes to a pastor who has been left behind by a congregation can serve as a powerful source for personal growth, especially as that pastor moves on and reaches out to others who are hurting.

Such feelings of self-doubt and humiliation are not known to the modern pastor alone. The Apostle Paul time and again expressed doubts and frustrations about his work and his lack of success, as did preachers of the gospel in the generations that followed him. The fourth-century priest, Gregory Nazianzen, was consumed with feelings of inadequacy when he entered his first parish fearing the task was "too high" for one such as himself who was unprepared to "guide and govern souls." Indeed, he became so overwhelmed with his incompetence that, barely ordained, he went AWOL ("he lost heart, deserted his congregation, and headed for the hills")—and not at a convenient time for the parish. It was Christmas. But after months of contemplating his cowardly deed, he returned—just in time for Easter. There was no warm welcome. In fact, the people were so upset with him they boycotted his preaching. In an effort to bring reconciliation, he wrote a letter confessing his insecurities. But now, he promised, he was back to stay—fearing a life of disobedience to God more than a life as a pastor.[14]

One could hope that Gregory settled down and became as beloved by his parish as the medieval priest in the prologue to Chaucer's *Canterbury Tales* must have been. Here we have a picture for all times of a left-behind pastor who is faithfully serving God:

> Wide was his parish, houses far asunder,
> But never did he fail, for rain or thunder,
> In sickness, or in sin, or any state
> To visit to the farthest, small and great,
> Going afoot, and in his hand, a stave.
> This fine example to his flock he gave,
> That first he wrought and afterwards he taught . . .
> There is nowhere a better priest, I trow.
> He had no thirst for pomp or reverence.
> But Christ's own lore, and his apostles twelve
> He taught, but first he followed himself.[15]

"A Stranger on the Earth"

One of the most famous left-behind ministers is known for his paintings, not his pastoral duties. But pain and failure in his short-lived ministry profoundly influenced his personality and his artwork. Many people who browse art museums do not know that Vincent van Gogh was not only the son of a minister but also a minister himself—though never ordained. Although his youthful life was surrounded by the church, his own interests lay elsewhere. But in 1876, at age twenty-three, while in England teaching at a school for boys headed by a minister, van Gogh's focus changed. He began an intense study of the Bible and underwent a religious transformation. With the minister's encouragement, he began speaking in the parish prayer meetings and at nearby, tiny Methodist churches. His real test for ministry came in his first sermon, one that amazingly has been preserved. It is difficult to evaluate a nineteenth-century sermon without context, but a psychologist would easily recognize some of van Gogh's struggles with depression coming through the text and even in his Scripture references.

The title of the sermon is "I Am a Stranger on the Earth," taken from Psalm 119:19. Life as a painful pilgrimage seemed to be the theme of his own life and this, his first sermon and the only one that has been preserved:

> Our earlier life might be compared to sailing on a river, but very soon the waves become higher, the wind more violent, we are at sea almost before we are aware of it—and the prayer from the heart ariseth to God: Protect me, O God, for my bark is so small and Thy sea is so great. The heart of man is very much like the sea, it has its storms, its tides and its depths.
>
> Does not every one of you feel with me the storms of life or their forebodings or their recollections?[16]

But Vincent van Gogh the preacher does not leave his listeners with fear and forebodings. He does not leave them hopeless. He sees the celestial city—perhaps not surprising in a work of art. His closing illustration is fitting:

> I once saw a very beautiful picture: it was a landscape at evening. In the distance on the right-hand side a row of hills appeared blue in the evening mist. Above those hills the splendour of the sunset, the grey clouds with their linings of silver and gold and purple. The landscape is a plain or heath covered with grass and its yellow leaves, for it was in autumn. Through the landscape a road leads to a high mountain far, far away, on the top of that mountain is a city wherein the setting sun casts a glory. On the road walks a pilgrim, staff in hand. He . . . goes on sorrowful

yet always rejoicing—sorrowful because it is so far off and the road so long. Hopeful as he looks up to the eternal city far away, resplendent in the evening glow.[17]

This sermon was a landmark event for van Gogh. "When I was standing in the pulpit, I felt like somebody who, emerging from a dark cave underground, comes back to the friendly daylight," he wrote to his brother Theo. "It is a delightful thought that in the future wherever I go, I shall preach the Gospel; to do that *well*, one must have the Gospel in one's heart. May the Lord give it to me."[18]

Soon after preaching this first sermon, Vincent van Gogh returned to Amsterdam, where he prepared for training in theological studies. Struggling with what some have conjectured was a learning disability, his progress was slow, and he failed to qualify for admission into an academic program. He later referred to this prolonged experience as "the worst time of my life."[19] Yet van Gogh refused to give up. He was convinced that God could use him in pastoral ministry. Through his persistence, the Dutch Reformed Church offered him a trial charge as an evangelist in one of the poorest districts in western Europe—the mining region of Borinage, Belgium. The duties, in addition to preaching sermons in a house church, involved caring for the sick and needy. His was what we might call *incarnational* ministry. He identified with the miners to the point of becoming one of them—giving away his possessions—and serving as a spiritual mentor. But his tenure was short—barely six months. His superiors were upset with his asceticism and released him from his duties. For his part, however, van Gogh refused to go away. He stayed on for more than a year—stripped of his official church duties—to serve the people and to *draw* the people. It was here that his art was born—depicting the poverty and pitiful conditions of the miners and their families.

Through his art, van Gogh painted the sermons he was not able to preach in church—painting sermons for generations of pastors who would follow, including Henri Nouwen, who was profoundly influenced by his fellow Dutchman. Of van Gogh, Nouwen wrote: "I experienced connections between Vincent's struggle and my own, and realized more and more that Vincent was becoming my wounded healer. He . . . gave me the courage to go further and deeper in my search for a God who loves."[20] Yet van Gogh had concluded that his ministry was over after he left Borinage. One of his works reflects his feeling of rejection as a pastor. In a painting entitled *Still Life with Open Bible, Candlestick, and Novel,* he sought to move beyond his failure in ministry. The symbolism was striking. The Bible lay open, but the flame on the candle alongside had gone out.

After little more than a decade as an artist, Vincent van Gogh's pilgrimage to the celestial city ended abruptly. "In a small village outside of Paris," writes Denny Gunderson, "Vincent Van Gogh, age 37, pulled the trigger on a revolver aimed at his heart and committed suicide [dying two days later]. The young man who wanted to be a pastor died penniless and in deep depression. It was only after his death that Van Gogh became famous as an artist and was recognized as an innovator of Expressionism, the idea of emotional spontaneity in painting."[21]

Pressure to Perform

For many pastors the pressure to perform is stressful— pressure from the congregation, from colleagues, and from unrealistic expectations generated by professors and mentors. This is the testimony of Douglas Brouwer, who served for twelve years as pastor of a large Presbyterian church in Wheaton, Illinois, and has since moved to a still larger church (more than 2,000 people) in Ann Arbor. In 1999 he reflected back on his almost twenty years of ministry and how that was shaped by "a beloved seminary professor" at Princeton:

> Start out, he said, on the staff of a large church. "If you go to a small church, people will always think of you as a small church pastor." Once you get to the large church, "learn the ropes" from a mentor.
>
> After a few years ("Don't stay too long or get too comfortable," he said, "or people might get the idea that you like being an associate pastor") you should look for "your own church," preferably a large one.
>
> And then, after a few years of hard work, the payoff, he said, would be the call to become pastor of Fifth Avenue Presbyterian Church in New York City. In my tradition at the time, Fifth Avenue

was the top of the heap in terms of membership and prestige. That was the prize for success in ministry.[22]

Numbers and prestige are part of the career path for the minister. But surely they are not enough. Ever so insidiously, spirituality has become linked to numbers and prestige. It is in the megachurches, we unconsciously imagine, where the Spirit of God is most evident. It is there that God is pouring out his blessings.

Pastoral Failure in Safenwil

The young pastor moved into the Swiss industrial town of Safenwil on July 3, 1911. The parsonage—one of 247 houses in the village—was old and musty and not the kind of place to show off to his fiancée, Nelly Hoffmann. But the minister was devoted to his calling, emphasizing in his inaugural sermon: "I am not speaking to you of God because I am a pastor. I am a pastor because I *must* speak to you of God." Here in this depressed and some would say "God-forsaken" place, Karl Barth, regarded as the greatest theologian of the twentieth century, began his ministry as a country pastor. The son and grandson of ministers, he might have expected a more prestigious parish, but, to him, this was where God wanted him: "I had a very lively time in every respect in this Aargau village. It was there that I first began at least to become aware of the full scope of the task of a Reformed preacher, teacher and pastor."[23]

For Barth, however, ministry was not without troubles. "I always seemed to be beating my head against a brick wall," he confessed, convinced that "going to church is contrary to the nature of the people of the Aargau." He tried not to despair over church attendance, "which was usually so sparse" that he was preaching to "gaping empty pews." He blamed himself for not being able to preach sermons that could speak to the divided mentality of his congregation, influenced "on the one hand by rationalistic ideas of progress and on the other by sentimental pietism." It was his fault, not theirs. "I was sorry for everything that my congregation had to put up with," he later lamented. "I am tormented by the memory of how greatly . . . in the end I *failed* as a pastor of Safenwil."[24]

6

Megachurch Mania

The year is 2005, as it was foretold fifteen years earlier by futurist and humorist Tom Raabe. In his book, *The Ultimate Church: An Irreverent Look at Church Growth, Megachurches & Ecclesiastical "Show Biz,"* he begins by picturing the biggest rage in church business after the turn of the millennium. The setting is southern California. The main character is Dr. Roy Dude, the pastor, with a strong supporting role played by Head Usher Simon Glibface, who is featured on the cover of *Christianity Today* and whose autobiography is titled *There's Life Beyond Name Tags*. First Ultra-Church of southern California "lays claim to 2.5 million souls"—increasing at the rate of some ten thousand members a month or "333 per day, 13.9 per hour, and one every 5 minutes." To keep track of those millions, "Dude has 166,279 cell groups, 172,346 deacons, and 12,820 full-time staff."

Church life in 2005 has moved far beyond the 1980s and 90s. First Ultra "makes the Crystal Cathedral look like a house church" by comparison. Tom Raabe, the author, in the company of other interested ministers, is visiting the church—and the tour guide is Usher Glibface. He is most impressed by the train system with stations at various points throughout the facility. More efficient than an airport, people are picked up from and returned to their parked cars a mile away. But even more remarkable is the "Cry

Room" with three thousand cribs. Glibface had the description and statistics on the tip of his tongue: "We have on hand 16,000 rattles, 4,000 dolls, 2,000 washettes, and 4,000 crib mobiles," and pointing to a huge bin, he said with a touch of pride, it "has the capacity to process 50,000 diapers a day."[1]

But First Ultra is not just about numbers, as Usher Glibface emphasizes. It's about land acquisition—like the present location acquired in 1995, when Dude purchased the Los Angeles Airport (LAX), with the airport relocating at a nearby landfill. The numerical growth and massive facilities did not come about by human endeavor alone, Glibface emphasizes. Prayer was critical, as is illustrated by the innovation of the rail system:

> "For five years we ringed the sanctuary with lots," Glibface said. "And when those were filled, we paved lots behind them, and more behind them. Finally, in 2001, attendance plateaued at 1.8 million. And curiously, our lots were only at 71 percent capacity. It was a crisis time for First Ultra. Dr. Dude prayed and fasted for a week on Mount Baldy, and when he came down, he imparted to us the Principle of Distance Strangulation: People will not willingly walk more than three-quarters of a mile from parking spot to sanctuary. At a ballgame, maybe. At church, no way. We had near-empty lots sitting a mile from church. . . . Dr. Dude toyed with purchasing surplus army helicopters—they seat fifty-five. But finally he chose light rail. We experienced a little backdoor loss from that—200,000 members. But we gained that number back in no time."[2]

What for Raabe is good humor, Os Guinness has found deadly serious. In his provocative title, *Dining with the Devil: The Megachurch Movement Flirts with Modernity*, he offers a sober assessment of superchurches. Written in 1993, the descriptions sound as though they were penned last week. But every decade has its innovations and media scoops. The megachurch that Guinness features is not the largest but rather the one that most symbolizes his concern about "dining with the devil."

The Mall of America opened to fanfare and frenzied media hype in the summer of 1992. It was billed as the largest enclosed retail and entertainment mall in North America. Everyone seemed to be awed, including my brother, who is anything but a shopper. But in an effort to impress his older sister with his beloved Twin Cities, he provided the transportation and I dutifully acted impressed. We went to "Camp Snoopy," with its seven acres of amusements, and took a ride on the roller coaster. What I did not realize at the time was that the mall also was home to a megachurch, an extension of Wooddale Church, held in the rotunda between Sears and Bloomingdale's. Six thousand came to the first service, which was dubbed "A Sunday Mallelujah" by the Minneapolis *Star Tribune*. When a press report described this new church as "a kind of mega-mall of surburban soul saving," one of the pastors agreed and added, "We're going to bring the mall a lot of business. We've suggested to our people that they wear comfortable clothes in which to do any shopping they have in mind after lunch."[3]

So what's the problem? Is Guinness overreacting? "The problem is not the presence of a church in a mall," he warns, "but the presence of the mall in the church."[4] There lies the problem for all churches—and particularly those, whether located in malls or not, that have become part of the consumer culture and all that goes with it. Indeed, malls have been labeled *cathedrals of consumption*, and churches are too easily reverse-labeled as *superstores of spirituality*.

For Guinness, the issue is much larger than a church in a mall. He warns of a "crisis of cultural authority" that is "sapping the very vitality of the United States." He argues that "Americans are no longer shaped by beliefs, ideals, and traditions as they once were."[5] But even worse is the fact that evangelical Christianity is part of the crisis—and perhaps more accurately, contributing to the crisis. Instead of standing as a countercultural force, the Christian church is joining in.

Was Guinness's warning heeded? Have things changed in the past dozen years, or has the headlong fall into the abyss only increased in momentum?

The *Meaning* of Megachurch

When I was growing up, we defined churches by denomination. They might be big churches (over two hundred) or medium or small, but the most important factor was whether it was a Baptist or Catholic or Lutheran or Pentecostal church. And we knew all the subdivisions as well. However, megachurches have little to do with denomination. They are all the same. *If you've seen one, you've seen 'em all!* Well, not really. But in most cases it would be very difficult to tell the difference between a Baptist or Methodist or Reformed or Assemblies of God megachurch—without first reading the fine print.

What is a megachurch? The term is readily bandied about, but no two definitions are alike—at least not as far as I have discovered in my research. The one definition I found most interesting—and perhaps most true to life—is offered by Leith Anderson, the minister of Wooddale Church, which sponsored the Sunday services in the Mall of America. He ought to qualify as one who knows the definition of a megachurch:

> Megachurches have 2,000 or more people at worship services each weekend. They are like large shopping malls offering a broad array of services to enormous numbers of people. Megachurches have large staffs, require expansive facilities, operate on multimillion dollar budgets, provide an impressive variety of services, tend to be leader led, and often have excellent preaching and music. . . .
>
> It is important to recognize that megachurches are not large versions of minichurches, just as a train is not a large car. They are different kinds of churches. They relate differently. They minister differently. They see themselves differently.[6]

Mega Marketing

Like any large corporation, a megachurch is involved in marketing. Marketing involves selling a product to more and more people so that the company can grow larger. Whatever a large company does to grow and bring in more revenue, so does the megachurch. There is advertising, trend analysis, product assessment, and headhunters in charge of securing top-notch managers—all in an effort to sell products or services. Ministers who once lamented the difficulties of managing an all-volunteer organization no longer face that situation in a megachurch. Here there is a large, paid staff that more closely resembles a large, nonprofit organization than a church. Elders and deacons no longer serve in volunteer capacities to conduct church business and minister to the disadvantaged. Instead, a board of directors oversees the paid professionals who work as employees. These employees often supervise large numbers of volunteers who serve with very little decision-making authority.

"Church marketers assume that marketing is a neutral process or technique that leaves the substance of the faith untouched." These are the words of Philip Kenneson and James Street in their book, *Selling Out the Church: The Dangers of Church Marketing*. When I read that sentence, I wished I had written it myself, and I wished I had hammered the truth of it into my students in my course last fall on Church Revitalization. We are always looking for the latest church growth methods, concepts, or fads—very often without any thought of how the very methods affect the gospel. "Said another way," the authors continue, "church marketers believe that marketing affects only the *form* in which the faith is presented, not the *content* of the faith itself. This assumption about the neutrality of marketing takes the church marketers off the theological hook."[7]

We too easily assume that we *do* church like we *do* other forms of marketing. I'll never forget coming back to my college church in Texas after having spent a summer selling encyclopedias. I had been the top student sales rep in the Minneapolis office and had been promoted to team manager. I had won some nice prizes and paid for my next year's schooling—all with a moderately good conscience. I was sometimes bothered that I had sold a set to someone who could not afford it, but I assuaged my guilt by remembering that I had emphasized that their monthly payments were less than the two-pack-a-day cigarette habit they appeared to have. Surely reading encyclopedias is a better activity than smoking. Returning to school, I assumed my sales expertise would be set aside, but word got back to my pastor about my success. He contacted me and asked if I would work with him in the door-to-door evangelism program the church was initiating. I agreed. Never did it occur to either of us that one would sell encyclopedias differently than one would sell the gospel. I taught the group all the little techniques of how to get a foot in the door, how to get someone to say *yes* when they really wanted to say *no*, and how to push a decision before someone was ready.

It embarrasses me as I reflect back. The gospel was not really the gospel as we went door-to-door selling it. *Form* has a strange ability to change *content* more than we could ever imagine. So it is with church growth techniques. "Marketing is a value-laden enterprise rooted in specific sets of convictions," write Kenneson and Street. "Having management techniques at one's disposal encourages one to see all people as objects to be managed and controlled, just as having marketing techniques at the center of the picture encourages one to view the entire world as a series of manageable exchanges."[8]

Yet the concept of *marketing* the church is widely touted by George Barna and other church growth experts. Indeed, Barna laments that the vast majority of churches in America do "not have a marketing perspective." Rather, they engage in "marketing by default" which "inevitably leads to failure by neglect." Churches fail for the same reason that businesses fail. "Sadly, research studies have shown that marketing [strategy] . . . is absent in more than nine out of ten evangelical churches. Most churches, by marketing standards, are failures: that is, they are not maximizing their potential for profit (i.e., ministry gains)."[9]

Mega Stats

For those fascinated by numbers, megachurch statistics can be most entertaining. There were only ten Protestant megachurches in 1970 (those with 2,000 or more in weekly worship services). Three decades later, there were more than five hundred, with a new one emerging every few weeks. This information was gleaned in 2001 by a reporter from the *Miami Herald*, a newspaper representing a city and state known for some of the country's largest churches. But according to an article in 2003 in the *Arizona Republic*, "California leads . . . with 101 megachurches attended weekly by 364,612 people." Arizona's megachurches, however, "are truly 'mega.' Attendance per church averages nearly 4,800 people, dwarfing California's average of 3,600."[10]

Megachurches make news. They are not good fodder for fiction and stories, but they serve up statistics with relish. And they serve as a benchmark for all other churches. Both pastors and laity look to the superchurches as a standard by which to measure success or failure. "Has this obsession with church growth and the megachurch been something that clergy have historically been enamored with?" asks Samuel Rima. "Or, is this actually a relatively new emphasis within the ranks of the ordained?" He answers his own question by stating that today—at least among evangelicals—the universal "sign of success is church growth." Many church leaders would insist otherwise, but Rima continues, "Try as we might to subdue the mega-church monster of success [it] constantly seems to stalk us. . . . The seminars in which we have been encouraged to participate have fed this obsession."[11]

Mega Mighty

What do you call a church that is bigger than all the other megachurches? There ought to be a name—one that has more class than *supersized* or *jumbo*. Size is everything when speaking in megachurch terms, and if size of membership is not at the very top, then size of stadium will do. So it is with Houston's Lakewood Church, which signed a thirty-year, $12.3 million lease on the Compaq Center, which in previous days was home to basketball and hockey. The costs far exceed the lease payment, when the renovation price tag approaching one hundred million dollars is factored in. But the property features more than "16,000 seats, two waterfalls, and an interior camera ready for Sunday broadcasts" and "a state-of-the-art hydraulic stage;" it also comes with "celestial bragging rights" as the largest church in America. But for how long? There are other stadiums being vacated across the country, and megachurch managers are visiting Lakewood and checking out the possibilities for their own expansion.

> That has made rejected sports arenas, faced with demolition, fertile ground for religious conversion. It may be a commercial real estate boomlet in its infancy. . . . Interest appears to be growing. Joel Osteen, the 41-year-old pastor of Lakewood Church, said half a dozen pastors from around the country had asked him how he went about signing the 30-year . . . lease. . . . Church leaders, he said, realize they have to be inventive these days. "You have to change with the times," he said. "If Jesus were here he'd change with the times. He couldn't ride around on a donkey."[12]

By 2004 statistics showed that there were some 850 Protestant megachurches in the United States, up from a mere ten in 1970.

Perhaps not surprisingly, four out of the top six are located in Texas. "Already the fastest-growing congregation in the country with more than 30,000 members, Lakewood in its new home will eclipse the 27,000-member Crenshaw Christian Center of Los Angeles as the biggest church in the nation—16,000 seats versus 10,000 or so at Crenshaw Christian Center's landmark FaithDome."[13]

As I was reading this story, the Astrodome kept crossing my mind. During my college days in the late 1960s, I attended a Billy Graham Crusade in that vast arena. It was a silly thought—until I read the following sentences on my computer screen: "There are some sports venues that have been discarded by pro teams but have yet to be made over as megachurches. Houston's multi-purpose Astrodome, for example, sits vacant." This 60,000-seat building is in good condition, but no church needs that much space. Osteen, who presides over Lakewood, is not so sure. "I think there could be a day when we see 75,000 [congregants] instead of 25,000," he says. "I think there's that potential."[14]

American churches are small, however, in comparison to the world's granddaddies of megachurches, some claiming member-ship into the hundreds of thousands—though numbers some-times appear to be rounded off to the nearest ten thousand. And some statistics on churches change almost overnight. "Churches which had an attendance of 300,000 a decade ago, such as 'Ondas del Luz y Amor' in Buenos Aires, now have 'only' 70,000." And some numbers are overstated. "Yonggi Cho's church in Seoul claims a membership of 773,000, but an attendance of 'only' 253,000 in the main church and most important satellites." This is the largest church in the world (according to the *Friday Fax* website) with three tying for second place—ones in Abidjan, Ivory Coast; Santiago, Chile; and Bogotá, Colombia.[15]

Just the other day when I was helping Sagarga, a new seminary student from Nigeria, with an Internet assignment, a website popped up on the screen telling about the third largest church in the world—Deeper Life Bible Church in Lagos, Nigeria. It numbers only 120,000 in average attendance—not apparently enough, how-ever, to confer its self-determined third place. Founded in 1973 by W. R. Kumunyi, a university math teacher, the church "on a recent Sunday . . . saw 74,000 adults worshipping together with 40,000 children meeting in a separate building across the street."[16]

After Sagarga left my office, I began searching for churches that were larger than the Deeper Life Bible Church, and I came upon the Hartford Institute for Religion Research, which listed in its megachurch database churches by alphabetical order. There right in front of me was the Ada Bible Church in Ada, Michigan (3,500 in attendance), with Jeff Manion listed as senior pastor. He was one of my good students years ago when I taught at Grand Rapids School of the Bible and Music—learned all his church history from me, I like to think. It reminded me again how common the megachurch phenomenon is today, and I wondered momentarily if that makes me a grandmother of sorts of a megachurch. When Jeff began as pastor, as I recall, Ada Bible was a little left-behind country church with some thirty in attendance.

A Mega Mentality

Although megachurches appear to easily buy into all that is cutting edge in contemporary culture, their theological tastes are decidedly conservative—evangelical and fundamentalist (including Pentecostal and charismatic subsets). According to Rob Marus, Southern Baptists are particularly tuned into the megachurch mentality because they, perhaps more than any other denomination, measure success in terms of numbers of baptisms or converts. "The more conservative and evangelical the church, the more important growth is," he argues. "It becomes almost a jockeying contest to see how many you can attract, how many you can convert, and how many you can baptize."[17] It is no accident that every one of the presidents of the Southern Baptist Convention in the past two decades has been a senior pastor of a megachurch.

Marus, who grew up in a large church in suburban Little Rock, is alarmed not only by such churches' often fundamentalist bent but by their tendency and capacity to grow at all costs, often to the detriment of the neighborhoods that surround them. In the case of churches like Hyde Park Baptist, he says, "It's an attitude of 'We want to be the biggest and the best and prove to everybody how special we are, and by the way, it's God's will because we're getting more people to know Christ.'" In reality, such churches may be stealing members from other churches that aren't doing as well. "It's a spiritualized version of the American idea of manifest destiny: it's our right, our destiny, and God's will for this expansion to happen," he says. But "in many ways, it's the most un-Christian thing in the world" for churches to pave over neighborhoods in order to expand.[18]

Yet these churches have incredible appeal, to which the numbers obviously attest. This is the conclusion of Kris Axtman, writing for the *Christian Science Monitor*: "Take the DeSelles, for instance. They have been coming to Lakewood for 16 years but at one point, grew tired of the 70-mile round-trip drive each Sunday." Finding nothing that could offer anything comparable to Lakewood, they returned for the sake of their teenage children. "On the stage below, the band cranks up as the Jumbotrons display a barrage of MTV-quality music videos produced in-house. The lights flash and the crowd rises to its feet, those in the upper balconies feeling 'just a little closer to the rapture.'"[19]

Black and Mega

The profile of a megachurch pastor in North America is a white male in his forties, and most of those who participate in megachurch worship are white. But in recent years, according to an article in *Ebony*, "stadium-sized megachurches have sprung up across Black America. They have emerged as the new spiritual symbols of the Black community, with thousands and thousands of members, popular television ministries and strong economic development programs." There are some one hundred such churches, mostly in the South:

> Among the largest megachurches are the Faithful Central Bible Church in Inglewood, California, the former home of the Los Angeles Lakers, which seats 17,505; the New Birth Missionary Baptist Church Cathedral in Lithonia, Georgia, which seats 10,000; the FaithDome of the Crenshaw Christian Center in Los Angeles, which seats 9,780; Jericho City of Praise Church in Landover, Maryland, which seats 10,000; World Changers Church International, which seats 8,900; and The Potter's House in Dallas, which seats 8,000. Also noted for their large seating capacity are Word of Faith International Christian Center in Southfield, Michigan,

which seats 5,000; the Apostolic Church of God in Chicago, which seats 4,500; and Christ Universal Temple in Chicago, which seats 4,000.[20]

Unlike the white megachurches, many of these have been "founded, or co-founded, by women, including Pastor Betty P. Peebles of Jericho City of Praise Church, the Rev. Johnnie Colemon of Christ Universal Temple and Pastor Taffi Dollar of World Changers Church International."[21]

Mega Messes

This obsession with church growth can create havoc in a church and leave it in shambles, as Rima testifies. He tells of a church in his neighborhood when he was in seminary in southern California. The pastor "was an extremely gifted preacher who was also a popular leader in local church circles." But the church was not growing. In an effort to spur church growth, he used the power of his position to push through a major building project—a new sanctuary. Those opposing the project had feared that the loan was a big risk for the size of the congregation. But he argued that "the building would be paid for with the help of those who joined the church as the result of the new sanctuary." Other churches in the area had undertaken building projects, and they were seeing growth. After the congregation voted by a small margin to launch the project, the work began. When it was completed, the church began reaching out into the community to publicize the event, but "their beautiful new facility was not attracting new attendees." Soon "the church was on the ropes financially and fighting for its life," writes Rima. "By the time I completed my seminary studies, the church was a mere shell of what it had been when I moved into the area."[22]

"Not . . . every church is called to be a large congregation." Those are the shocking words of Gene Appel and Alan Nelson, in their book, *How to Change Your Church without Killing It.* "Through history," they write, "people have taken a new thing God was doing and elevated it to an unhealthy level, so much so that their affections became attached to the method instead of to God."[23]

Rima, too, is convinced that church growth is far more than a set of principles or a "star" pastor. It is a matter of God's sovereign will, and sometimes when personal dreams and desires for success get mixed into the equation, the result is painful failure. In his own experience as a pastor, Rima had effectively planted a church that had grown to nearly eight hundred. He felt confident and successful in his ministry, when one day he received a fateful phone call.

On the other end of the phone was a member of a call committee of a prestigious church with a long history. The caller was asking if Rima would consider candidating as senior pastor. The church had been in slow decline and needed a successful pastor to turn it around. Rima turned down the offer. But before the caller hung up, he requested a videotape of Rima's preaching. A phone call two weeks later led to conversations and visits and finally, after about six months and a nearly unanimous vote from the congregation, Rima agreed to become the church's new pastor. "I had accepted this position to succeed," he writes. "I didn't move my family across the country . . . just to survive and maintain the status quo." But despite his best efforts, the progress was slow:

> Up to this point in my life everything I had attempted in ministry had been successful. . . . But in spite of my record . . . I ended up leaving that church after just six years of feeling like an unmitigated failure. In fact my failure at this church left me wounded and shaken to my very soul. During my final years of ministry there, I became so depressed my wife finally convinced me to see a psychiatrist to get help. . . . Sadly, the reason for my feelings of failure was that I had not achieved the level of success I had envisioned for myself and that church, and the little success that we did see was not happening fast enough for me. . . . So I left with my tail tucked between my legs, my confidence shaken, feeling that my successful ministry track record had been tarnished.[24]

In a situation like this, there is plenty of blame to go around. Any pastor who is leaving in such a state of anxiety is not being affirmed by the people—whether they are other staff or church leaders or members of the congregation. And perhaps with good reason. But more than individual flaws, failures, and sins, it seems that in this case, like many others, it was the system that overturned what should have been fruitful pastoral ministry with a faithful community of Christians.

Form does matter. The competitive corporate core structure of the church affects the *content*. Marketing is not a neutral formula that leaves substance untouched. Perhaps some would argue that *substance*, for whatever reason, needs to be changed. And surely the case for the megachurch has been ably made by its many defenders. But that these defenders would claim that form does not affect substance amounts to a superficial analysis at best. And that the megachurch *form* would find its rationale largely based on the failure of the typical left-behind church is an argument that does not fly. All Christians are admonished by the words of Jesus that the last shall be first and by the words of Paul that by weakness we are made strong. Form that flies in the face of bedrock Christian principles must be challenged.

7

Literature, Seminars, and Theory of Church Growth

The contemporary *church growth* movement traces its origins to the 1980s and the theories and strategies of Donald A. McGavran, sometimes referred to as the "father of Church Growth." But long before McGavran, there were church growth gurus whose megachurches drew media attention. The Spurgeon brothers, Charles and James, were noted for this in late nineteenth-century London. There were nineteenth-century megachurches in North America as well, including slave-born Charles Tindley's 4,000-member church, Tindley Temple, in Philadelphia. More and more of these large churches dotted the landscape as the decades of the twentieth century rolled on.

In the 1930s, Oswald J. Smith founded the Peoples Church in Toronto, a church that he would bequeath to his son in later years. At the same time in Atlanta, the Reverend Mike King was turning Ebenezer Baptist Church into a megachurch. A poor, struggling church (with a respectable attendance of 400) in 1931 rose in attendance to some 4,000 by 1940—spurred on by the often dictatorial and always calculated and shrewd leadership of the pastor.

A decisive turning point during this period of church growth for Ebenezer Baptist was a sabbatical excursion to Europe, Africa, and the Holy Land that the church gave King in 1934. In Germany, inspired by the legacy of Martin Luther, he decided to legally change his name and that of his five-year-old son from Michael to Martin. If a mere monk could change the course of religious history, so also could an up-and-coming Black preacher in Atlanta.

Church growth did not initially come without conflict. But "if Mike King had his critics, they were soon silenced by the church's dramatic financial recovery as well as the irrefutable passion with which he willed one thing: the advancement of Ebenezer. Whether by Machiavellian business instincts or blunt-edged buffoonery, Mike King got his way." Such a description is amazing considering his heritage as the son of a drunken sharecropper:

> A near illiterate, he was determined to break into Morehouse College and to become a refined pastor. At age twenty-one he was a fifth-grader in a remedial school in Atlanta. For several years he served a tiny church in Atlanta called Traveler's Rest where he labored with a reading ability "barely beyond a rank beginner" and preached to deacons who "didn't know the alphabet." A member of the lowest caste of rural Negroes (his schoolmates had taunted him unmercifully for smelling like a mule), he set his cap to marry the princess of Ebenezer, the boss's daughter, Alberta Williams. A poor man with dung on his boots, he dreamed of living in a brick house with a fine porch and shutters on the windows.[1]

Marrying the preacher's daughter set the stage for King to succeed his father-in-law—a transition that took place in 1931. Immediately the younger man began consolidating the finances of the various church auxiliaries so as to have more direct control over expenditures. In order to increase giving, he implemented a system of publicizing "each member's contributions—amounts plus names." He "also established birth-month clubs whose members engaged in friendly fund-raising competitions to the benefit of the whole congregation." But he did not stop at merely shaming people into giving or coaxing them through competition.

> King's shrewdest financial maneuver he learned from the successful insurance companies on Auburn Avenue. Because their

clients were not able to afford large policies, insurance salesmen collected small premiums on a monthly or even weekly basis. King recruited the insurance people as members who in effect became collection agents for the church. The salesmen acquired a new field of customers, and the church benefited in many ways from a new system that not only increased contributions, but also created a network for communication and home care.[2]

King's *purpose-driven* church and life would have ranked along-side the best of today's megachurch CEO preachers. And he, like some of them, was driven to rise above his meager birthright and do something big for God. The style of leadership and church growth tactics have changed, but the burning zeal to rise higher and higher and to preside over bigger and better remains the same.

The Father of Church Growth

King served as both a theorist and model for church growth, as do many other ministers of the mid-twentieth century. But the ideas and tactics behind the movement churned in the head of a missionary and theoretician, not a church pastor. Donald A. McGavran is the uncontested *father* of Church Growth, but the movement quickly attracted followers—and self-described *leaders*. The movement displayed a strong current of pragmatism founded in the discipline of sociology—concepts that "sound as if they were invented by a frustrated sociologist whose idea of a wild and crazy Saturday night is rearranging his sock drawer," writes Tom Raabe. Their books, he continues, flaunt "mundane titles like *Understanding Church Growth*, *How to Grow a Church*, *I Believe in Church Growth*, and *Strategies for Church Growth*." And their *doctrines*? Even the specialist is easily confused: "The homogeneous unit principle; the Resistance-Receptivity Axis; composite church membership; multi-individual, inter-dependent decision; E-2, 3-P evangelism; etc." Who then was McGavran? According to Raabe, from his mission post in India McGavran "sent forth a phalanx of researchers marching behind the banner of the Great (Growth) Commission: 'Go ye therefore and study growing churches and find out what works.'"[3]

100

If there is one common element of church growth in all its varieties, it is *pragmatism*. The underlying rationale is that it is our responsibility to bring as many people to Christ as possible. A world is dying without the gospel, and if we don't reach them, who will? William Booth, who with his wife, Catherine, founded the Salvation Army, illustrates this mentality. The story is told of how Rudyard Kipling, poet and fiction writer, watched General Booth boarding a ship, accompanied by a band of tambourines. Kipling, more attuned to traditional music and liturgy, complained to Booth about how offensive he found this *noise* to be. Without hesitating, Booth responded, "Young man, if I thought I could win one more soul for Christ by standing on my head and beating a tambourine with my feet, I would learn how to do it."[4] So it is with the church growth movement. Pragmatism rules the day. If we don't stand on our heads, they may be left behind at the judgment. The end-*times* justifies the means.

McGavran's team of researchers did not confine their research to the *mission fields* of the world. In fact, North American ministers quickly answered the call to grow, and the church growth movement of the 1980s melded into the megachurch movement of the 1990s. What McGavran did as a theoretician in the foundational stages of the movement, George Barna did as a statistician as the movement developed.

The Pollster Man

George Barna is a pollster. He is to the evangelical church industry what George Gallup is to the news industry and politicians. His appeal has been due in part to what some people might term cocky confidence. His principles are based on quantitative research and statistical analysis—and *statistics don't lie*. Most of the literature and seminars related to church growth apply to new church development or continuing growth for a church that is moving full steam ahead. This is where Barna has focused. While there is no shortage of advice for churches that are declining, there is little room for optimism. Indeed, their future is grim. Statistics show and Barna concludes: "Without being unreasonably optimistic about the chances of a once-healthy church being turned around after a severe decline, our research demonstrates that there is relatively little reason for such optimism. . . . In many cases, trying to revitalize a declining church is probably a wasted effort."[5]

But for churches that are determined to regain their health, what is the key turnaround strategy? Barna's answer is unequivocal: "The first step may be the most important. To turn around a church, *a new pastor must be brought in* to lead the revolution. . . . An entrenched pastor who has lived through the heart of the decline is unlikely to command the respect and to have the necessary energy not only to apply the brakes to the skid, but also to determine how to reverse the fortunes of the church."[6]

It would be unfair to argue that the church growth industry and its subsidiaries have nothing to offer those who are concerned about the condition of contemporary Christianity. But it is irresponsible for a pastor or a congregation to simply accept the basic premises without challenge. Much of the church growth industry has followed cultural patterns—those related to consumerism and marketing on the one hand and to self-help and therapy on the other. "The producer/consumer market model turns possible vice into virtue," writes David Kelsey, "by generating its own growing and lucrative market for experts and consultants who analyze religious customers' felt needs and help churches package their products in effective ways." He names George Barna as the leader of these marketers, citing his book *Marketing the Church*, where Barna argues that "the major problem plaguing the church is its failure to embrace a marketing orientation in what has become a market-driven environment."[7]

Church Growth, Pride, and Jealousy

Is the church growth *addiction* fueled by that most foundational sin of all—pride? Many critics hint as much if they do not say it outright. But there is the opposite accusation as well. Why is there such animosity toward megachurches? Is it jealousy? Both accusations point to motives. How can I judge another's motives, especially those of a Christian brother or sister? But we question motives all the time—in murder cases and financial rip-offs and political scams. That a minister would couch motives in will-of-God terminology should not automatically sanctify the circumstances.

Eugene Peterson, a longtime minister of one congregation, addresses the matter of motives in many of his writings. He was tempted on more than one occasion to move on to greener pastures. Such temptations, he realized, spring from a human tendency toward sin and pride—and ministers are tempted at every turn. The harlot of success is ever paraded before them. Sometimes they are simply innocent bystanders trying to fulfill their calling, as Eugene Peterson suggests:

> Some propagandists in the land are lying to us about what congregations can be. They are lying for money. They want to make us discontented with what we are doing, so we will buy a solution from them that they promise will restore virility to our impotent congregations. The profit-taking among those marketing these spiritual monkey-glands suggests that pastoral gullibility in these matters is endless. Pastors, faced with the failure of these purchased procedures, typically blame the congregation and leave it for another.[8]

Gordon MacDonald agrees. "As a new pastor, it seemed that every week someone from some new organization blew into town with a new program to sell me." For someone frustrated by the lack of practical training served up in seminary, the temptation to buy the program is real. "The opening pitch rarely varied," writes MacDonald; "the church was dying, pastors were desperate, and here is a program (anointed by God) to save it all. Somewhere in the country (usually California) was a church that had adapted the program and was now growing by the 'thousands.'" Sometimes the pressure came from church members who had attended a conference, "saying, 'You won't believe what God is doing there' or 'You've got to attend their . . .' or 'You've got to start this . . .'" There is a downside to all of this, MacDonald insists: "More than a few young pastors (myself included) have gone to seminars that promised big stuff, come home with enthusiasm, expecting that something close to a reformation will break out in their town. A year later some are in the process of leaving their ministries, heartbroken, rejected, defeated. Casualties of heart can be high."[9]

Superpreacher or Shepherd

There is a strong temptation for pastors to attend conferences and seminars and to look up to the superpastors as models. And why shouldn't the pastors of the megachurches be called superpastors? We have supermodels and superstars—designations for those who are at the top of their profession. Why not superpreacher? "A growing number of pastors have modeled their style after the megachurch pastors," writes H. B. London. "They think, *If it is good enough for them to be a CEO, why can't I?*" But London goes on to point out that in North America there are some one hundred thousand churches with an average attendance of fifty or less and that 80 percent of pastors will never serve in a church of more than two hundred. "If that is true, then the need for CEOs is not so critical."[10]

London argues that it is more important for a pastor to be a shepherd than a leader. On graduating from seminary, he was "assigned to a church on the wrong side of the street in a Southern California community." The odds of his being able to pull his "little charge out of the doldrums" were slim. With no surefire solutions, he fell back on a simple strategy: "I had learned from my heritage how important it was to love people. So I did. . . . The church grew. The folks began to believe in themselves. . . . Word got out that ours was a church where love was genuine. . . . That was forty years ago. I went on to pastor three more churches before becoming a 'pastor to pastors' at Focus on the Family, but my style never changed."[11]

Loving a congregation is not necessarily as easy as it sounds. Many pastors simply do not love their people, particularly when they are out with the *boys*—their fellow ministers—and each one is telling war stories to top the other. Or, as Kevin Ruffcorn warns, "we can get caught up in the Fat-and-Ugly-Congregation Syndrome"—a congregation "to be endured rather than loved." Ruffcorn, pastor of Grace Lutheran Church in Oconto Falls, Wisconsin, was convinced that in comparison to what other pastors were saying about their congregations, his must be on the high end of the bell curve. On impulse, he revealed his feelings one Sunday morning:

> "Many of you do not have the opportunity to visit other congregations," I began. "Based on my observations I want you to know

that I think you're a great congregation, and I feel privileged to serve as your pastor."

The congregation was a bit taken aback. Then smiles lit up their faces, and they broke out in applause. It was a spontaneous celebration of who they were and a thanksgiving to God. From that moment I realized that praise was important.[12]

Formulas for Success

There are an infinite number of formulas for ministry success that have been touted over the past several decades. Like many pastors, Samuel Rima confesses that he "tried numerous surefire methods down through the years that promised to produce significant church growth, only to be left frustrated and even at times angry with the congregation God had called me to serve." Indeed, he testifies that while he was involved in new church development in the 1980s, "there was a literal smorgasbord of church-growth formulas from which to choose." One of those programs was called "The Phone's for You." It virtually guaranteed that for every one hundred "dial-ups," there would be a favorable response. So if the church's goal was one hundred new people, all they had to do was dial up ten thousand people. "I conducted this program at least twice during my tenure as a church planter," recalls Rima. "Though we never came near to the results that the program creators promised, we did receive some positive benefits. . . . However, the people that responded to our phoning efforts generally tended to wander off after only several weeks of attendance."[13]

For many ministers, the never-ending parade of church growth programs—whether purpose-driven or natural growth—has a debilitating effect. The comparisons with other pastors and their ministries are as demeaning as they are draining. Neil Sims from Queensland, Australia, writes:

I bought into that culture of success. It was all around me. After 15 years and four placements I began to wonder if I would ever be a successful pastor. At a church growth seminar, we studied the quality of life in the early Church and its growth. . . . If we followed this model, growth was virtually assured! . . . There was a phase where lots of congregations across Queensland came together to learn and implement "12 keys to an effective church."[14]

For Sims, this culture of success was depressing and stressful: "He continued to carry out his pastoral duties, but the joy of serving the Lord had been sucked out of him." He was in a church where numerical growth was going in reverse—as was his self-esteem. "How could I come to terms with the fact that I might never be a successful pastor?" This low point prompted "a lot of soul-searching."

Unlike many ministers, Sims's soul-searching did not lead him out of the ministry. "I came to realise how egocentric it was to want to be a successful pastor. That had nothing to do with God's call of me, and everything to do with my concern about my public image. It had more to do with meeting popularly accepted standards than with being embraced by grace."

It was through participating in a spiritual retreat—not a church growth seminar—that brought him back to equilibrium: "I had been a pilgrim on an Emmaus Walk. One of the daily celebrations of Holy Communion is called 'dying moments.' . . . It's an act of personal confession, of giving up something that interferes with God's call. On a later Emmaus Walk, . . . I knew that my dying moment needed to be, 'to die to success as a pastor.' My desire to be a successful pastor had intruded on my faithfulness to God's vocation for me."

Sims speaks for many ministers. He concedes, "It doesn't look good to be the minister of a church where worship attendances are falling and offerings are declining." But he asks a rhetorical question that should be posed to all church growth experts: "If only a handful of congregations in our Synod are growing in number, does that mean that most ministers of congregations are failures?"[15]

Many of the church growth gurus would concede that not all churches ought to aspire to be megachurches. But the literature often leaves little doubt that effective pastors will lead churches that will grow by addition and multiplication and eventually turn into superchurches. "Not every church can or should be a shopping-center church," writes Leith Anderson. "The shopping centers of America have certainly had their critics. These malls have contributed to the decay of inner cities and the loss of economic and social stability in neighborhoods. . . . Frankly, similar criticisms may be launched at shopping-center churches that have drawn parishioners away from smaller churches and accelerated the decline of neighborhood relationships."[16] But these drawbacks do not dim his enthusiasm.

Anderson writes about many varieties of churches in his book, *The Church for the 21st Century,* but his choice is clear:

> There is validity to these and other critiques, but don't allow the negatives to overshadow the significance of the shopping-center church phenomenon. Recognize that shopping-center churches will be the major ministries and primary pacesetters for the twenty-first-century church. Just as downtown cathedrals, Sunday schools, and frontier chapels greatly influenced all churches of earlier generations, so will shopping-center churches influence this generation.[17]

The Reality of Church Growth

The literature and the lectures make church growth sound all too easy. Whether twelve steps or ten principles, the work of the Lord is more than selling shoes or selling encyclopedias or selling furniture. I was a hotshot encyclopedia salesperson, and my son, Carlton, followed in my footsteps as a hotshot furniture salesperson. I was number one in the regional Minneapolis office in book sales, and he at age nineteen was number one (out of more than fifty) in a large store in Grand Rapids. For him, the first-place rating came in the month of December when others wanted time off with their families. Carlton is competitive, and he was on duty every hour the store was open. His rating did not endear him to the other sales associates, but he had all the sales skills to make it to the top. Carlton's style was very different from mine. Back in the 1960s as a college student, we were taught to put on the pressure, and I did. Carlton, by personality and training, was laid-back. No pushing. No pressure. Just friendly, easygoing banter—and listening. People would come into the store looking for a lamp, and before they left, they had purchased an entire bedroom suite. It is in his blood, and he's good. If he were a minister, who knows, he might be presiding over a megachurch.

But not all ministers possess the sales skills that Carlton does. For them, the task of church growth is as difficult as rating number one in sales at a big furniture store—perhaps more so.

How difficult is it to effect significant church growth in a left-behind church? Is it an impossible task? E. Stanley Ott suggests that it is impossible—or nearly so. Yet he is convinced it is necessary. He begins with what seems like an impossible task: "Imagine that at some time in the future you are Pastor Hybels' successor at Willow Creek, with its thousands of worshippers. Suppose you are given the mandate (for whatever surprising reason) to change the Sunday morning 'Seeker Service' that defines the Willow Creek culture into a Mozart- and Bach-based service—without losing anyone." Such a mandate is rarely discussed at church growth seminars, but Ott argues that such is the expectation of many ministers today. "Many of us face that challenge in reverse in mainline churches today: how to expand the scope of our ministries to attract people of different tastes while keeping those members we have—without burning out or being taken out in the process. That doesn't necessarily mean that we will introduce 'seeker services' into our congregations, but it does mean that reaching people today will require many of us to make major adjustments in our ministries."[18]

In order to make such changes and open the windows of a dusty old church to new ideas, it requires gifts and abilities in dealing with people and, yes, even some savvy sales skills. But ranking *number one* in church growth is not a goal that ought to capture the dreams of ministers. Jesus set a standard that sets us apart from the world:

> Jesus got them together to settle things down. "You've observed how godless rulers throw their weight around," he said, "and when people get a little power how quickly it goes to their heads. It's not going to be that way with you. Whoever wants to be great must become a servant."
>
> Mark 10:42–43, *The Message*

8

Left Behind with a Woman's Touch

Did you hear the joke about the woman preacher? . . . There are a lot of woman preacher jokes going around. My favorite is about the woman who accepts a call to a small-town church despite grumbling and opposition from church members. But within weeks she's won their hearts. She preaches better sermons than her male predecessors, she offers better pastoral care, she is more efficient in organizing meetings, and she's more welcoming to visitors. She's a perfect match for their little church. They're all convinced—except for one grumpy old man. He doesn't agree. And besides, she doesn't fish. The previous preachers went fishing with him. "Well, ask her to go fishing," a deacon admonishes. "She'll probably turn out to be a better fisherman than any of the others."

So the old man extends a halfhearted invitation, and she joins him in his boat. But she can't even bait the hook. After he shows her how to do that, he has to explain how to cast the line, and when she finally catches a fish, he has to help her pull it in. But it gets worse. They're out in the middle of the lake and she starts shivering. Seething with anger, he agrees to go back to shore so she can get her jacket from the car. "No, no," she insists. "I'll get it myself." She stands up in the boat and steps out and walks toward the shore. He shakes his head in disgust and mumbles to himself, *"She can't bait a hook, she can't cast, she can't pull in a fish, she can't stand the cold, and she can't even swim!"*

A Personal Perspective as Pastor's Wife

Back in the 1960s and 70s, during my college and graduate education when I was contemplating *the will of God for my life*, a ministerial calling was not an option—especially in the fundamentalist circles in which I was groomed. The closest I would ever come to this calling was ministry as a pastor's wife. But such a ministry has lost its savor. The feminist movement has changed things. As Barbara Bush faced protesters in her role as First Lady (by women students from Wellesley College where she had come to speak), so have I. Not that I have actually encountered picket signs. But as one who has ministered as a pastor's wife, I'm not considered a legitimate professional. Like Mrs. Bush, how dare I speak as a wife to women who aspire to the job my husband filled? Yet we both have important things to say.

Like many left-behind pastors' wives, I worked alongside my husband in ministry. Both churches in which we served truly got two for the price of one—though in actuality the pay did not even amount to *the price of one*. I did not preach, and I did not attend council meetings. But my role in pastoral care and other activities was a full-time job. "I have enjoyed the challenges that come with the territory," I write in *Private Lives of Pastors' Wives*. I enumerate these challenges: "the satisfaction of having a young person seek me out for counsel *because* I am the pastor's wife, the fulfillment in helping plan the first annual missions conference [an idea that was my own], the satisfaction of hearing a sermon illustration from a magazine article that I shared with my husband."[1]

For better or for worse, there was very little that went on at the church in which I did not have a hand. I know the ins and outs of a left-behind church through the eyes of a pastor's wife, which in many cases may be a more perceptive perspective than that of the pastor himself. I was the lively conversationalist in home visitation; I made hospital visits and phone calls, contacted missionaries, and designed bulletins and bulletin boards—all that besides my volunteer ministries of teaching Sunday school, Vacation Bible School, children's clubs, youth groups, women's Bible studies, mission societies, and serving on various committees. But having said that, the role of pastor's wife is secondary. Suggesting sermon illustrations and hymns and biblical texts to the pastor is not the same as preparing sermons and preaching and leading worship oneself. And even if the wife's role is equivalent to that of the pastor (as it often was in some Pentecostal churches), marriage to a minister is neither an option nor a desire for many women who are called to pastoral ministry.

A Reformation Role Model

Yet the role of pastor's wife from a historical perspective has much to say to women ministers today. Church history is a long narrative of denying ministry to women—the very gender that had so much opportunity for ministry in the New Testament era. Palestinian Jewish culture severely restricted women in every area of life, as was true in neighboring cultures; yet women are everywhere in the New Testament carrying out tasks that one might expect to be appropriate for men only. Women were not ordained for ministry then, but of course neither were men. The prominent involvement of women in the church continued for generations following the close of the Apostolic period, but as the church became more organized and hierarchical—especially following Emperor Constantine's reign—women's roles decreased. With the growth of monasticism during the medieval period, women entered monasteries, though they were usually cloistered and often silenced.

The Reformation was a time of great advance for women. True or false? For most historians, that question is a no-brainer. Catholic women in the late medieval period had significant opportunities for education and humanitarian service and even diplomatic endeavors through monastic religious orders. Protestants, who often violently closed down these convents in areas under their domination, offered no such ministry for women. By renouncing the vow of celibacy, Catholic priests turned Protestant preachers did open the door to a new ministry—that of pastor's wife—but that role from the beginning was restricted. Only by pushing the boundaries did women become ministers in their own right, but even then they served without official sanction and always in what could be termed *left-behind* situations.

Katherine Zell, who married a Catholic priest turned Protestant preacher, served alongside her husband for many years in Strasbourg during the early years of the Reformation. After his death, she was accused of aspiring to become Dr. Katrina and take his place in the pulpit. She did not do that, but she did serve in leadership capacities that rivaled that of some of the late medieval Catholic abbesses. She also preached and ministered to small groups, but never with official sanction. As a Reformer, Zell demonstrated that women do not duplicate or mirror the ministry of men. Her insights and agendas were different from those of her male counterparts. She focused on humanitarian ministries and called for religious toleration at a time when persecution and execution were the preferred tactics. "Why do you rail at Schwenckfeld?" she demanded of a Lutheran leader. "You talk as if you would have him burned like the poor Servetus at Geneva. . . . Anabaptists are pursued as by a hunter with dogs chasing wild boars. Yet the Anabaptists accept Christ in all the essentials as we do."[2]

Katherine Zell was also deeply concerned about individual and community spiritual formation. Although she was a self-educated theologian and conversed with the likes of Ulrich Zwingli and John Calvin "so intelligently that they ranked her above most doctors,"[3] she was not consumed with matters of doctrinal precision, as were many of the Reformers. Her ministry was one of pastoral care. Zell organized a vast refugee relief program, compiled a hymnbook, and wrote countless letters that served as tracts, complete with biblical commentary and application. Her ministry was unique among the Reformers but no less significant. Yet she is largely forgotten today. She would not be listed among the leading Reformers. Women must succeed by male standards or they do not make the cut.

Gender Difference and Ministry

Similar standards for success hold today—standards that permeate the church growth movement and the minds of many male ministers. "I once attended a church service in a small Midwestern town," writes Anne Wilson Schaef. "Afterward, I told the minister how pleased I had been with the prayer and sermon meditation. He nodded and immediately launched into a discussion of church attendance and how few people were there on communion Sundays during summer. I had commented on the quality and content of the service—and he had responded with numbers!"[4]

I am surely not the first woman to notice that the vast majority of church growth literature is written by men. Women are, likewise, rarely featured at church growth conferences—and no doubt with good reason. Many of the featured speakers are ministers whose own churches have mushroomed to megachurch size, and such women ministers are rare. That is true of the emergent (or postmodern) church movement as well. Jenell Paris challenged Brian McLaren (author of *A New Kind of Christian*), who has become known as the guru for the emergent church movement, on his failure to cite women as authorities or models of ministry in his books.[5]

Other women have taken up the cause and have organized meetings specifically geared for women. Heather Kirk-Davidoff tells of her efforts to bring more gender equity to this new movement and how her involvement began: "In March 2003, I flew with three other women pastors to the first Emergent Convention in San Diego, California. I was excited to introduce my friends to a conversation that I had found so energizing, but soon found myself apologizing for the near total exclusion of women's voices from the main sessions of the conference."[6] Since that time, women have met together, but they are still rarely profiled at larger conferences related to church growth and revitalization.

But what difference does it make? Of course, women want equal rights, but church growth is church growth, whether the principles come from a woman or a man. In the early years of the modern feminist movement, this was the attitude most often assumed: that women and men were essentially the same, except for obvious anatomical differences. The apparent disparities between the sexes were attributed to nurture, not nature. But in recent years that doctrine has been almost universally rejected. Women, plain and simple, are wired differently than men.

Studies show that women coach athletic teams very differently than men do. The same is true in business. Their leadership styles, many observers insist, have a feminine or female touch. We are cautioned about making too much of these differences, but the old accusation of "stereotyping" is no longer automatically marshaled forth by feminists. Contemporary feminism is far more at ease with gender difference.

Most books and articles written about women in pastoral ministry focus on the novelty of such a situation—and with good reason. The first woman preacher in a particular denomination elicits interest—as does the *problem* of women in ministry. The difficulties they face among colleagues and parishioners have been told in many ways.

But viewing women ministers as models for effective ministry is not yet a literary genre—in part because their numbers are so few. Models for ministry are typically equated with success, and success is typically equated with numbers, and when numbers are high enough, you have a megachurch. But in this category we search in vain for women who are top-dog preachers. The names are Rick or Robert or Bill or Jack or Charles or Tony (or Kim or Park or Jin So), minus the Marys and Megans and Beths.

But the numbers of women in left-behind churches has grown rapidly in recent years, and studies are beginning to show that they offer a leadership style that models effective ministry to other women and, perhaps more importantly, to their male counterparts. Unfortunately their voices are not being heard. The vast majority of articles in the "professional preacher magazines" are written by men, as are the books.

The most obvious asset that a female left-behind preacher lacks, in comparison to her male counterpart, is a wife. As a one-time left-behind preacher's wife, I know how important my place was in two struggling little churches and how important this role has been historically. Women such as Susannah Spurgeon, Emma Moody, and Ruth Peale were vital to the success of their husbands' pastoral ministry. Such partners, in male form, are rarely found among women preachers.

A Preacher of Righteousness

Traveling through England and Scotland last summer, one of the stops I most wanted to make was at Epworth and, more specifically, the Epworth rectory where Susanna Wesley held forth as lady of the house and, in the words of her famous son, John, "a preacher of righteousness." As we strolled through the sitting room and kitchen and up the staircase to the bedrooms, I sensed the spirit of Susanna. I even thought I heard the voice of this lady preacher who refused to leave behind a left-behind church. Of course it was in my imagination, but surely her spirit lingers there and wherever the message of Methodism has been carried. This mother of nineteen, including John and Charles, the fathers of Methodism, however, was not a Methodist herself. As a teenager, she turned away from the Nonconformist beliefs of her parents and decided on her own to return to the Church of England. As a young adult she married Samuel Wesley, an Anglican priest, and it was in the capacity of a minister's wife that she served as a minister herself.

The Anglican parish in Epworth was a left-behind church—at least during the tenure of Samuel Wesley. He was not what people wanted in a pastor. His rigid discipline and lack of relational skills created animosity in the church and the community. Indeed, so hated was he that he was the target of vandalism and violence. "They burned his flax crop, taunted the Wesley children, pried the hinges off the rectory doors . . . stabbed his cows so that they gave no milk and once even tried to cut off the legs of the house dog."[7] On one occasion in 1705, when John was still a toddler, the Wesleys were threatened in their home by an armed and angry mob. Soon after that Samuel was arrested and sent to debtors' prison for not paying a debt to one of his parishioners.

Life was not easy in the Wesley home, and the voice of Susanna that cries out from the grave speaks for other ministers' wives through the generations. But Susanna was determined not to let the church self-destruct, even if her husband did. During the winter of 1711–1712, while Samuel was away for an extended time—leaving the parish with no vicar—she took charge. Far from trying to make a statement as a woman preacher (as the Quakers did), her concern was that the people not be without spiritual guidance. Initially she confined her ministry to her own children, but as neighbors got wind of what was going on, they sent their children to learn under Mrs. Wesley. And as their children came home and reported what they were hearing from the lips of this wise woman, the parents came to the rectory as well. As Susanna tried to explain in a letter to her angry husband:

> Other people's coming and joining with us was merely accidental. One lad told his parents: They first desired to be admitted; then others that heard of it begged leave also. . . . I chose the best and most awakening sermons we have. And I spent somewhat more time with them in such exercises, without being careful about the success of my undertaking. Since this, our company increased every night; for I dare deny none that ask admittance. . . . Last Sunday I believe we had above two hundred. And yet, many went away, for want of room to stand.[8]

Samuel was not happy and made himself clear in a return letter to Susanna. He had never attracted such crowds, and he apparently thought she was making him look bad in comparison. Her response was the response of one concerned about the church: "I cannot conceive, why any should reflect upon you, because your wife endeavors to draw people to church. . . . For my part, I value no censure. . . . As to its looking peculiar, I grant it does. And so does almost anything that . . . advance[s] the glory of God, or the salvation of souls."[9]

Susanna Wesley, the "preacher of righteousness," serves as a model for men and women today who would "value no censure" for safeguarding the church no matter how peculiar their efforts may appear. Like many women before and after her, she served without official sanction. But that in no way lessens her distinction as a preacher of righteousness.

Church growth concepts were not present in Susanna's rationale or motivation for carrying on with ministerial duties, so far as I can discern from the sources. She simply served the congregation in humility and in subservience to the gospel message. She was a strong, confident woman, but she knew her place (in eighteenth-century England), and that place was not in the pulpit. She accepted her role as preacher only with a deep sense of unmerited grace. That is exactly how all ministers should approach their calling. Both men and women can learn from this woman who represents a left-behind gender in a left-behind church.

Nursing Sick Churches

That women as pastors are able to revitalize even the sickest churches is not a new phenomenon. For women, however, the end result has sometimes been heartbreaking. In the aftermath of the Great Depression, during World War II, for example, many women "were taking on struggling and defunct churches, rebuilding them, and then seeing them taken over by men once the congregations were revitalized."[10]

This phenomenon also happens in church planting—as was the case in the little country church where I grew up. Once Miss Salthammer and Miss Cowan had planted and nurtured their work to the point of moving from *mission* to *church* status, they moved on. To imagine, however, that they felt exploited or used is to transpose our own cultural sensibilities back on them. Some people feel uniquely gifted in the ministry of church planting, as these two women very well might have.

Perhaps it is saying too much to argue that a left-behind gender is in a unique position to serve in a left-behind church. And for some women, such an argument is condescending. Women, like their male counterparts, should be filling the most prestigious pulpits. But if our theological foundations are in place and we really believe that the highest form of ministry is the lowest and that the ideal of simplicity and humility is more grounded in true Christian discipleship than the ideal of size, numbers, and prestige, then the ministry of women ought to be studied for what it brings to the pastoral profession.

Dr. Rose

Some women may appear on the surface as anything but humble, and they may easily adopt tactics identified with church growth strategies and systems. But the feminine *style* is nevertheless evident.

"Have a country church with waning membership, a dilapidated building and no hope? Don't call the coroner; call Dr. Rose." Dr. Rose Grindheim Sims is a name that is familiar to many Methodists—especially those who lament the closing of thousands of rural churches in recent decades. Recipient of the

Circuit Rider Award for church growth, she confronted not only dying churches but also church officials who were uneasy with a gutsy, retirement-aged woman. Yet she was confident that she was doing the work of God, and she would not be deterred.

Dr. Rose has served as a doctor to dying churches—working to counteract the wave of church closings especially in rural Methodist parishes where thousands have been given last rites in recent decades. Where others see desolation, she sees hope. When she was at Trilby United Methodist Church in rural Pasco County, Florida, she found a run-down, turn-of-the-century-vintage sanctuary with a rusty roof and a ramshackle lean-to. The small membership indicated the church was barely hanging on. But she saw hope not despair. "From the minute I walked in," she recalls, "I saw it filled with people."

Within five years after she arrived the church had turned around. Trilby had "a new, debt-free plant built with volunteer labor and valued at $400,000. . . . The old building has been refurbished and turned into a fellowship hall, the lean-to has become a church parlor." It is a church that serves the community with clothing distribution, a health clinic, a dinner theater, adult education, senior citizens' activities, Boy Scouts, and "a thriving singles' group which packs up and distributes hundreds of pounds of food monthly to needy families."[11]

The story of Dr. Rose, like so many stories of left-behind churches, defies statistics and common sense. "Almost all of the turnaround pastors [we studied]," writes George Barna, "assumed the pastorate of their church before they had reached the age of 45. . . . The task is so spiritually demanding, so emotionally and physically draining and so taxing on one's family and relationships that only a person of relative youth can succeed."[12]

Dr. Rose has a unique personality distinguished by vigor and energy that few ministers can match. She stands as a monument and model for all women and men who would seek to revitalize a left-behind church.

St. Andrew's Reverend Veronica

There are other women ministers, however, who do not raise the bar so high. Anne Lamott tells about the woman's touch in

her left-behind St. Andrew Presbyterian church. But even before the woman's touch, God had touched her life through the
ministry of men.

"If I were to give a slide show of the next ten years, it would
begin on the day I was baptized, one year after I got sober," writes
Lamott. "I called Reverend Noel at eight that morning and told
him that I really didn't think I was ready because I wasn't good
enough yet. Also, I was insane. My heart was good, but my in-
sides had gone bad. And he said, 'You're putting the cart before
the horse. So—honey? Come on *down*.'"

How this utterly left-behind church attracted ministers, she
doesn't say, but there would be a succession of them during the
next decade while she as a single mother raised her son. "There
would be thousands of slides of Sam and me at St. Andrew," she
continues. "I think we have missed church ten times in twelve
years. Sam would be snuggled in people's arms in the earlier
shots, shyly trying to wriggle free of hugs in the later ones."
Through these years ministers came and went, but "none was
the perfect fit until Veronica came. This tall, gentle African-
American woman won their hearts—especially as she shared
stories of her childhood."[13]

One important aspect of Veronica's storytelling was the power
of a left-behind church—power that Anne understood well in her
own pilgrimage. The Christian life is not defined by a single or
a spectacular experience. It is rather defined by a relationship
to God, one that comes primarily in community through God's
people, otherwise known as the *church*. Anne relates a story
Veronica shared and then adds her own postscript:

> When she was about seven, her best friend got lost one day. The
> little girl ran up and down the streets of the big town where they
> lived, but she couldn't find a single landmark. She was frightened.
> Finally a policeman stopped to help her. He put her in the pas-
> senger seat of his car, and they drove around until she finally saw
> her church. She pointed it out to the policeman, and then she told
> him firmly, "you could let me out now. This is my church, and I
> can always find my way home from here."
>
> And that is why I have stayed so close to mine, because no
> matter how bad I am feeling, how lost or lonely or frightened,
> when I see the faces of the people at my church, and hear their
> tawny voices, I can always find my way home.[14]

House-Church Ministry

Small is better. Such a motto would not be suitable for a church growth slogan. But for Tillie Burgin, it is a motto that fits her ministry. In 2000 she was inducted into the Texas Women's Hall of Fame. Her contributions to her community included "a medical clinic, a dental clinic, a crisis counseling office, a day shelter, job training, an adult day care facility, and summer camps for inner city children." Hers is a massive program known as Mission Arlington that started out less than two decades ago as two weekly Bible studies.[15]

Burgin had served for more than a decade as a missionary in Korea and then returned to the United States and became a school administrator in Texas. But as she looked around and saw all the needs of the community, she became convinced that she had not actually left the "mission field." Indeed, the mission field was all around her. She was not dreaming of starting a big-time evangelistic association. And she did not even have an organization plan or statement of purpose—except to take the church out into the streets to people who did not attend church. Her rationale was as simple as it was profound: "to hang out and hover around John 3:16."[16]

What started as one Bible study and then another has today developed into a house church movement with more than two hundred house churches, averaging fewer than twenty people in each church. A ministry outreach center spreading out to fill a square block, with numerous types of services, reaches deep into the community. But the focal point of the ministry is found in the homes and apartments, the house churches. The extent of this outreach is summarized on the ministry website:

> Each day hundreds of people come through the center with various types of needs which are addressed at the center. Then, these folks are followed up through the geographically located churches. Last Thanksgiving, Mission Arlington fed 9,000 people in their homes, having realized that people would rather eat with their families and friends than in a center somewhere. . . . Last year over 16,000 people came through their Christmas Store, heard the Christmas story and then selected gifts. . . . One little boy chose a brooch and then had it wrapped as a gift for his mother. He was seen unwrapping it and then getting back in line with the

same brooch to have it wrapped again. This cycle was repeated a few times. . . . He said he had never been treated so nice as those people were treating him and so he got in line just to feel the love![17]

The Shady Lady

Left behind with a woman's touch brings tranquility and triumph in the Lord's work. Does it, indeed? The answer is, not necessarily. Women preachers encounter as many demons as do their male counterparts, and sometimes those demons are all too close to home. So it was with Mother Fannie Bee Jordan, a self-styled African-American minister of Holy Family in New Orleans, a left-behind church with an evangelical-spiritualist blend. She ran a tight ship—some would say she was a tyrant—in a style that sometimes triggered mutinies. For mothers like Ottie Mae Youngblood, Mother Jordan and Holy Family offered security—a place where a young boy would be schooled on the straight and narrow. "Part of the appeal was the way church filled all the hours, with prayer services on Tuesday and Thursday, a choir performance on Wednesday, the Junior Missionary Society for the children on Saturday, and two services and a live radio broadcast on Sunday." But besides the structured programs there was the "hoodoo" factor, a spiritualist feature scorned by educated blacks that at the same time extended a "backhanded compliment of acknowledging its African roots."[18]

Here in the heart of New Orleans was a mix of African traditional religion, biblical beliefs, and Western Christian forms. Mother Jordan's little congregation was comprised of women and children who were prohibited from "drinking, dancing, and cussing." Her followers were called *saints* and "wore robes and veils to indicate their echelon, from missionary to evangelist to reverend mother." The lengthy Sunday meeting "operated within the conventions of black Christianity, but on the weeknights there was no mistaking the Spiritualists for anyone else. . . . Sweet incense hovered in the air. . . . They were a gathering of shadows and forms, voices lifting in praise, arms extending in appeal, heads lolling in reverie [often going until] past midnight."[19]

The story of this tiny, left-behind church of some ninety people would have faded into obscurity were it not for Mother Jordan's star apprentice, Johnny Youngblood, who would go on to serve as a community leader and prominent minister of St. Paul Community Baptist Church in New York City. As a "boy preacher" he was "the star attraction of Holy Family's radio show on WYLD," and from that base he built his own youth choir of more than thirty members who traveled to neighboring states to perform. He was rewarded with pocket change and treats—incentives that could never offset Mother Jordan's abuse. "Mother Jordan wielded a left hand that her charges talked about the way fight fans of the era talked about Sonny Liston's," writes Samuel Freedman. "And nobody suffered that left more often than Johnny. Mother Jordan hit him for talking in church, chewing gum, laughing aloud, missing assignments. . . . Once she hauled Johnny before the congregation and beat him till he wet his pants. As he trembled, damp and stinking, she directed the faithful to withdraw the 'right hand of fellowship' from him."[20]

In his late teens, as Mother Jordan was verbally excoriating him, Johnny walked out and never returned to the church again—until nine years later when he came back to offer a eulogy for her. In the meantime Johnny joined Reverend Eli Wilson's church "in a large measure to dash the fear that if he died, Mother Jordan would perform his funeral." Here he found the male role model he had been longing for and an opportunity to enter the world of rhythm and blues.

As a leading minister in his own right in Brooklyn, Johnny Youngblood would turn Mother Jordan's all-women's spiritualist church on its head. In his church, men who have never before darkened the door of the church are not only invited to come in but to come in and take over the leadership as *real* men. Men were soon seen heading to St. Paul on Sunday mornings. "Reverend Youngblood was no longer their wives' surrogate husband, no longer their own caricature of the 'jackleg preacher,' one hand in the collection plate and the other down a woman's blouse."[21]

Yet despite all the differences he had with Mother Jordan and in spite of all her deficiencies, Johnny Youngblood gleaned more from those years of her dysfunctional discipline that would shape his life than he could have possibly imagined at the time.

The Female Factor

How have women in pastoral ministry fared compared to their male counterparts? A study on the impact of women clergy offers some interesting insights: "Predictions of large-scale withdrawal of church members in response to a woman pastor failed to come true. More often than not members with women pastors tended to report slight increases in attendance, memberships, and financial contributions due to the influence of the clergy woman's work."[22]

Women often encounter difficulty in securing a pastoral call, but once they settle into ministry, their level of contentment often far surpasses their male counterparts. In the left-behind church, pastoral care and personal skills are in high demand, and women, especially those who enter the ministry, are more comfortable in such situations than men. Yet women, like their male counterparts, are often overwhelmed by the duties and time and expertise demanded of them—yes, the very soul of which the left-behind church so easily lays claims.

Jean Newstead offers tips to both male and female pastors that have helped her maintain balance and a sense of satisfaction in her parish. Three things in particular have been essential for her survival. The first is to get out of town "for at least one week every three months" whether for committee responsibilities, study, or vacation. The second is openness with the congregation "about who I am and what I am about." This is self-serving as much as it is a courtesy. "I announce plans for vacation, visits of family and friends, and other unusual events in my life in groups of people wherever it is appropriate, so as many people as possible get the same story at the same time and can later correct each other's misinterpretations." Her third tip is her ability to maintain a sense of humor, "especially a willingness to laugh at my own situation, mistakes, and expectations." Beyond those, she is active in a local ministerial group, and she has "two cats who help lower my blood pressure when life gets out of hand."[23]

Physical and emotional health is tied directly to spiritual health. "In the course of this ministry," writes Rebecca Hazen, pastor of a left-behind Presbyterian church in Eagle Creek, Oregon, "it has become obvious that the spiritual health of the congregation is directly related to my own spiritual health. As

I grow in my own faith and speak of it in practical ways, the congregation seems to do likewise."[24]

Well, duuhhh might be the only fitting response to such a confession, except for the fact that so few pastors actually internalize and come to grips with such an obvious truism. *Leadership* has become the watchword for seminary training today. More emphasis on leadership is the consensus recently acknowledged by the editor of the journal of the Association of Theological Schools. But what kind of leadership? For Hazen the focus is on spiritual leadership. Though a generation younger than many in her congregation, she is perceived as a spiritual mentor and model. "The longer I am here, the deeper it seems become the levels of trust and sharing," she writes. "It seems that as pastor and parish we could now weather a substantial crisis, due to the quality of our relationship." Do all pastors have opportunities for this kind of spiritual leadership? Not necessarily, would be Hazen's understated response: "I believe that in a small church this type of bonding might involve a higher proportion of the congregation than in a large one."[25]

A smaller church frequently affords the pastor more opportunities for spiritual leadership and mentoring than does a megachurch. For a pastor who wants well-rounded ministry, a left-behind church can be an ideal situation. Many women like Rebecca Hazen discover this to be a perfect fit.

9

Left Behind in Community

It is difficult to imagine someone writing a series of best-selling novels about the sterile confines of a megachurch. There is something appealing about a vine-covered left-behind church with a bell tower, an appeal that is entirely lacking in its giant sister church with its executive pastor and dozens of staff members of varying degrees of prominence and power. Perhaps the time will come for a detective series that captures all the conspiracy and intrigue that must surely transpire in a church of 17,000, but it will be a different genre of literature than the traditional *church* story. It is the smaller church that grabs the attention of novelists. Here the story often revolves around the rector or minister and key people in the parish *family*. The appeal may be community as much as anything else.

That spirit of community permeates Jan Karon's stories in the Mitford series. The main character is Father Tim Kavanaugh, the priest of a small-town Episcopal parish, the Lord's Chapel. "While persons in rural ministry may find him too good to be true, too effective, and too fortunate," writes Gary Farley, "we ought to take some comfort in the fact that tens of thousands of persons have read about one of our colleagues."[1]

But more than anything else, readers of the Mitford series are reclaiming a lost time in their memories or their fantasies.

The longing for community is the attraction—an attraction that cannot be duplicated in the superchurch. Indeed, this focus in the Mitford series has drawn people to the Christian faith and has drawn walk-aways back to faith. Lauren Winner speaks of this longing and her own conversion. In her spiritual memoir, *Girl Meets God,* she tells how she converted from Judaism to the Christian faith and how "Jan Karon's Mitford novels . . . about a kind of community" played a role: "I think this vivid portrayal of a community organized around one's faith was very appealing."[2]

Jan Karon's grasp of community in the small-town church was drawn from observations from her childhood. She knew the church through power struggles that often occur, but she also knew it through the mundane aspects of community life. Reflecting on another best-selling church fiction writer, Susan Howatch, who "deals with the politics of the church," Karon points out the difference in their stories: "I deal with the casseroles. I like to get right down in the kitchen, to the volunteerism and the bane and blessings sale, and I get into the politics of the human heart, how people interact with one another on a very simple level because that's just a microcosm for the larger church." Her themes correspond with her own memories—memories of a church community as the center of her social life:

> Raised by my grandparents, I sat in the front row at the Methodist Church. I was listening to the preacher. I was looking around to see what people were doing, how they were dressed. I was seeing their stockings rolled down below their knees. It was wonderful. Just to watch people and watch their faces. I enjoyed church, but it was a social outing for us because we lived in the country and we were very sheltered. I never had an overnight party . . . I never did anything social [except for church].[3]

Good as well as bad things happen at the Lord's Chapel, and Father Tim is always the center of the action that sometimes seems to slow to the pace of a southern drawl. The characters are regular folks trying to come to terms with life in a small town that occasionally rubs against the bustle and blare of a larger world. But central to all the goings-on is community.

A Definition of Community

What is *community*? It's a word that is bandied about; everyone is for it. But do we really know what it is? I think about the term a lot as it relates to my childhood memories and to my adult life, especially in relation to the church and workplace. Whatever the word means, I know I have rarely experienced it in adult life with the exception of my marriage to John, which is a wonderful combination of community and intimacy.

This concept of marriage and community is thoughtfully developed by Lauren Winner (in a review of Wendell Berry's novel *Hannah Coulter*). Her reflections help define the term *community* and are applicable to the concept of church as community. "Both of Hannah's marriages are models of something good and rare," she writes. "Both show us that love is a room, a place, a habitation. And both show that marriage is a communal venture, not a lonely, if romantic, twining of two atomized individuals." In Winner's description of marriage, there are analogies with the church of our generation. Hannah Coulter stands as a model for the Christian in community. "Both of Hannah's marriages are powerful rebuttals to glossy magazines and to Hollywood, which tell us at every turn that marriage is about individual fulfillment and pleasure, and that when fulfillment and pleasure disappear it's time to pick up and move on to someone else."[4]

Winner goes on to say that this novel is "like much of Berry's prose and poetry, a meditation on community, and on decline."[5] Small-town America is in decline, and Berry's Port William, Kentucky, for all practical purposes is more nostalgia than reality. So too the small community churches. But the ideal of community must not die. It is as fundamental to Christianity as it is to marriage. It is *a room, a place, a habitation*, and it cannot find substitution in glossy magazines or Hollywood. Much of our focus on numbers, size, and performance in our churches flies in the face of community. This is the challenge we face. Is it possible to have true Christian community in our churches? Is it possible to have true community in marriage instead of imagining that marriage is about individual fulfillment and pleasure?

Rodney Clapp argues that church (as community) should be regarded as our *first* family—first in relation to our biological or nuclear family, which he maintains is second. I disagree with

Clapp. I believe his use of the term *family* for church is misplaced. The two terms are similar in many respects, but family is family and church is faith community. But even if his thesis is seen as an ideal, is it workable? In reality it seems an impossibility—at least in North America. As in marriage, "when fulfillment and pleasure disappear" many people "pick up and move on" to another church. Moreover, the mobility of the family does not lend itself to church as first family. And from a more theoretical (and theological) consideration, can and should a church come before the family (or marriage) community?

But Clapp certainly does challenge the church on matters of community. His call for love and care beyond blood ties is well placed. He rightly emphasizes responsibility, loyalty, and accountability to a body of believers who live and interact in close physical proximity. A father (or mother) who uproots the family simply to follow a job promotion is defying the very foundational notions of community. Such a radical change that affects family and church, it would seem, should be made only after serious and prayerful deliberation, with the knowledge that the family and church community involved will be severely altered.

In most cases, however, the church community is hardly considered in the face of a geographical move. And perhaps for good reason. Most churches are not faith *communities*. The family is not bound to a church community but rather *attends* church, and there will always be another church to *attend* in a new city where the salary is higher and the house is bigger.

Intergenerational Community

Community in the left-behind church is intergenerational, unlike that of the megachurch I visited in a suburb of Denver. There the youth had their own sanctuary—"The Cave"—where hundreds of them met together without having to endure the wearisome monotony of adult worship. In the megachurch, separate youth worship is often taken for granted. But there are some who would strongly question the long-term spiritual benefits. "It is a sad fact of life that often the stronger the youth program in the church, and the more deeply the young people of the church identify with it," writes Ben Patterson, "the weaker the chances are that those same young people will remain in the church when they grow too old for the youth program. Why? Because the youth program has become a substitute for participation in the church. . . . When the kids outgrow the youth program, they also outgrow what they have known of the church."[6]

Some churches are so small they don't even have a youth group. A pastor of such a church was embarrassed by this "deficiency." But when he was questioned further, he revealed that there actually were young people in his church, each of whom he knew by name. He cheered for them at their sports events and found other ways to interact with them on a regular basis. He pitched in when a single dad was planning a surprise birthday party for his daughter. And yet the pastor said he did not have a youth group.[7]

Intergenerational community is more than multiple generations sitting in pews together on Sunday morning. A left-behind church in many cases cannot function without the help of everyone from fourth graders to grandparents. Sometimes this involvement serves both youth and adults better than age-specific activity does. In his book, *Family-Based Youth Ministry*, Mark DeVries tells of a pastor of a small church in Texas who apologized for not having a young people's program. Yet all but three of the eighteen young people were involved in teaching Sunday school or nursery, ushering, singing in choir, or participating in worship in other ways. "If this church is ever able to create a 'successful youth program,'" writes DeVries, "it may destroy its youth ministry."[8]

Open Doors

If a church is truly a community of believers that serves the wider neighborhood community, church doors will be left open. *Oh, but you don't know our neighborhood* is a standard reply. True. I don't. So I take back (while letting it stand) that unqualified statement. All churches should deal with the matter of open doors. There are ways to secure offices while leaving the sanctuary open, and there are other means of dealing with security matters without locking the doors. Perhaps there is no alternative to locked doors, but such an alternative should not be assumed without serious discussion and deliberation. Kenneth E. Kovacs, a Presbyterian minister in Maryland, tells of visiting New York City, where he "stumbled into an Episcopal church on West 46th Street, the Church of St. Mary the Virgin." The first thing he noticed was a "sign on the sidewalk that read, 'Church Open.'" There was no official function taking place and no security guards watching for riffraff.

> I walked into the sanctuary and found a number of people there. The doors open into the sanctuary on both 46th Street and 47th Street, just one block from Times Square. It's a very high Episcopal church, very ornate, quite beautiful. To my amazement the doors were left open, with not one church official in sight keeping watch! There were people lighting candles, kneeling, praying, walking around in a contemplative manner. On the pews in the back of the church homeless people were sleeping. As I walked and looked (trying to find the church office) . . . I realized, *This is a great church*, truly welcoming the children of God.[9]

Kovacs goes on to say, "A great church is not characterized by the numbers on its membership rolls, the size of its budget, the beauty of its sanctuary, or even the effectiveness of its preaching. A small, struggling, country church might be greater than the rich, megachurch in the suburbs."[10]

Nor is a great church characterized by the *quality* of its members. I will never forget coming back to church, after having been away traveling for a number of weeks, and hearing the minister not so subtly take a jab at his critics. Apparently some had criticized his leadership, and he was smarting over an assessment review. From the pulpit, during the time for announcements, he said, "Anyone who doesn't think the Lord is blessing the ministry in this church ought to look at the quality of people who are joining today." He then made reference to the bulletin, which listed *quality* people: families with the fathers' professions listed—a doctor, two attorneys, a business owner, a salesman, and a college professor. There were no menial laborers and, God forbid, no homeless, single mothers. As with our cars and the furnishings in our homes, we recognized *quality*.

Community and Solidarity

There is solidarity in community, and sometimes that means that the pastor and people stand together against injustice. Such was the case with Karl Barth, serving as a Reformed pastor in a tiny, Swiss industrial town in the 1920s. He soon realized how impoverished the people were, due to low wages and lack of benefits. He was convinced that he had no other choice than to come to their aid and help them organize by lecturing to the local Workers' Association. His lectures were sermons of sorts. He "drew a contrast between the church, which for 1800 years had failed to deal with the social needs, and Jesus Christ as the partisan of the poor, for whom there had been 'only one God, in solidarity with society.'" He faced opposition from the wealthy manufacturer, but he refused to be deterred. He vowed continued support of the workers. "I regard socialist demands as an important part of the application of the gospel, though I also believe that they cannot be realized with the gospel."[11]

Now retired from decades of pastoral ministry, Eugene Peterson, known for his biblical paraphrase, *The Message*, attends a left-behind church in his hometown of Flathead Lake, Montana. It is a church that has little to offer by megachurch standards, but it models *community*. "In church last Sunday, there was a couple in front of us with two bratty kids," he tells an interviewer. "Two pews behind us there was another couple with their two bratty kids making a lot of noise." This was going on in a congregation of mainly gray heads, who might be expected to react very negatively to what Peterson describes as "not very good worship." But after the service, people came up and greeted the children and expressed empathy with the mother. "Now why do people go to a church like that when they can go to a church that has a nursery, is air conditioned, and all the rest?" he asks. His answer is as revealing as it is perhaps tongue-in-cheek. "Well, because they're Lutherans. They don't mind being miserable! Norwegian Lutherans!"[12]

What these Lutherans do well is simply being Christians. They do not have a state-of-the-art sound system or a first-rate worship team, and they are not growing by leaps and bounds. But they recently welcomed a single mother who requested baptism for her little ones with different fathers. "She's a Christian and wants to follow in the Christian way." In that little church, she now has godparents for her children and friends who check in on her during the week. This might seem like an unlikely place for a struggling young mother to find a home and a sense of inner joy. Indeed, this is the very question Peterson raises and answers: "Now, where is the 'joy' in that church? These are dour Norwegians! But there's a lot of joy. . . . I think there's a lot more going on in churches like this; they're just totally anticultural. They're full of joy and faithfulness and obedience and care. But you sure wouldn't know it by reading the literature of church growth, would you?"[13]

The left-behind church remains the best hope for community and family connectedness in today's world. *Left behind* does not mean hopelessly mired in the past. It does not mean a no-growth graph. It does not mean stiff formality or fundamentalist separation. But it does mean holding on to traditions, hymns, liturgy, and intergenerational togetherness.

The downtown church of which I am a member is an old church by western Michigan standards. Although its numbers are increasing, it is purposefully out of sync with today's purpose-driven religious environment. There on any given Sunday morning we might hear Zachary's voice before we spot him: "Papa! MiMi!" And Mitchell and Ashley are never far behind. And we wave to brother Jim and Darlene up in the balcony. For some families, it's four generations. Such connectedness with tradition and family makes it harder to pull up roots when the megachurch comes to town.

Church Shopping

For Grand Rapids, Mars Hill came to town less than a decade ago, and within days it was boasting ten thousand members. Well, maybe not that fast. But one church after another lost families to Mars Hill. Many of those churches were caught up in megachurch fantasies themselves.

Today it is too easy to leave one church for another—much easier than it was in past generations, though church shopping has a long history. Martin Luther had no designs on starting a new denomination, but he incited a revolution that has reverberated through five hundred years of history. Any unity there may have been among those first protester Protestants quickly dissipated. "The next thing you know," writes Tim Stafford, "we had 20,000 denominations worldwide—and counting." Stafford illustrates this propensity for religious individualism and restlessness with a cute story that has appeared in many guises:

> A man is rescued after 20 years on a desert island. His rescuer is astonished to find that the castaway has built several imposing structures.
> "Wow!" the rescuer says. "What's that beautiful stone building overlooking the bay?"
> "That is my home," the castaway says.
> "And what about that building over there, with the spires?"
> "That," the castaway says, "is my church."
> "But wait!" the rescuer says. "That building over there, with the bell tower. What is that?"
> "That is the church I used to belong to."[14]

In speaking of "seeker-sensitive" churches, Stafford writes: "I admire the evangelistic spirit behind this. It has attracted many people into a church building who would probably not otherwise attend. But I think it has exaggerated a sense that the church must adapt to the general public, not the other way around."[15]

Evangelical Individualism

Today's individualized *designer* spirituality is an outgrowth of the individualism imbedded in evangelicalism since the mid-nineteenth century and that continues to this day. When I contemplate this kind of individualism, I remember the stories I grew up with—stories that featured the heroes of the faith. D. L. Moody was such a hero, and it may be that modern evangelical individualism began with him. "Perhaps the line most frequently attributed to Dwight L. Moody (and spoken by his character in the only film on Moody's life) is the famous quotation: 'The world has yet to see what God can do with a man fully consecrated to him. By God's help, I aim to be that man.'"[16] We were inspired to emulate him and *be that man.* I do not remember hearing a challenge for us to multiply our gifts and abilities through community and collaboration.

The "great man" theory of leadership has also strongly influenced the concept of individualism—one that is not celebrated in Scripture. Surely we cannot deny the Hebrews Hall of Faith in chapter 11 that calls to our attention individuals, but it is the *faith* not the individual that we are to imitate. That is true in the case of Isaac: "By faith Isaac blessed Jacob and Esau in regard to their future" (Heb. 11:20). Paul is a "great man," but he repeatedly refers to his coworkers, both women and men. And Jesus himself is in community with the Twelve as well as the larger group of disciples, both women and men. As a historian I find it much easier to write history according to the "great man" (or woman) model, but in real life the Christian faith is best represented in community rather than by individuals.

A church is a community of faith, and it should also be "the 'community of memory' in which members are nurtured in tradition," writes Richard Lischer. But in our individualistic culture this kind of community "has given way to the 'life-style enclave' in which convenience and common mode of consumption are the most important factors."[17]

Countercultural or Contextualized?

An important issue for any church to wrestle with as a community is whether the church is one that emphasizes *contextualization* with the culture around it or whether it sees itself as being *countercultural*. The philosophy behind many megachurches is that of contextualization—reaching out to the postmodern generation(s) in culturally relevant ways. One of the hallmarks of church growth is the church's ability to make someone on the outside feel comfortable on the inside. And that is surely not all bad. In fact, *contextualization* has been the buzzword for cross-cultural missions for decades, with a long history that goes back through the Jesuits to those early mission ventures authorized by Pope Gregory the Great in the sixth century and before that the Apostle Paul, who was "all things to all men that I might by all means save some" (1 Cor. 9:22 KJV). But at the same time the early church was very countercultural in standing apart from the worldliness *around* it.

And it is on this side of the equation that the left-behind church is often better equipped to radiate the *good news* that stands in stark contrast with the *bad news* of the world around it.

But the *good news* should not be misconstrued with the good feelings that are easily manufactured in a North American *contextualized* church. Our culture is one characterized by materialism and the cult of therapy, self-absorption, and political correctness. This was not the way of Jesus. Jesus was countercultural even as he so seamlessly contextualized the gospel. His listeners understood, except when he purposely perplexed them. To follow Jesus was to step out of the crowd and be different. Jesus continually spoke of the uniqueness of the kingdom of God as opposed to the world at large. But on the surface at least, it was not the good life. Yes, there was life more abundant and for the weary there was rest, but there was also a cross to bear, one the world knows nothing of. And even this kingdom would not erase a sense of God-forsakenness—the very lament of Jesus on the cross. Nor should we be rid of such feelings of lament and God-forsakenness today.

Community of Shared Sorrow

"The use of [the] 'psalms of darkness' may be judged by the world to be *acts of unfaith and failure*," writes Walter Brueggemann, "but for the trusting community, their use is *an act of bold faith*, albeit a transformed faith. It is an act of bold faith on the one hand, because it insists that the world must be experienced as it really is and not in some pretended way. On the other hand, it is bold because it insists that all such experiences of disorder are proper subjects for discourse with God."[18]

I remember well some years ago when I was a member of a church of several hundred people that was introducing new ideas for contemporary worship. People were excited. We had a praise team and an acting troupe—and a new worship leader. Music and skits were tied into the theme of the season or the chosen Scripture passage. For what they lacked in raw talent, they seemed to make up for in enthusiasm.

It was Thanksgiving morning—our usual Thanksgiving service. The theme was thankfulness, with a skit attempting humor and plenty of praise songs. But like many other members, I had come with a heavy heart. The local news headlined an accident the evening before. A truck ran a stop sign and a man was killed, one of our dear, old-time members. But the worship had been planned. Almost twenty people had set aside precious time for practice, and a Thanksgiving theme is not easily postponed and used as an Advent theme. The show must go on. And it did.

It was not until halfway through the service when there was a time for "open mike" for people to stand up and say what they were thankful for that someone stood and, with a quivery voice, made mention of the deep grief we were feeling. Most megachurches—or megachurch wannabes—do not want to ruin the upbeat feeling with sorrow and weeping. Had we been *left behind in community*, we would have stopped and canceled the show before it got started, and we would have raised our lament to God.

A megachurch or a megachurch wannabe has no room for lament—and perhaps for good reason. A megachurch is too big for lament. Every week there are sorrows and tragedies. Church growth requires a spirit of optimism and elation—certainly not one of sadness. "At Saddleback, we believe worship is to be a celebration," writes Rick Warren, "so we use a style that is upbeat, bright, and joyful. We rarely sing a song in a minor key."[19]

"We avoid life's darkness because we do not let God be God," writes Marva Dawn. "We try to control the darkness ourselves, or we must ignore it because our worship does not proclaim God's sovereign control." She tells of her own darkness and lament, "one health crisis after another—crippling of a leg and hands, hearing and vision losses, frequent wounds that won't heal, intestinal dysfunctions, immunity deficiency, nerve deterioration, cancer." God, she writes, too easily becomes small in her personal worship. "I need public worship to bring me a holy and merciful God who shows me my sinfulness and yet offers the possibility of repentance and forgiveness. I need worship that lets me lament and find in that cry God's caring presence. I need an assembly of people who ask God to be God in their lives."[20]

Churches—regular churches, not megachurches—have continued through the centuries to be community centers. From Ontario to Appalachia, from Maine to New Mexico, churches have served for generations as community gathering places, safe havens during times of hardship and sorrow as well as times of celebration. In *All Over but the Shoutin'*, Rick Bragg pays tribute not only to his mother but also to his heritage in the South, and the church was a key element of that heritage. "My mother and father were born in the most beautiful place on earth, in the foothills of the Appalachians along the Alabama-Georgia line," he writes. "It was a place where playing the church piano loud was near as important as playing it right." It was a life of poverty, where "men paid for their plain-plank houses and a few acres of land by sawing and hand-lifting pulpwood onto ragged trucks for pennies a ton." To make even a subsistence living, "their women worked themselves to death, their mules succumbed to worms and their children were crippled by rickets and perished from fever." Yet in the midst of all this there was hope. "Every Sunday morning The Word leaked out of little white-wood sanctuaries where preachers thrust ragged Bibles at the rafters and promised them that while sickness and poverty and Lucifer might take their families, the soul of man never dies."[21] Nevertheless, God exacted a high price for life on this planet with church community a solace in an otherwise laborious life.

> It was as if God made them pay for the loveliness of their scenery by demanding everything else. Yet the grimness of it faded for a while, at dinner on the ground of the Protestant churches, where people sat on the springtime grass and ate potato salad and sipped sweet tea from an aluminum tub with a huge block of ice floating in it. . . . The hardness of it softened in the all-night gospel singings that ushered in the dawn with the promise that "I'll have a new body, praise the Lord, I'll have a new life," as babies crawled up into the ample laps of grandmothers to sleep across jiggling knees.[22]

Inclusive Community

Community is the theme of *Home to Harmony*, best described as autobiographical fiction, by Quaker minister Philip Gulley. Told in first person, Gulley returns to his hometown of Harmony "sorely depressed," and for good reason: "Thirty-eight years old, married with two children, and living with my parents." But when the local Quaker minister was hit by a truck and killed while jogging, Gulley's fortunes changed. He was asked to fill the void for Easter Sunday. Within weeks he was the minister of the very church in which he had grown up—and not only minister but the one who was expected to "open the church doors, shovel the walk, and mow the grass." Harmony is a small town, and without the Harmony Friends Meeting House, the little town and its environs would have been much poorer.[23]

The reality of community is best illustrated in routine acts of kindness. The story of Paul and Judy is one example. "It wasn't unusual for our church to have visitors," writes Gulley. "What was odd about Paul and Judy Iverson was that they came back a second time." When they announced that they would be going to China to adopt a baby girl, church members busied themselves in transforming a closet into a nursery. Rarely had there been such excitement. "A baby! Just think of it. A baby in the meeting. In our very own nursery. A little girl with a good tan and dark hair. In our nursery."

The Iversons left on Tuesday. When a long-distance call came to the meetinghouse on Friday, Frank, the church handyman, picked up the phone. Listening through the static, he was sure he heard "Siamese twins." Then the line went dead. "Frank didn't know what to think. He walked into the nursery and looked at the crib. . . . It won't be big enough, Frank thought. . . . I must build a new crib. A big crib. A crib for the Iverson Siamese twins." When Paul and Judy returned with their twins—Chinese twins—Frank welcomed them into the nursery with the big crib.

On Thanksgiving Frank invited Paul and Judy (and his beloved twins) for dinner. It was his first since he had been widowed. He prepared the turkey not realizing he should remove the bag of giblets. Instead of eating turkey still frozen on the inside, he took them to McDonald's. When the minister stopped by later that afternoon to check on Frank, he commented: "I sure hope the Iversons stick with us. . . . Hope they don't go to that new church out by the interstate. You know, the one that shows music on the screen and has a children's minister."

Frank said, "They're not looking for a children's minister. They're looking for love. I think they'll stick."[24]

Many left-behind churches get failing marks on the matter of *community*. Indeed, the small church is sometimes far less conscious of community than the megachurch. One woman, in describing her church situation, summed the situation up in terse sentences: "What really rattled my cage was the hypocrisy of it all. Here we'd been talking for some years about community and love and bearing each other's burdens. Then, when the going got tough, everyone got going—out the back door—because it was tough. No community, no bonds of faith."[25]

Community surely does not mean uniformity. Some churches display uniformity, though often at a cost of creativity and originality. Individuals are forced to conform to the system. A healthy community encourages differences and new ideas while at the same time fostering unity, though many pastors would testify that maintaining unity is an exercise as exasperating as herding cats. "From the outside, church congregations can look like remarkably contentious places, full of hypocrites who talk about love while fighting each other tooth and nail," writes Kathleen Norris. "This is the reason many people give for avoiding them. On the inside, however, it is a different matter, a matter of struggling to maintain unity as 'the body of Christ' given the fact that we have precious little uniformity. . . . We can do pretty well when it comes to loving and serving God, each other, and the world; but God help us if we have to agree about things. . . . [like] that Holy of Holies—the church kitchen."[26]

The community of the left-behind church, it must never be forgotten, includes the community of the dead. Woe be the pastor who imagines the *community of the dead* in the cemetery are no longer considered part of the church community. This tension between congregation and pastor is very cleverly captured by Father Peter J. Surrey, rector of St. Paul's Episcopal Church in Savanna, Illinois, in an article entitled, "Changes in the Small-Town Church." He introduces the article with an old Episcopal saying:

> Be we High or Low
> The status is Quo.

The entire text of Surrey's article is a letter (that sounds more real than fictitious) from Mary Walsh, who is writing him to set him straight about church life and to chastise him about his shortcomings. She begins by referring to the recent meeting he had with the Women's Guild:

"You began by remarking on our low Sunday attendance," she reminded him. "Then you reviewed the budget, especially the many bills. The main explosion was provoked by your innocent comment—or was it that innocent?—on the old furnishings of the sanctuary. 'All that old stuff,' you said, 'is so dreadful that it looks as though it had been handmade by the monkeys in Noah's ark!' In case you did not know it, that set was given many years ago by the family who founded this church. Oh, we all know their bodies are out in the cemetery, but . . . these people in a very real, spiritual sense are still with us."[27]

A left-behind church is a community—a community where the living mingle with the dead. There is shared sorrow. But the dearly departed often linger on in the traditions and memories of the congregation, masking their *dead and buried* status in the nearby cemetery. By its very nature this community is a counter-cultural entity that radiates the countercultural message of the gospel if it is truly following in the footsteps of Jesus.

10

Left Behind with a Sense of Humor

"That's sacrilegious!" I'll never forget the accusation, though at the time I had never before heard the term, and I've long since forgotten the context for it. I had graduated from a small-town public high school and was enrolled in Bible college in St. Paul, Minnesota. I hadn't had the benefit of a *good Christian family* as my friends had, and I didn't know how to play the game. Well, maybe I did. But I've always been what some people describe as edgy, and I am easily enticed by offbeat humor, the likes of Michael Yaconelli and the *Wittenberg Door*. I love irony. Whether political or religious, irony is for me a key survival tool in this old, troubled world. But we evangelicals, I've always maintained, take ourselves way too seriously. We are fodder for humor, no doubt. Turn on late-night comedy for proof of that. But we rarely recognize these quirks in our own subculture.

Why are the most recognizable comedians Jewish—the Marx Brothers, Jack Benny, Milton Berle, Lenny Bruce, Jerry Lewis, Jonathan Winters, Alan King, Woody Allen, Joan Rivers, Jerry Seinfeld, and Jon Stewart, host of *The Daily Show*? It is estimated that about 80 percent of comedians in North America are Jewish, though Jews comprise only 3 percent of the population. Why aren't evangelicals, whose numbers rank high in population statistics, recognized as the comedians of our time? Don't we claim special *giftedness* from God? Isn't *humor* listed among the spiritual gifts?

Though accused of starting college on the wrong foot, when I graduated (from another Christian college), I was voted by my classmates as having the "best sense of humor." That alone is proof enough of how desperately deficient evangelical humor is.

Laughter at what we cherish most is deemed sacrilegious because the subject is considered too sacred. But is anything too sacred for laughter? Or are we too stuffy to laugh at what is truly funny? The French philosopher Voltaire playfully suggested that Christians were disparaging their Creator by their somber manner. God, he said, "is a comedian, playing to an audience too afraid to laugh." Nothing is worse than folded arms and a stern expression when laughter is called for. Is it possible that we are grieving the Spirit by our refusal to laugh?

Perhaps no topic offers more fodder for humor than the left-behind church. The term *left-behind* when describing a church is not one that I use in a negative way. But the term surely holds that connotation in its most widely recognized religious usage: that of being left behind when the rapture occurs.

I grew up in a left-behind church in which warnings came with regularity about the fate of the unsaved who would be left behind. This was an era when bomb shelters offered little security against the ominous threat of Soviet communism. Armageddon was but a nuclear strike away. It was a time that predated the church growth movement, when megachurches were few and far between and neighborhood churches dotted the landscape. It was before the mass distribution and enormous popularity of evangelical books, magazines, and music. In the world of the 1950s, almost everything that was associated with fundamentalist or evangelical was deemed *left behind*. We were left behind and we knew it. But our time was coming. When the rapture came, we would not be left behind.

Left-Behind Rapture Humor

We were among a wide spectrum of fundamentalists influenced by Nelson Darby and the Plymouth Brethren, who took very seriously the end-times succession of events—events illustrated and brought to life on linear charts starting with the first day of creation in 4004 BC and culminating at the end of the thousand-year millennium.

But it was the rapture that most captured our attention—an event that was imminent. It could happen any moment. There were, however, signs of the times, as the book of Revelation combined with news stories from the St. Paul *Pioneer Press* surely confirmed. "This World Is Not My Home"—we sang it with gusto. But we also had our doubts. Were there some among us in our left-behind earthly condition who would also be left behind at the rapture? Waiting for the thief in the night can be nerve-wracking. Along with every other fundamentalist child, I feared the rapture at one time or another. Garrison Keillor, himself Plymouth Brethren in background, expresses it best through his autobiographical, albeit fictional, humor. He picks up the story of his adolescence as he is sneaking peaks at a girly magazine, *High School Orgies*:

> I am going to spend eternity in hellfire for what is twitching in my mind right now.
>
> Here I am in my room, weeping for my carnal sins, on a warm summer night, and what if the Second Coming is scheduled for nine-fifteen p.m. Central Time and in exactly five minutes the saved of earth will rise into the stratosphere and I will find myself left behind with the heathen?
>
> This could be the case. What if I tiptoe downstairs *right now* and Daddy isn't lying there on the daybed listening to the Millers on the radio—what if all the Sanctified Brethren have whooshed up to the sky, Sugar and Ruth and Al and Flo and LeRoy and Lois, and I am left behind with the Catholics and the atheists and the drunks at the Sidetrack Tap?[1]

Keillor has made a career (and a fortune) poking fun at regular Christian folks who are left behind. His style of poking fun at himself and his heritage ought to be the standard of all left-behind churches. If a church is left behind without a sense of humor, it is in a sad state of affairs.

A Safe Space for Fun

The pastor is a key element. I say this from personal experience not as a pastor but as a professor. I have long believed that if a class runs an hour without at least one good, hearty belly laugh, I have failed. Sometimes I make a comment or string together a clever comeback that draws laughter. But more often it is one of my students who recognizes an atmosphere that welcomes humor. A pastor or professor is in the position to set the stage for this kind of environment.

The *gift* of humor is truly a much underrated "spiritual gift." There is so much talk these days (and in days past) about *identifying one's spiritual gifts*, as though such identification automatically paves the way for utilizing those gifts to transform the individual or the church. Most *gifts*, such as those of humor, are obvious. Everyone knows it if the pastor has a quick comeback or a hearty laugh or a dry sense of humor or is one who does not take himself or herself too seriously. And if the congregation is so fortunate to see this in their pastor, they are blessed. There is so much anger, angst, hostility, and fear that can be quickly dispelled by humor. How much better board meetings are when a little humor is employed. The same goes for the building committee and the pleas for more funds. Laughter truly is the best medicine. This *gift* was given to one species only (though my mongrel Rafiki was on many occasions, I swear, *amused*). We often utterly fail to recognize its importance in the matter of church health.

Humor over Happiness

When we think of the church, if we are theologically oriented, the term *ecclesiology* comes to mind. Ecclesiology is that aspect of theology that seeks to bring Scripture to bear on matters of church order, focusing on church organization, governance, and guidelines on matters from discipline to deed ownership. Issues of church size, substance, and self-esteem fall outside the parameters of ecclesiology. Yet these things are often deemed the very *stuff* that defines a church.

But a church is first and foremost a *story*. Far more than it is a set of rules and regulations or even size or social standing, *story* is the essence of a church. The rules, to be sure, are necessary, as are the doctrinal and biblical foundations that give grounds for the church's very existence. But they form the skeleton. The *body* is an ongoing narrative and life of people—flesh and blood and warts and all—and the people, for better or for worse, are what others see. Churches are *bodies* with personalities that are far more obvious to outsiders than the skeletal framework.

In assessing the personality, perspective, and appearance of a church, it is sometimes tempting to concentrate on superficial qualities. Church growth literature emphasizes friendliness, and along with friendliness comes a smiling, happy demeanor. Radiating a sense of excitement and enthusiasm is also high on the list, as is cultural sensitivity, particularly in worship style. If hymns are "outdated" it is a sure sign of being left behind.

Sometimes the suggestions for improving appearance are as "design-oriented" as those of the realtor who is listing my house. For a house to sell quickly, he insists, bathrooms and kitchens make or break the deal. For the church the requisites are similar. Indeed, churches are taking cues from upscale homes and fine restaurants and are turning toilets into ladies' powder rooms with exquisite décor. The appearance of the nursery and the children's worship space is also high on the list, at least for young families. This formula is substantiated by statistics. An increase in attendance is the proof of success.

But should the left-behind church be focused on superficial cosmetic changes? If not, what kind of personality and appearance should distinguish the church? Many would say that the personality should shine forth with smiles, friendliness, and happiness that defines the Christian life. But what about authenticity? Does not authenticity sometimes fly in the face of a happy and friendly demeanor? I sometimes catch the news by tuning in to the *Imus in the Morning* program, the host of which rails against the competing morning network TV news programs. "They're too happy," he fumes. "They're all phonies. No one can possibly be that happy." He himself appears to be the least happy person in the news media. But what distinguishes him and fuels his ratings is his humor.

Phony happiness is easily detected and quickly rejected. Humor is not happiness. Indeed, it is often a means of coping with the troubles and sorrows of this world. And two things that left-behind churches typically have in ample supply are troubles and sorrows. The left-behind church is a gold mine of humor. Raw material oozes in abundance.

Taking a Cue from Keillor

Garrison Keillor's *left-behind* church humor is drawn most personally from his own Plymouth Brethren background. But his spoofs do not end there. Indeed, some claim that as host of *A Prairie Home Companion* and the author of *Lake Wobegon Days*, his homespun humor parodies left-behind Lutherans most of all. According to a *National Post* editorial, he has singled them out as representative of all that is peculiar about Scandinavians transplanted in Minnesota. "Are Lutherans funny?" asks Robert Fulford. Most people would not imagine that they would be fodder for comedy. But Keillor's genius lies in turning mundane eccentricities and self-righteous conceit into spoofs that poke fun at human nature. When we laugh at the Scandinavian Lutherans, we are laughing at ourselves. "This strikingly original idea dominates much of his writing and talking," Fulford continues. "'Lutheran' is Keillor's best punchline, the Lutheran church the site of his best stories, the Lutheran ethos a favorite object of his satire."[2]

But having grown up among the Plymouth Brethren, Keillor reserves some of his funniest lines for them. PBs are representative of a host of fundamentalist denominations and independent churches. Though much of Keillor's humor is fiction, there is a not-so-subtle autobiographical slant to what he writes. He reflects back on his own childhood formed by his extended family, all part of this fundamentalist subculture. Only in such left-behind churches can one get "saved . . . at a gospel revival at the Green Lake Bible Camp" to the singing of "Lord, I'm Coming Home" and "Come into My Heart, Lord Jesus." But even before the altar call is over, he is having trouble with the assurance of his salvation:

> Brother Rowley said anyone who wanted to accept Jesus Christ as Savior should come forward—and I didn't go. I didn't care to be a tree toad on his knees, bawling, for everyone to gawk at. So I sat in my seat and quietly invited Jesus into my heart. But did He come in? Or did He say, "If you're too scared to come down front, then, why should I walk all the way back there?"
>
> Condemned to eternal perdition because I was too shy to walk fifty feet! What a fool! . . .

I sit every Sunday morning with the Sanctified Brethren in Aunt Flo and Uncle Al's living room, the Body and Blood of our Lord Jesus Christ on a card table in our midst, and listen to the men pray their long expository prayers ("O Thou Who didst pass over the dwelling places of the children of Israel, so too watch over us, Thy Church, Thy Faithful Remnant, as we seek to uphold Thy Word in the midst of great spiritual darkness").[3]

Shared experiences like Keillor's combine to make up our church story. A megachurch filled with corporate transients does not have comparable shared experiences and has less potential raw material for comedy. Any effort to create an environment for humor is aided by this fertile soil indigenous to the left-behind church. Left to its own devices, the church with a pastor who cultivates this soil will reap a harvest of goodwill. Humor serves effectively as a preventative measure in avoiding normal flare-ups that often occur during stressful times, including those precarious times when a church is involved in remodeling or major building projects.

"Shingles for the Lord"

I was reminded of that this morning as my husband read to me (as he does most mornings) William Faulkner's short story "Shingles for the Lord." There is good reason why Faulkner is recognized as one of America's all-time great Southern writers. He is a skillful humorist who, with all his senses, captures the essence of life with his pen. This short story is about a left-behind church that needs a new roof and in the end will get much more than that. Here we recognize quickly how our own stubborn sinfulness can get the best of us in a church building project. And every church building committee and congregation—before committing to the project—should read "Shingles for the Lord."

The story, as told by a boy, starts out with the frustration of the boy's "pap," a down-home, low-class, hardworking farmer trying to get to the church early in the morning to begin the job of re-shingling the church. He has in good faith made a commitment, but he is foiled by old man Killegrew, who was out all night and into the morning fox hunting and thus not home to lend pap his froe and maul, the tools he needs for the job. So pap arrives two hours late, much to the irritation of Reverend Whitfield. The Reverend is supposed to be supervising his volunteer parishioners, two of whom arrived on time: Solon Quick and Homer Bookwright were "setting on two upended cuts" waiting for pap "with their froes and mauls and axes and wedges" lying idle. An argument ensues about his being late and the lost time that has elapsed. Infused in the dispute over the delay is a theological wrangle. Says pap, "I reckon the Lord will forgive it. He ain't interested in time, nohow. He's interested in salvation." To which Whitfield responds: "He ain't interested in neither! Why should He be, when he owns them both? And why He should turn around for poor, mizzling souls of men that can't even borrow tools in time to replace the shingles on His church, I don't know either. . . . Maybe He just said to Himself: 'I made them; I don't know why. But since I did . . . I'll roll My sleeves up and drag them into glory whether they will or no!'"

Finally the project gets started—that of cutting new shingles and removing old shingles for more volunteers who will be coming the next day to nail them on the roof. Pap works at twice the speed of the other two, but in the eyes of the others he can in no way redeem himself for the lost time. He is "six units short," as counted in WPA (Works Progress Administration) time. The haggling over units continues endlessly. Then Solon makes an offer. He will make up the six units if pap gives him his half share of his mixed breed bird dog. Pap is incredulous. So that is what Solon was up to all along, manipulating the situation so as to acquire the dog. Now the argument turns to "dog units" and how much the dog is worth in man hours. Pap, to the horror of his son (the narrator), agrees to trade the dog for work, plus a handsome sum of two dollars cash, which Solon gives him. But pap has a maneuver up his sleeve. He figures he will get the best of Solon, ending up with both the cash and the dog, if he comes back after dark and finishes his "work units."

After chores, pap and the boy return with a lantern, and pap is up on the roof tearing off the shingles when he, in haste, inadvertently pulls a section of the roof itself down. The lantern falls into the sanctuary setting off a conflagration. "It was an old church, long dried out, and full of old colored-picture charts that Whitfield had accumulated for more than fifty years." Pap is knocked cold (and wet) as he tries to hoist a barrel of water onto the flames. Neighbors—those to whom this little church belonged—gathered to watch. "And then there wasn't nothing but jest pap, drenched and groggy-looking, on the ground, with the rest of us around him, and Whitfield like always in his boiled shirt and his black hat. . . . He looked around at us. . . . 'I was wrong,' [he] said. 'I told you we would meet here tomorrow to roof a church. We'll meet here in the morning to raise one.'" They all immediately volunteer, including pap, who points out, however, that "there's some of us done already give a day or so" of work.

Whitfield turns down the offer with the hiss of "arsonist." Others will rebuild the church but not pap. "Not one hand shall you lay to this new house until you have proved to us that you are to be trusted again." Pap is livid. They all go home. The night is late as he crawls into bed. "Then he set up in bed and drawed a long, shuddering breath." Speaking of Whitfield, he fumed, "If him and all of them put together think they can keep me from working on my own church like ary other man, he better be a good man to try it. . . . Work units. Dog units. And now arsonist. . . . What a day!"[4]

This story truly must be required reading for any left-behind church embarking on a building project that is most often accomplished by volunteers. Such projects are accidents waiting to happen, and they are prime fodder for fratricidal church fights. But the story is more than merely a lesson in avoiding brawls. It is a story of church ownership. As much as these men resented the Reverend, and as much as they sniped about tardiness and work units, they were ready to pitch in. And more than that: no one, including the Reverend, had the right to deny any one of them the right to help rebuild his own church. That is and must be the spirit of the left-behind church if it is determined to carry on.

Enjoying Canned Jokes

Church building projects, for all the conflict they spawn, need humor. Canned jokes are better than no jokes at all, even if they rate low on the laughter scale.

So the minister announces the latest fund-drive numbers to his Sunday morning congregation. "I've got good news and bad news," he reports. "The good news is that we have enough money to pay for the new addition, free and clear. . . . The bad news is that it's still out there in your pockets."

So how does the minister get the money out of their pockets? He waits until the first Sunday in July. He announces that there will be a time for pledging immediately following the sermon—a sermon that carries a combination stewardship and patriotic theme. When he is finished, he asks all who are willing to pledge an extra thousand dollars to please stand. And then he nods to the organist to begin the hymn—"The Star-Spangled Banner."

There are an infinite number of preacher jokes, and the preacher who can pass them along will pave the way for good feelings.

The elderly, retired minister goes in for his annual physical, and the doctor tells him the tests are negative and that his heart is pumping like that of a sixty-year-old. He's in good shape except for his eyes—now dimmed by cataracts. But the Lord, the minister insists, takes care of him, indeed, in the most miraculous ways. He tells the doctor how God provides light when he most needs it. In fact, he reports that when he gets up in the night to go to the bathroom, "poof" God gives him light, and when he's done, "poof" the light goes off. The doctor is puzzled, wondering if the old gentleman might have some sort of optic nerve condition. He calls the wife aside and mentions this unusual claim to her. "Oh, my gosh," she moans. "He's peeing in the refrigerator again."

Boring sermon jokes are a dime a dozen.

Gladys Dunn was new to the community, and after settling in, she visited the little church down the street. She liked the old hymns and the choir, but the sermon was long and tedious. It dragged on past noon. Finally the service was over. As she got up to leave, she turned to the man next to her, extended her hand, and said, "Gladys Dunn." He shook his head and sighed in relief, "You and me both!"

And then there are the redneck church jokes. You know that you're a redneck church if . . .

- the collection plates are hubcaps from a '79 Chevy.
- the choir is known as the "OK Chorale."

- the congregation numbers 200—with only five last names in the church directory.
- the deacons think the "rapture" is what you get when you lift something too heavy.
- the baptismal font is a #2 galvanized watering trough.
- the purchase of a chandelier is voted down because nobody can play one.
- the pastor calls on Bubba to take the offering and five men come forward.
- the restroom is outside.
- the only reason to lock the car is to stop neighbors from leaving bags of zucchini.

Every denomination has its own jokes as well. You might be a United Methodist if . . .

- your "heart is strangely warmed" after eating that third piece of pie.
- you know that a circuit rider is not an electrical device.
- the *Upper Room* is as essential to your upstairs bathroom as the toilet paper.
- you have at least one pair of cross and flame boxer shorts in your drawer.
- you consider the monthly potluck a church sacrament.
- UMW has more to do with women than with United Mine Workers.

And of course there are the top ten jokes—*Late Night* style. What are the top ten remarks the left-behind pastor longs to hear?

10. Yes, of course, the country club membership is part of your benefits package.
9. I was so engrossed, I didn't even notice your sermon went a half hour overtime.
8. Personally, I find witnessing much more enjoyable than golf.

7. To feel at ease with the professionals in town, you'll need to drive this loaner BMW.

6. Can I be the permanent teacher for the junior high Sunday school class?

5. Just kidding about your job description including the janitorial and lawn duties.

4. Do you mind if I bring all the ladies in my garden club to church next Sunday?

3. Pastor, we'd like to send you on this spiritual retreat in the Bahamas.

2. Hey! It's *my* turn to sit on the front pew!

1. New furniture? Sure. Just put it on the church account.

Another genre of humor that a left-behind church produces in abundance is *actual church bulletin announcements*. The megachurches have well-paid office staff—managers, secretaries, editors, proofreaders—and perfect church programs. But in the left-behind churches, bad grammar and typos come with the territory, and bulletins are often as amusing as the soloist or the sermon:

- Remember in prayer the many who are sick of our church and community.
- For those of you who have children and don't know it, we have a nursery downstairs.
- The ladies of the church have cast off clothing of every kind and they may be seen in the church basement Friday.
- Thursday at 5:00 PM there will be a meeting of the Little Mothers Club. All wishing to become little mothers, please see the minister in his study.
- This being Easter Sunday, we will ask Mrs. Lewis to come forward and lay an egg on the altar.
- At the evening service tonight, the sermon topic will be "What is Hell?" Come early and listen to our choir practice.
- Pastor is on vacation. Massages can be given to church secretary.
- Eight new choir robes are currently needed, due to the addition of several new members and to the deterioration of some older ones.

- Scouts are saving aluminum cans, bottles, and other items to be recycled. Proceeds will be used to cripple children.
- The Associate Minister unveiled the church's new tithing campaign slogan last Sunday: "I Upped My Pledge—Up Yours."

Holy Laughter

"A church that knows God's grace ought to know how to laugh," writes Steven L. McKinley, a pastor of House of Prayer Lutheran Church in Richfield, Minnesota. "Conjure up for yourself a few pictures of the first becoming last and the last becoming first—what can you do but laugh?" Yet we so easily rule laughter out of order in church. Most of us have no concept of, no category for, holy laughter.

> The Lutheran church carries the name of a man famous for enjoying a good time. Martin Luther was plenty serious about his ministry, but he never forgot how to laugh. Unfortunately the church that bears his name sometimes forgets how to laugh. We take ourselves with deadly seriousness and live as if the world's salvation is our responsibility. . . . Because we take salvation seriously we don't have to take ourselves so seriously. We give life our best shot, but when all is said and done, God is still in charge, not us. So we can laugh.
>
> Our laughter isn't just the gentle laughter of bulletin bloopers and the cute things the little ones say during the children's sermon. . . . Rather, the church's laughter is the deep kind that grows out of knowing how this human story ends, knowing that in the sense of the classical theater, it's a comedy, a story with a happy ending.[5]

We easily take ourselves altogether too seriously, and some of the best laughter comes at those very moments. Beth Quinn tells a story of her childhood when "an altar boy's gown caught on fire during a Christmas service." That such an incident had not occurred before is amazing, considering the explosive mix of "pre-adolescent boys, flammable gowns, and candles." He was not injured, but the fracas created much-appreciated animation in an otherwise tedious Christmas pageant. "The priest was the first to notice the flames," she writes. He "knocked the startled altar boy to the floor and began rolling him around to put him out. The other altar boys got involved in variously inept ways, ranging from throwing their own bodies on their smoky cohort to racing for holy water." The drama on the platform, however, was soon upstaged by drama in the pews. The boy's mother fainted. The ushers moved in and revived her "by fanning her with their collections baskets—while the son [looked on] stripped down to his skivvies."[6]

Memories simply don't come any better than that. Such incidents, if treasured with fond amusement, can carry a left-behind church through difficult times.

11

The Messiness of the Left-Behind Church

"There is a balm in Gilead," but there are also toxins. Marilynne Robinson, who wrote about balm in *Gilead*, wrote an earlier novel, *Housekeeping*,[1] a story of two adolescent sisters who struggle to make their way in a little town after their mother has drowned herself. In reviewing the book, J. A. Gray writes, "In this diluvian world the little church where grandmother used to sing in the choir is a source merely of unwelcome and finally fatal intrusions. The ladies of the congregation bring to the girls' crumbling home not the good news of salvation but only casseroles and coffeecakes that are left untouched and uneaten." It is not as though they mean them harm, but "their well-meant meddling incites the book's climax, when the young women set fire to their house and flee across the lake into a life of endless wandering. The people of the church and town suppose them to be drowned—as indeed they are, spiritually. In the contest of life and grief, grief has won."[2]

Even in the novel *Gilead*,[3] there is not all balm, as Robinson profoundly portrays. This is the story of three generations of preachers whose sins are as subtle as they are plainly visible, including the grandfather's terrible sin against his ten-year-old son and the father's early retirement that was actually a cover-up for his loss of

155

faith. Indeed, both sins are so concealed "that a reader who blinks may miss them." But there is a balm, not the least of which is proffered by a wife's tender care. John Ames, the novel's protagonist, late in life experiences a "domestic resurrection by a wayward young woman" who has "rolled back the stone behind which he had buried his heart." The book offers a fresh slant on spirituality and spiritual formation. "In this new access of feeling, he is dimly aware that some of the warmth of his pastoral compassion derives from the old, banked fires of anger toward his father and grandfather that lie within."[4] True spiritual understanding often sprouts out of compost—or out of the stench of horse manure.

Faltering Saints

For its small size, the left-behind church has its full share of sin and sadness. For many of us, there are nostalgic, spiritual memories of the white, steepled church of a bygone era. But we also know that there are as many skeletons in the proverbial church closet as there are in the churchyard cemetery. That is one of the reasons that makes the neighborhood church an interesting subject of fiction. The utter fallenness of God's people—especially in a small-town setting—offers tensions and twists that the much more anonymous megachurch does not possess. To be sure, there are as many sins and failures per capita in large, thriving churches as there are in urban storefronts or rural chapels, but size and sophistication—whether corporate industry or corporate church—can mask transgressions that cannot be concealed in a church *family*.

"We are not saints," writes Frederick Buechner. "Much of the time our faith is weak and the God we have faith in seems far away if not absent altogether. But we go to church nonetheless in *hope*—hope that God is truly God even so, hope that God will mend us where we are broken, and forgive us where we have a hard time forgiving ourselves, and breathe into us new life when the lives we are living seem empty."[5]

Going to church in hope of forgiveness is most difficult, especially when the ones for whom *our* forgiveness is most needed are among the ninety-four people gathered together and are sitting two rows ahead and across the isle. Such forgiveness is difficult, but it is possible. When the offended one, however, is among six thousand and attends the Saturday night service, I can carry on with worship and volunteer ministry without ever seeing him or her. Sometimes we assume that the smaller church where personality clashes and emotional stress are out in the open is more corrupt and dysfunctional than the megachurch. But the potential for dysfunction can be greater when troubles are suppressed. Professional, glossy worship combined with size and anonymity can easily masquerade for church purity.

God's Grace amid Sinfulness

"If we were to insist on the purity of the church, where would it end?" asks Richard Lischer. As the pastor of a country church, he tells the story of Heather, a young woman whom he told not to participate in communion because she was involved with a married man. "Tears the size of rain drops began to fall" down her cheeks. She loved the church, and "she cried because she was *ex-communicated*." Not long after his encounter with Heather, he "ran into a hateful old bird"—a man "whose everyday speech was riddled with complaint and innuendo about 'the colored.'" Lischer told him that he disapproved of his views, but he treated him differently than Heather. "I didn't bar him from the Eucharist or threaten to do so. Why not? Did his routine racism pollute the body of Christ any less than Heather's adultery?"[6]

The question is one that churches face every day. Do we demand purity in the church, and if so, does the racist stand on the outside with the adulterer? These issues can tear apart any church, but the left-behind church with its small size and sense of community is particularly vulnerable. Sins quickly rise to the surface. Heather may have never been challenged about her adulterous affair had she been in a megachurch. And sins of racism are not confined to redneck, left-behind churches. Though often expressed in more politically correct terminology, they are alive and well in the superchurches.

Some sins, such as racism, were not considered sin by most Christians a generation ago. Other sins, like alcoholism, have lost their edge. One of the most unforgettable poems of the late Stanley Wiersma (aka Sietze Buning) is entitled "Excommunication." In this poem we meet Benny Ploegster, who was no doubt referred to as a "drunkard" in many good Christian Reformed households. "For three years Benny had been under discipline: first a silent censure, then a more public censure that initially left his name out of the matter," writes Scott Hoezee. "Later it was announced publicly that it was indeed Benny who was under scrutiny. Three years is a long time to work with someone, and so finally Benny's persistent struggle with the bottle led the church (and God, too, apparently) to run out of patience."[7] This is the backdrop for the poem. Here is Benny, a man who had been given ample opportunity to repent. He is standing before the church, accepting his excommunication.

Benny could have avoided the public embarrassment and simply stayed home. Indeed, writes Wiersma, he could have said, "Churches are full of Pharisees," and never darkened the church door again. But Benny (perhaps middle age, and probably not the sharpest pencil in the drawer) stood up as his father sitting next to him wept silently. "And why shouldn't Benny stand up?" continues Wiersma. "One stands for confession of Faith, and excommunication is its reverse. . . . Why shouldn't Benny stand up? Jesus himself had set up the procedure, followed by St. Paul, John Calvin, and other fathers Benny respected. Why shouldn't Benny stand up?"[8]

Benny was part of the church. He knew that. Yet he had been excommunicated. He never again took communion, but he faithfully attended until he died of cirrhosis of the liver. Like Jacob wrestling with God, he was saying, "I will not be cut off as though I do not exist. I am God's child, all right, God's naughty child, but still God's child: Benny." Benny stood and accepted his discipline. The poem ends with Wiersma asking whether he or anyone else in that congregation had any more right to be sitting in those pews than Benny did. "Was Benny excommunicating me?"[9]

Amazing Grace

"If grace is so amazing, why don't Christians show more of it?" asks Philip Yancey. "I believe that grace is the Christian's main contribution to the world. . . . The world can do anything the church can do except one thing: it cannot show grace."[10] Whether or not that is true is debatable, but surely the church should have a reputation for showing grace. The church should be known for living out the theme of John Newton's hymn, "Amazing Grace"—amazing grace that saved a wretch like me. We blithely sing the words while figuratively pocketing all the grace for ourselves with none left for Heather or Benny. The left-behind church has the opportunity to show God's grace in the midst of sinfulness. There is often a fine line between where grace ends and discipline begins, but in the midst of church discipline, we all are confronted with sin.

In a megachurch it is easy to get lost and to be anonymous. People look clean on both the outside and the inside. True, there are a host of special needs groups and ministries where one can let it all hang out, so to speak, but there Mary is identified as a substance abuser, one of many in the group. In a left-behind church it is hard to get lost, a factor that carries both pros and cons. In many cases, the one who is struggling with obvious problems is rejected and leaves, and the church takes one more step backward. But in an authentic community of believers, everyone is sullied with flaws and failures. There Mary is a multifaceted person, albeit a substance abuser. There she struggles with her demons within the community.

Last night I read an obituary of a thirty-nine-year-old woman survived by both parents. Brief details of her death over the New Year's weekend had appeared the day before. I had taken particular notice because her body was found less than fifty yards away from commercial property that I own with my son. She had apparently frozen to death. But there was more to the story. According to the obituary, Kristin "was a very caring and compassionate person who loved art and nature." Yet she battled with problems that defied a diagnostic label—problems that no one fully comprehended, perhaps least of all herself. The last lines of the short column spoke volumes—or did they barely offer a clue? "Even though she lost her battle against alcoholism, she never gave up hope and trust in the Lord."

When I read those words, I thought of Anne Lamott and the little, left-behind church that rescued her during a difficult time in her life. It was a church that lived out Newton's hymn. What if Kristin had found community in a similar church, I wondered. Perhaps she did. Perhaps it was offered and she rejected it. But bottom line, any left-behind church that is struggling to find its way in a megachurch world needs to recognize and reach out to the Kristins in their midst or the Kristins standing outside in the dark. That very Kristin may be an angel or an Anne Lamott.

Anne, the daughter of atheists, was thirty when she encountered the left-behind church that would change her life—a life that seriously needed changing. She was both a writer and a substance abuser—cocaine and alcohol. Often on Sunday morning, pregnant and still with a hangover from the previous night, she would wander over to the flea market:

> I could hear gospel music coming from a church right across the street. It was called St. Andrew Presbyterian, and it looked homely and impoverished, a ramshackle building with a cross on top, sitting on a small parcel of land with a few skinny pine trees. But the music wafting out was so pretty that I would stop and listen. I knew a lot of the hymns from the times I'd gone to church with my grandparents. . . . I couldn't believe how run-down it was, with terrible linoleum that was brown and overshined, and plastic stained-glass windows. But it had a choir of five black women and one rather Amish-looking white man making all that glorious noise, and a congregation of thirty people or so, radiating kindness and warmth.[11]

That was in 1984. Her conversion experience, related in her book *Traveling Mercies*, followed soon after, and in the ensuing years she became actively involved in a still left-behind but growing church. In 1998 the church moved to a new building, and she helped develop a church school. "There's often up to 30 kids," she says. "There used to just be Sam" (referring to her own son). On Sunday mornings "she sits near the front of the sanctuary . . . and herds the children up for the children's sermon and then off to their classes. She makes sure there is a teacher in each class, often teaching herself or recruiting on the fly on Sunday mornings." She also reaches out with others in the congregation to minister in a nearby convalescent home. Then in 2000 Anne accepted additional responsibilities in becoming a church elder.[12] Hers is a story of receiving amazing grace not only from God but also from a group of left-behind believers.

Pastor as Prosecutor

The messiness of a left-behind church often involves the pastor—if not as a participant, at least as an active bystander. But in most cases, the role of bystander is less than adequate. The left-behind church, as opposed to the megachurch, is a community in which the pastor assumes multiple roles, one of those roles being mediator. This task should not necessarily be viewed as burdensome, especially if the pastor has established a ministry in the church on principles of justice and fair play. It was this aspect of ministry that the sixteenth-century English minister George Herbert insisted was embedded in the work of a country parson. In his volume *Country Parson*, he argued that "justice is the ground of charity," and it was a proper area of concern for the minister. "The Countrey Parson," he wrote, "desires to be all to his Parish, and not onely a Pastour, but a Lawyer also." Indeed, the parson should study law, and Herbert recommended helpful books.[13]

Herbert's ideas did not arise only out of his own interest in law. He pointed to the Apostle Paul as model—Paul, who scolded the Corinthian Christians for suing each other in court instead of bringing the matter before arbiters in the church (1 Cor. 6:1–8). In pointing to Paul, Herbert was encouraging other parsons to keep parish matters out of court. In his effort to "be all to his Parish," the minister should be available so that not "any of his Flock should go to Law; but in any Controversie, that they should resort to him as their Judge."[14]

By seeing himself as judge, Herbert was not magnifying the position. Indeed, most of the cases were incredibly petty, though significant enough to create dissention in the church. At times Herbert seemed exasperated by the kind of *law* he was practicing: "Nay, to descend yet more particularly, if a man hath wherewithall to buy a spade, and yet hee chuseth rather to use his neighbors, and wear out that, he is covetous. Nevertheless, few bring covetousness thus low, or consider it so narrowly, which yet ought to be done, since there is a Justice in the least things, and for the least there shall be a judgment. Country people are full of these petty injustices, being cunning to make use of another, and spare themselves."[15]

Herbert's advice is valid for today among churches in which matters of justice and discipline are often swept under the carpet. He did not envision the parson working alone but rather with the help of "three or four of the ablest of the Parish." But the pastor makes the final judgment. He is concerned about property rights, thus ordering "the poorest man of the Parish" to give back a pin he has taken from "the richest," but the parson also calls upon the rich man to be charitable.[16]

Today the squabbles are less likely to revolve around the stealing of a spade, but they are no less trivial. This is evident in the First Church of Ruin, Texas. Cyrus, the pastor narrator of Jeff Berryman's novel *Leaving Ruin*, encounters many difficulties, including his wearying elders. "I don't know how much longer the First Church of Ruin will have two elders to serve them," he laments. "Yesterday, Jack came to my office and said he wanted to resign as an elder. It's not the first time he's offered, but Roland never lets him get away with it. But these days, Roland's fading as well, and who knows, I think they might both walk if given the chance. They're tired men."[17]

Roland and Jack have served together for a long time—"known each other over forty years, and like brothers, they bicker and fight." Roland is not as strict as Jack is, and how the church functions, for example, in regard to women, can create an explosion. Jack "stormed out" of a meeting "upset over Roland's idea to let Beatrice speak at the church meeting on the twenty-eighth." Such a decision was more than a mere innovation; it challenged not only tradition but biblical interpretation. "Roland said he already promised her, which sent Jack through the roof, and lots of old, unfinished business came spewing into the room." Cyrus is caught in the middle. "At one point, Roland stopped just short of calling Jack a lying SOB, but I shouted him down, telling them they had to stop it, that they were going to have to get past this petty stuff—jealousies, turf issues, whatever—before God could do anything with this church." But Cyrus's words had little effect. "Jack grabbed his coat and hat, furious, tears right on the surface, and walked out, saying over his shoulder that he resigned, and to go on and let Beatrice be pastor." So it was with an elder's meeting in Ruin. All Cyrus could do was sigh. "Roland and I sat there, exhausted, not stunned at all."[18]

Many pastors have high expectations of what *shepherding* a flock involves. They imagine members of the congregation falling behind them in line, eagerly volunteering to do all the dirty work of the parish. But such is rarely the case. "Pastoring consists of modest, daily, assigned work," writes Eugene Peterson. "It is like farm work, involving routines similar to cleaning out barns, mucking out stalls, spreading manure, pulling weeds. . . .

There are no wonderful congregations. . . . Every congregation is a congregation of sinners."[19]

Pastor as Defendant

George Herbert wrote in an age when ministers were accorded far more respect than they are today. Indeed, in this litigious era it is difficult to imagine a minister having the standing to serve as a mediator or judge. More likely, the pastor is at the other end of the spectrum, flailing about as a defendant. "I remember the pain and abandonment I felt," writes Steve Bierly, "when I found out that a small-church board, with whom I felt I had a good relationship, had been having secret meetings for some time about 'what's wrong with the pastor.' They had been smiling and patting me on the back for months, while at the same time trying to get rid of me."[20]

The story of secret meetings and trying to get rid of a pastor is the entire plot of *Leaving Ruin*. The reader is like a fly on the wall during the grueling final weeks of a minister's tenure at a dysfunctional, left-behind church. No one single sin has led to this awful ordeal. Rather, it was the usual assortment of failings, some of which would be considered assets in a church of a different denomination or personality. There was no scandal that shamed the pastor out of town in the dead of night—no sordid stories in the newspaper that fed the town gossips. Yet the pain was no less real.

In fact, sometimes those most guilty suffer the least. So it seems with the scandal of the century involving a celebrated nineteenth-century minister.

Henry Ward Beecher did not preside over what could be considered a left-behind church. Park Congregational in New York City was large and prestigious by any standard. His fall into sin, like that of many ministers before and after him, was occasioned by his love for a woman, Libby Tilton. She was married to a wealthy and prominent church member who traveled on business. During his long absences, Libby poured her heart out to her counselor and pastor about her feelings of loneliness and neglect. What went on behind closed doors remains a mystery—a mystery that was not resolved in what

came to be known as the "trial of the century." Sued by an en-
raged husband, Beecher was in the end found not guilty. But
the jury of public opinion was not so sure. Whether people
believed they only kissed or crossed the line into adultery depended on which one of Libby's conflicting accounts seemed
most truthful.

Sometimes the sin of the minister does not make the newspapers. But the effect can be just as great, as in the case of the left-
behind church in Nathaniel Hawthorne's *The Scarlet Letter*. The
adultery covered by the dark of night for the Reverend Dimmesdale
cannot be concealed by the pregnant Hester Prynne. She serves a
prison term and is stamped with the letter *A*. She goes on to raise
her little girl and to reach out in deeds of mercy to the needy. But
the minister's prison sentence is far worse. His is the imprisonment
of the soul. "He was broken down by long and exquisite suffering"
and "his mind was darkened and confused by the very remorse
which harrowed it."[21] When I contemplate Reverend Dimmesdale,
I'm reminded that there truly is no such thing as "secret" sin in a
left-behind church.

In Peter De Vries's *Slouching Towards Kalamazoo*, it is the
pastor's wife who becomes enmeshed in an affair with her doctor, though it is the pastor who loses his faith. He challenges
this very doctor, an atheist, to a debate. "They were both wind-
bags," writes the narrator son, "and perfectly matched. People
streamed into the auditorium by the hundreds, expecting a show,
and they got one. Each had rooters hoping to see him mop
up the floor with the other, which he did." But in the end, the
judges voted the contest a draw. And the folks in the left-behind
church returned to their lives, convinced that their minister had
properly defended God. "In the days that followed, my father
listened to personal and telephone congratulations of friends
and strangers alike" and "he went for solitary walks." He had
brilliantly defended the faith, but in the process, he lost it. His
opponent had won. "He persuaded me," his father lamented.
"He's right. There is no God. Or none justifying the religion I've
been preaching."[22]

To you who think you stand, writes Paul, take heed, lest you
fall (1 Cor. 10:12). To the left-behind church who thinks its pastor stands, take heed. . . . To the left-behind church who thinks
the church stands, take heed. . . .

Circumstances of Messiness

Sometimes circumstances breed messiness. The economy or the weather can open up wounds that have never fully healed. Our Christian faith ought to make us less susceptible to conflict, but sometimes church fights are the bitterest of all.

Left-behind churches are certainly not immune to infighting and nasty disputes that are sometimes exacerbated by a left-behind mentality in an entire community. Yet even in the midst of spiritual dysfunction and disarray, good things can happen. The evidence of this struck me as I read *Amazing Grace*, by Kathleen Norris. She tells of moving back to South Dakota from New York City, returning not just to her geographical roots but also to her spiritual roots. But her grandmother's little hometown Presbyterian church was going through difficult times.

> During the "farm crisis" of the 1980s, the church included in its membership both a bank president and a farmer who was being prosecuted by that bank (and eventually sent to jail) over a bankruptcy proceeding. It is enormously difficult for a small-town church to contain such serious disputes among its members; what often happens is that the pastors, as the hired help, are scapegoated, and forced out. This is a scenario that was played out in many small towns of the western Plains during the 1980s. When the population of our county dropped twenty percent between 1980 and 1990 (other nearby counties lost a full third of their population), it was easier to focus blame on "outsider" professionals than to accept the reality of change. Institutions such as schools and churches became particularly vulnerable to turnover.[23]

So how do we process the *problem* of sin, of messiness in the left-behind church, or in any church for that matter? Dutch missiologist Hendrik Kraemer argues that "the Church is always in a state of crisis and its greatest shortcoming is that it is only occasionally aware of it." This condition he sees as part of the nature of the church, that "according to the testimony of history . . . [the church] has always needed apparent failure and suffering in order to become fully alive to its nature and mission."[24]

To the left-behind church, the Apostle John admonishes us: "If we confess our sins, he is faithful and just to forgive us our sins, and to cleanse us from all unrighteousness" (1 John 1:9 KJV).

12

Spiritual Memories
of the Church in the Valley

> There's a church in the valley by the wildwood,
> No lovelier spot in the dale;
> No place is so dear to my childhood,
> As the little brown church in the vale.
>
> William S. Pitts

Those words are ones I sang decades ago in a little white clap-board church that was dear to my childhood.

Write a song; revitalize a church. This is one slogan that has not been suggested in any of the books that I have read on church revitalization. But it worked for William Pitts, who penned lyrics about a little brown church in Bradford, Iowa. The song was sung at the church dedication, and a year later in 1865 he sold it for twenty-five dollars and used the money to enroll in medical school.

But by the turn of the century, Bradford, Iowa, was little more than a ghost town, having been bypassed by the railroad, and the dilapidated brown church was closed. But the song lived on and was made popular by a traveling team of Canadian musicians. In the years that followed as the song became more popular, people began making pilgrimages to see the little church. It was reopened and became a favorite church for weddings—more than 70,000 performed in the remaining years of the twentieth century.

I told that story to one of my classes and Jeff in the back of the room howled out, "That's the church where my mom and dad were married!" Today that student serves as a pastor in a little Midwestern town himself. The ripple effect of the little churches that dot the North American landscape is impossible to calculate. How many of us would not be where we are today if it were not for a left-behind church somewhere in our background? And many of us look back to these places of worship with more than nostalgia. These churches laid many a foundation for a lifetime of spiritual formation.

William Pitts's "Church in the Wildwood" was not the only left-behind church that inspired a hit song. There is a fascinating story of a Texas church that inspired the hit song "Crying in the Chapel," which was written much earlier by Artie Glenn. "My Dad," recalls Larry Glenn, "wrote the song after he prayed and repented at the Loving Avenue Baptist Church." His father, a songwriter who also played guitar and bass fiddle in country bands, was in the hospital recovering from back surgery. There he vowed that he would turn away from his life of sin and commit himself to God. After he returned home, he went to the church nearest his home on Loving Avenue in Fort Worth, Texas. It was a humble little chapel—"built in 1936 using lumber from an abandoned mule barn." Artie Glenn later told his wife that he "walked to the front of the church with tears rolling down his cheeks," and then the sentimental words flooded his mind, never imagining anything would come of it. In 1953, when he was seventeen, Darrell Glenn, Artie's oldest son, recorded the song. It quickly became a hit—especially as he toured with Bob Hope. The song was recorded most recently by Sonny Till and the Orioles and was playing in the background in one of the scenes in the movie "Just Cause" starring Sean Connery. Throughout the years, some two dozen singers, including Ella Fitzgerald and Eddy Arnold, recorded it in their own soulful renditions.[1]

My own familiarity with the song, however, comes from one of my Elvis CDs. He recorded the song in the 1960s, with a million copies selling in two months and going to the top of the chart in Britain. He sings it with a depth of expression and feeling as only he can:

> You saw me crying in the chapel.
> The tears I shed were tears of joy.
> I know the meaning of contentment.
> Now I'm happy with the Lord.[2]

These are sentimental and syrupy lyrics, but they represent the power and influence of the left-behind church. Church growth experts can effortlessly dismiss such communities of faith with statistics and graphs, but they live on in memory and reality.

The Power of Memory

Many of us look back to a time that was simpler, when God was more approachable, and the questions of mature faith had not yet defied ready answers. I reflect with fondness on the little church that gave me my religious underpinnings, even though I would no longer find the straightlaced atmosphere conducive to worship. Yet much of who and what I am today as a Christian was formed in that country church. And today as I struggle with doubt and unbelief, I often go back to my religious heritage, recalling my tradition, knowing that this life of faith will continue as long as I have breath, ever prodded by spiritual memories.

"Remembering helped," writes Kathleen Norris in relating her story of moving from New York City back to her ancestral home in a small town in South Dakota. Part of returning home to live was returning home to her religious roots, though the effort was through fits and starts of "coming to terms with my religious inheritance."[3]

> Remembering helped; it helped enormously. Believing in God, listening to Bible stories, and especially singing in church on Sunday mornings had been among the greatest joys of my childhood. And when I would remember that, a modicum of faith would enter my heart, a conviction that the God who had given me all of that would be likely to do so again. But if I had to find one word to describe how belief came to take hold in me, it would be "repetition." . . . Repetition as in a hymn such as "Amazing Grace."[4]

168

In his book *Growing Deep in the Christian Life*, Charles Swindoll, who served as the pastor of the First Evangelical Free Church in Fullerton, California, for twenty-three years, fantasizes about what he would do if he had one wish: "If God allowed me to be in charge for just twenty-four hours, I'd do *one* thing. . . . *I'd change people's opinion about the church.* I would remove all prejudice about the church. I would erase all church scars and heal all church splits, all church bruises, and all hurts that came from church gossip. . . . I would have everybody see only the values of the church." But having not been granted that wish, he challenges his readers to pause and remember the church with only positive thoughts:

> Let's go back to our childhood. Let's go way back. Let's go all the way back to when we first heard the hymns. . . . For many of us, it was a country church with a steeple, located in a rural part of the state where we lived. . . . That was my church: little country town, little country church. But what a place! To this day I cherish healthy memories about that little house of worship. . . . It was there you gave yourself to that first group of people. They became a part of your life. You saw them every week, and you laughed with them, you wept with them, you celebrated with them, and you grieved with them. Just a little pocket of people. And because of them, the seasons had new meaning. Easter, Thanksgiving, and Christmas took on new color—even the new year gained purpose and significance. You thank God upon every remembrance of those people who were partners with you in the gospel. You and I have the church to thank for all those rich childhood memories.[5]

But he reminds us that there are other memories as well: "Remember when grief struck you at the deepest level? Remember when your loved one was put in a casket? . . . Who was there when the flowers wilted? . . . The people who surrounded you and gave you hope to go on were church people. They understood your world, they brought light to your darkness. That's the way God designed the church." Swindoll continues to move on through life—the high points, the crises, the big decisions. In many cases, the church was there as a guide through life. He certainly concedes that there are many negative memories as well as nightmares associated with church, but for those of us who have positive memories, our spiritual lives are richer, and we do well to cultivate that part of our past.[6]

For Susan Fleenor, who began her ministry at a small Presbyterian church in California, *remembering* was a key aspect of her call to ministry. After graduating from seminary, she was urged to take a staff position at a larger church. "I could have followed such counsel," she writes, "but I would not have been faithful to my experience, gifts, or identity. The small church was all I knew, and I couldn't imagine being anything but a small church pastor." As they dim over time, memories play tricks on people—sometimes exaggerating the pain and difficulties or, as the case may be, the pleasure and enjoyment. For Fleenor, the past invigorated her ministry. "Many memories are blurred now, but the ones that are most vivid center on the experience of the church as extended family. When I recall these memories and picture myself in that time and in that place, love and devotion for that small country church and its people well up. It was there, in the life and ministry of that church, that I felt most at home." These cherished memories, she says, "shaped my vocation in the church and my style of ministry as a small church pastor."[7]

The Smithville Methodist Church

Spiritual memories of the church of a bygone era sometimes ambush an individual when least expected. I'm reminded of this every time I read Stephen Dunn's poem, "At the Smithville Methodist Church." He and his wife had permitted their little girl to attend Vacation Bible School—for the arts and crafts. She came home happy with her new friends and her new songs—and her "Jesus Saves" button—a not-so-subtle clue that confirmed to them "what art was up, what ancient craft." But they reasoned, what harm could one week do, and after all, "Jesus had been a good man."

Yet when their daughter came home singing "Jesus Loves Me," they wondered how they might balance the propaganda. "Could we say Jesus doesn't love you?" It had been a long time since they had sung such songs—"so long since we needed Jesus," so long "that we thought he was sufficiently dead." For their children, Jesus would be another Lincoln or Jefferson.

But the little girl was already singing the songs, and "you can't teach disbelief to a child, only wonderful stories, and we hadn't a story nearly as good." They had, of course, the scientific explanation, but "you can't say to your child 'Evolution loves you.' The story stinks of extinction and nothing exciting happens for centuries." At the end of the week there was the usual VBS program. The children sang their songs, including "one in which they had to jump up and down for Jesus." Their little girl "was beaming. All the way home in the car she sang the songs occasionally standing up for Jesus." What was a parent to do but "drive, ride it out, sing along in silence."[8]

The poem speaks of memories that double back when least expected. And the poem speaks of a heart's longing that is often suppressed. In my book *Walking Away from Faith*, I quote those who testify of a hymn or a memory from a childhood church that brought back a childhood faith after many years of thinking Jesus was sufficiently dead. For one man, it was the singing of "Great Is Thy Faithfulness" that brought him back to faith and ministry after twenty years of wandering.

Memory and the Return to Faith

Spiritual memories have the power to bring people back to faith or to make them realize that God had never abandoned them, even in their darkest moments. This is the testimony of "the Preacher," whose website and recent book go by the same title: RealLivePreacher.com. Here Gordon Atkinson, who is the pastor of a small church in San Antonio, tells about his struggles with prayer and faith in God. He had been raised in "a devout Baptist family in Texas," and "felt 'the call' to ministry after high school," a call that was "a strong desire to be of service to God."

After seminary Atkinson served as a hospital chaplain. It was then, he says, "I met Jenny. 30 something. Cute. New mother with two little kids. Breast cancer. Found it too late. Spread all over. Absolutely going to die." He had prayed before for people with such a prognosis, and they all died. But Jenny's prayer request was different: "I know I'm going to die, chaplain. I need time to finish this. It's for my kids. Pray with me that God will give me the strength to finish it." Her request was that she would have time to finish a needlepoint pillow with apples and alphabet blocks. "She knew she would not be there for them. Would not drop them off at kindergarten, would not see baseball games, would not help her daughter pick out her first bra. No weddings, no grandkids. Nothing." But she wanted her little ones to remember her, to feel her presence, with that pillow. "I was totally hooked," writes Atkinson. "We prayed. We believed. Jesus, this was the kind of prayer you *could* believe in. . . . A couple of days later I went to see her only to find the room filled with doctors and nurses. She was having violent convulsions and terrible pain. I watched while she died hard. Real hard. As the door shut, the last thing I saw was the unfinished needlepoint lying on the floor."[9]

That experience was the final straw. "The hammer fell and preacher came tumbling after. . . . I don't remember the walk back to the office. . . . I looked in the restroom mirror and said, 'I do not believe in God.'. . . I was an unbeliever." The unbelief continued, but it only brought despair. While others testified how they walked away from faith with gladness, for Atkinson, it was anguish—pure hell. Finally, he says, "I decided not to give up without a fight." It was then that the spiritual memories came back. It was then that he realized how much he was losing by turning his back on his faith in Christ.

> My parents were and are gentle Christians. . . . We lived near the border, and my parents were actively involved with a group of Christians who were constantly throwing their resources at the piteous poverty that co-existed with us just on the other side of the Rio Grande.
>
> I was exposed early to the real stuff—Top Shelf Christianity—Deep and Old Christianity. This kind is practiced by people who work until they stink and take life in great draughts. Their hands are as rough as their hides, and they DO their faith in secret, hiding their good works in obedience to Christ. . . .
>
> These Christians don't want your money and they don't advertise.[10]

These spiritual memories were the bedrock foundation that supported Gordon Atkinson in his darkest hours of unbelief.

The Spiritual Pilgrimage

In medieval times Christians took pilgrimages to the Holy Land to visit holy sites as a means of spiritual formation. And even today Christians, particularly Catholics on pilgrimage, visit shrines, though the Holy Land is more a tourist mecca than a true pilgrimage destination. We should not demean such instruments of spiritual development. Nor should we limit holy sites to the Holy Land. There are places in our own spiritual heritage that ought to bring back memories of times when we felt near to God and in community with others of like mind.

Last summer I was with a friend as we went back to an old brick building—now remodeled—that had been a holy site in our spiritual formation many years ago. She has since moved on—far beyond those times—in belief and lifestyle. But I'll never forget how somber her mood was and how she walked away by herself and touched everything she could find—banisters, windowsills, and old oak doors—that were part of that previous era in her life. For a few moments she was back to a time that she could only recapture in her memories.

Herbert Brokering writes of this kind of experience in an Advent devotional:

> I know a country church which is like the birthplace of Christ for me. It is where I would invite you to see "Jesus in my town." We all know such a place. There are ways to take people there by true stories about people and events. The white country altar is what I would show you. There is Christ with outstretched hands. Today, the old church is gone; the altar is in a warehouse in a nearby town. Yet I will always know that humble, holy site.[11]

For Ken Bradbury, the memories were similar—memories that allowed him to take a "spiritual trip" back to his youth. He revisited a little church after many years away:

> The small rural church was just like I remembered. . . .
> The musty smell of worn hymnals was the first reminder of coming here as a youngster. . . .
> . . . I could see the scuff marks of grandpa's church shoes . . .
> I began to look for the one thing I most wanted to see again . . .
> the picture of the Savior kneeling in the garden, looking straight

173

up into the light of His father. You can get copies of that print, but the light will never shine on his face the way the sun hits it through those old south windows.

That little church. It was the first place past home we came after we were born . . . the last building we entered when we died.[12]

Balm in Gilead

"There is a balm in Gilead, to make the spirit whole. There is a balm in Gilead, to heal the sin-sick soul."[13] Gilead, in biblical symbolism, is a place associated with many well-known names, including Jacob, Saul, David, and Elijah. It was also noted for its spices, myrrh, and balm. And the old Negro spiritual tells us there is soothing relief—a balm—in Gilead.

Gilead is the fictional name of a town in Iowa, home to the elderly and dying minister, John Ames, the narrator of Marilynne Robinson's novel, *Gilead*. The old preacher is passing on memories and advice to his young son, and in doing so, he describes the town and spirit of Gilead. "There have been heroes here, and saints and martyrs," he insists. Yet "to look at the place, it's just a cluster of houses strung along a few roads, and a little row of brick buildings with stores in them. . . . But what must Galilee have looked like? You can't tell so much from the appearance of a place." Gilead, Iowa, was a place that many thought when "looking back . . . from any distance" seemed like "a relic, an archaism."[14]

There is a balm in Gilead, a factor that is too easy to forget—by both pastor and people—when we are living in Gilead. Yet it was here that John Ames and others were able to heal their sin-sick souls. The book is a lesson for all of us.

When he was still a boy, John Ames's older brother Edward, who had walked away not only from Gilead but from faith, said to him: "John, you might as well know now what you're sure to learn sometime. This is a back-water—you must be aware of that already. Leaving here is like waking from a trance."[15]

After John Ames went away to college and seminary, he returned to this backwater town to serve as minister as his father and grandfather had done before him. It was here where he truly found God, even amidst times of pain and depression.

The light in the room was beautiful this morning, as it often is. It's a plain old church and it could use a coat of paint. But in the dark times I used to walk over before sunrise just to sit there and watch the light come into that room. I don't know how beautiful it might seem to anyone else. I felt much at peace those mornings, praying over very dreadful things sometimes—the Depression, the wars. That was a lot of misery for people around here, decades of it. But prayer brings peace. . . .

In those days . . . I'd think how pleasant it was to walk through the streets in the dark and let myself into the church and watch dawn come in the sanctuary. . . . The building has settled into itself so that when you walk down the aisle, you can hear it yielding to the burden of your weight. . . . After a while I did begin to wonder if I liked the church better with no people in it.[16]

As I read *Gilead*, my own memories were stirred—memories of times and places long past. My Gilead is my balm in good times and bad.

13

The Church in the Valley
of the Shadow of Death

There is a profile of a dead left-behind church. The artist's sketch is comprised of older people in an older building in the shadow of a megachurch where things are happening. But this picture is not the one that has always come to mind in times past. The *dead* church was often one that was dead not by competition but rather one that was dead in its cold formalism. Such was the state of the church in Victorian England, at least in the minds of many observers. Charles Kingsley, a well-known Victorian novelist, wrote a poem in 1848 by the very title, "The Dead Church."

> Wild wild wind, wilt thou never cease thy sighing?
> Dark dark night, wilt thou never wear away?
> Cold cold church, in thy death sleep lying,
> The Lent is past, thy Passion here, but not thine Easter-day.
>
> Peace, faint heart, though the night be dark and sighing;
> Rest, fair corpse, where thy Lord himself hath lain.
> Weep, dear Lord, above thy bride low lying;
> Thy tears shall wake her frozen limbs to life and health again.[1]

Charles Kingsley (1819–1875) is as fascinating as any of the characters in his novels. A parish priest in left-behind churches most of his life, he supplemented his income by writing both fiction and nonfiction. In all his activities, his heart was for the poor, and he became one of the founders of Christian socialism. Later in life he served as chaplain to Queen Victoria and held other royal posts as well as a professorship at Cambridge. But with all his honors, concern for the poor remained his chief focus. The church must care for the *least of these* if there is any hope of waking "her frozen limbs to life and health again."

Since those lines were penned, the church in many areas of the English countryside has been resurrected. Her frozen limbs have awakened to life and health again. True, there are some churches that are little more than corpses. But as my husband and I visited churches while traveling through Warwick, Lancashire, Northumberland, Yorkshire, and Essex, we found many of them alive and well. The Alpha course was widely advertised, and ministry to the needy came in every shape and size. And generations after Kingsley's lament, the Evangelical Alliance has taken up his cause in following Jesus into the poorest neighborhoods. This is the largest Christian organization in the United Kingdom, representing more than a million Christians from dozens of denominations and hundreds of organizations.

But even during the dark, dark nights when the very light of the gospel seems to have burned out, there are flickering lights on the landscape that poets sometimes miss. This was certainly true during what seemed to be the darkest nights of nineteenth-century England.

Archeologists and Dead Churches

The dead church today in North America is not the universal church gone dim. Indeed, archeologists and historians will look back at this era of the church as one of vitality and virility, an era when churches mirrored shopping malls. But they would find only miles away from the ruins of these giant structures small religious communities that were slain in the battles of worship wars or ones that simply decayed and died of old age. Here the archeologist would unearth stained glass and choir robes and

wooden pews with hymnbooks along with telltale signs showing declining attendance and in some cases, locked doors, and
boarded windows. Why did some small churches succumb to
the strength of the giant, these historians will ask, while others
prevailed like David against Goliath?

This is the question we ask ourselves as we contemplate *dead*
churches. Why does one left-behind church thrive and the other
die?

There is power in the gospel, but sometimes that power is
nowhere evident in the left-behind church. It almost seems as
though every drop of lifeblood has been drained out and there is
no hope of regaining the energy that once animated the people,
programs, and plans for the future. George Barna tells of such
a church that declined from a regular attendance of four hundred down to as low as fifty, all in the space of five years. Bill
Cochrane's response to questions of *why* were telling: "My sermons were okay. . . . The programs were adequate. . . . I just didn't
have the umph left to rekindle the flame. . . . I guess I gave up."
What is so amazing about this precipitous decline is his seeming
obliviousness to it: "One reason the numbers were down was
because everybody but me knew that we were on the decline."
When it suddenly dawned on him how serious the decline was,
he quit: "That's when I handed in my resignation." Comments
from members were equally dismal: "It was awful." "People were
discouraged." "Today, this church is just a skeleton of what it
was." "I must be crazy to keep attending that church."[2]

How do we respond to such a situation? Is there any hope
for this church? One church leader whom Barna interviewed
responded that "some [churches] are full of emotionally crippled
people. . . . We should leave them alone and start another church
full of people who want to grow. Don't kill the old church. It'll
run down and kill itself over time."[3]

If we read only statistics, Barna and the experts are right.
Let the emotionally crippled churches die. But if we read the
stories—sometimes between the lines—we often see a different
picture. We often see that there are reasons for this church to
live—even in some cases when the pastor has given up. God
works amid flaws and failure and dying flames. There is power
in the gospel even when it appears as though the circuits have
all been shut off.

Awakening Frozen Limbs

One powerful example of this power is the St. Paul Community Baptist Church in Brooklyn. The story is told in *Upon This Rock: The Miracles of a Black Church* by Samuel Freedman. A *New York Newsday* review describes the book as "the story of the Rev. Youngblood's personal and professional odyssey as he struggles to turn a half-dead Brooklyn church into the epicenter of a ravaged community."[4] Here is a church that in Kingsley's words wakened "her frozen limbs to life and health again."

When he came as the minister in 1974, Reverend Johnny Ray Youngblood found fewer than a hundred people who considered the church their home. Fifteen years later there were 5,000 who looked to him as their pastor. But church work for Youngblood, in this oasis in the midst of poverty, is personal. He relates to individuals not to thousands. Parents are regularly reminded to "lend him their children's report cards so that he can read their grades from the pulpit." His philosophy has not been merely to turn around a church, to turn a left-behind church into a megachurch with a focus on numbers. Rather, the power of the gospel has turned around lives (and report cards) and has begun to turn around left-behind, crime-ridden neighborhoods in Brooklyn.[5]

Why do some churches thrive and others die? Today's *Grand Rapids Press* carried a story with a few details about a dead church. Identified only as the Stittsville Church, named for the unincorporated crossroads of Stittsville, north of Cadillac, Michigan, "it is getting a new lease on life." Does this new lease mean a minister is moving into the community? Or is the church moving out of the community? "Built in 1889, seldom used since 1990 and decaying, Stittsville Church didn't appear to have a prayer." According to the Associated Press reporter, this new lease is a move for the church: "Today, it is scheduled to be moved more than 20 miles to Wellington Farm Park, a living history farm southwest of Grayling." The move, costing $50,000, funded by "private donations, grants and a series of chicken dinners," paves the way for this church to turn into a museum.[6]

The cause of death was not noted in the article. Is this what Kingsley meant when he wrote: "Rest, fair corpse, where thy Lord himself hath lain. Weep, dear Lord, above thy bride low lying"? Will the dear Lord's tears ever "wake her frozen limbs to life and health" again? Perhaps. "Weddings, christenings and other religious ceremonies will be held at the church after renovations are completed, although regular worship services will not be held."[7]

Why do some churches thrive—or limp along—and other churches die?

Funeral Rites for a Church

Many church specialists rightly emphasize the importance of the minister in the matter of revitalization. Certainly it is difficult to overestimate the significance of a Johnny Ray Youngblood in the recovery of what appears to be a terminal case. But without regular folks taking ownership, a dead church cannot be resuscitated.

The story is told of a new minister reporting for duty at a little left-behind church in Oklahoma. He visited those on the membership roster reminding them to come out for the Sunday morning service. But the next Sunday the church was nearly empty. Frustrated, he placed an obituary in the local newspaper announcing that the church had died and that there would be a funeral the following Sunday. He sent word to members that they should show their respects and give the church a proper burial. Curious about this strange event, crowds filled the church the following Sunday. There in the front of the church was a coffin with floral arrangements and wreaths. The minister offered a eulogy and then opened the casket for parishioners to view the "body." Attached inside the coffin was a mirror. What the people saw was their own reflection.

This little hoax could well be duplicated in many left-behind churches. When the *body* is dead, there is nothing left. A funeral is warranted. But in many instances, the body is tired or just plain lazy. In such cases, a stunt might do the trick. But the truth that this little hoax reveals is that the church cannot survive without regular folks. More than warm bodies, a church that is truly alive is identified by disciples of Christ whose commitment is demonstrated by their love for each other and a needy world outside their doors.

Many left-behind churches, however, are on their last legs, so to speak. They are going through the valley of the shadow of death. Old age has set in, or perhaps a terminal illness. They go through the motions of living. Churchly functions continue. But "in the meantime," writes Jane Newstead of her church in Iowa, "the question that colors all our issues is, 'Can these bones live?' No, we are not yet dried up and scattered in the desert, but the fear we all hesitate to articulate is that we will be in twenty or thirty years." For a remote left-behind country church, these fears are far more than paranoia. "In three years there have been two baptisms in the church and two weddings (both couples moved out of the area). In one two week period last fall, we had five services of witness to the resurrection. But we call them funerals."[8]

So also with funerals of churches. The dry bones of countless left-behind churches have been scattered. Only the memories linger on. The ripple effect of this once living organism, however, will continue on through eternity.

Funerals are not always sad times. I'm reminded of that when I reflect on the deaths of my mother and father. Mom was killed in an auto accident at fifty-seven. The pain was indescribable, and thirty-five years later it still hurts. Dad died at eighty-nine, his mind dimmed and his body wracked by a long illness. His funeral was not a sad time. He was no longer suffering. I delivered a spirited eulogy with a touch of humor. Likewise with some churches. We should let them die in peace and offer eulogies to their once thriving ministries.

Dying with dignity. Living will. These are terms we hear more and more as the population ages. Under what circumstances should life support not be administered? This question plagues many denominations as well as individual churches. The tensions run high as financial expenditures are weighed against family and community considerations. For some people—particularly those with a lifetime of memories—a church closing is less a matter of withholding life support than it is administering a lethal injection. If there is a doctor close at hand who is prepared to step in and offer healing ministrations, the failing patient might be brought back to life.

Can These Bones Live?

So it was with a hopelessly weathered old United Reformed church located in a slum near Birmingham, England, standing in the gray shadows of the Winson Green prison. There were fewer than two dozen members, and the final recommendation for its closing was on the agenda of the denominational council.

On the day of the meeting, a seventy-year-old returned missionary was substituting as chair of the council. The decision should have been easy. But not for this man with a missionary heart. "If the Church abandoned such areas in order to settle in the relatively easy circumstances of the suburbs," he argued, "it would forfeit the claim to be a missionary Church." He passionately argued his case, and he convinced the other members of the council, on the condition that he would serve as minister. Without pay. So at age seventy Lesslie Newbigin found himself back in ministry again; no longer in India where he had served so many years, but in an urban setting in his homeland where there was a large Asian and Indian population.[9]

Newbigin did not accept the position without some concessions on the part of the council, however. He convinced the denomination to provide for a young Indian pastor to join him in the ministry. "Together they went door to door in the run-down neighborhood, and Newbigin got a ground-level introduction to how far from Christian his England had become." But this change that had occurred since he had left his homeland many years earlier to serve in India was not a negative factor in his effort to revitalize the church. "While Asian immigrants almost always welcomed him and Rahi in for tea, Anglo neighbors often slammed the door in their faces." Such experiences led to him to rethink the whole mind-set of mission outreach and to put his thoughts into what would become his landmark book, *Foolishness to the Greeks*, a work that launched him into a postretirement career as a much-sought-after writer and speaker.[10]

Newbigin in a very real sense got caught in his own trap. But some people feel called by God to the resurrection business. Oscar Grindheim was one such individual (married to Rose Grindheim Sims, who carried on in the calling after he died). In 1966 he was awarded the designation as the "Outstanding Rural Minister in America" by the American Baptist Convention. But the work was often painfully slow and difficult. Sometimes the work seemed impossible—"opening church doors shut as tightly as great coffin lids, after the mourners had gone." But he effectively used the gifts he believed God had given him:

> Time and again, three years after Oscar had stood at a tightly barred door, the church would lead the state in professions of faith and missions. Lives were miraculously changed by his undaunted faith in the Master Builder.
>
> Then, because churches of the quality he forged were always in demand, a full-time pastor would be appointed. Once again we would be standing at a lonely, nearly forgotten, nailed-shut church door. Time and time again, over twenty-seven years, Oscar proved that renewal could happen anywhere fishermen dared to battle the elements of neglect and discouragement and put out their nets for a catch.[11]

Celebrating Death

For some churches, turning off life support is probably the most humane act, and some would figuratively counsel to go a step further by administering a lethal injection. Philip Yancey tells of returning as an adult to attend the burial of the church in Georgia in which he grew up. The sign out front identified with key words its place in the broader realm of American Christianity—words employed to exclude outsiders as much as to safeguard the faithful: "New Testament, Blood-bought, Born-again, Pre-millennial, Dispensational, Fundamental, . . ." Defense of *the truth* was its role in the community.

"Our little group of two hundred people," writes Yancey, "had a corner on the truth, God's truth, and anyone who disagreed with us was surely teetering on the edge of hell." It was *truth* that was naturally blended with racism, and it took years, by Yancey's own testimony, "for God to break the stranglehold of blatant racism in me." During his childhood, the church had moved away from what had become a racially mixed neighborhood, and it was again facing the same situation with its membership declining. "In sweet irony, it was now selling its building to an African-American congregation." The minister of forty years was there to celebrate God's faithfulness throughout those decades of contending for the truth.

> During the expanded service, a procession of people stood and testified how they had met God through this church. Listening to them, I imagined a procession of those not present, people like my brother, who had turned away from God in large part because of this church. I now viewed its contentious spirit with pity, whereas in adolescence it had pressed life and faith out of me. The church had now lost any power over me; its stinger held no more venom. But I kept reminding myself that I had nearly abandoned the Christian faith in reaction against this church, and I felt deep sympathy for those who had.[12]

It is difficult to assess such funerals. With some individuals, there comes a sigh of *good riddance*. Yet for others the church, rigidly fundamentalist and even racist though it may have been, brought them to faith in Christ. Am I the arbiter who judges their faith to be no more than "wood, hay, and stubble"? We all, individually and collectively, are infected by sin, and our sin affects others. Does that cancel the entire ministry of the church? I can rejoice that the building will serve as a church in racial harmony with the community. But this church too is capable of distorting the pure gospel with sin.

Deathbed Choices

When and how does the left-behind church decide to amputate a leg and live or refuse amputation and die as a *whole* person? That is one of the most difficult issues a church in the shadow of death confronts. Can the church make a significant change without compromising its history, traditions, and sense of community? Ralph Bauserman, a former Methodist minister now serving on the General Board of Discipleship for that denomination, tells a story that shows his own sense of ambivalence toward the left-behind church. By his own testimony, he served as pastor for "two long appointments in large, fast growing churches." Yet he emphasizes that the small church is still close to his heart.

"As a young man, I joined a Methodist Church that was a part of a four-point circuit," he writes. "Our pastor came every other week for 'preaching,' and we had Sunday school each Sunday. On an average Sunday, about thirty-five of us gathered to share fellowship and faith. It was this church that gave me a wonderful wife; it was here that our first son was baptized; and it was from this little country church that we received the call to ministry." For these and many more reasons, he continues, "there will always be a special place in my heart for the small church."[13]

But he also sees problems with this and other small churches that he served in a circuit as a seminary student—they "shared one thing in common; they lacked vision." Referring to those churches he served in a three-point circuit, he laments that "each of these churches over the years has grown older and much smaller. In fact, one has closed its doors. It is painfully ironic that this decline has occurred in the midst of substantial growth in the communities." But worse than merely declining was the fact that they refused the medicine they needed to stay alive and vibrant. He tells of a "young student pastor" who one evening "cast his vision" to a group of "the most influential leaders of the four churches." He challenged these leaders "to unite as one church and to get serious about being in mission in the community." He was not without a plan. A family had offered to donate several acres of land near a major highway. On this highly visible site, the young pastor envisioned "a building that would not only serve as a worship and spiritual formation center for our people but as a center to serve the youth and other needs of the community." But the vision fell flat. The leaders regarded the young pastor as little more than a dreamer. So the churches remained as they had been—except that nothing ever stays the same.

Indeed, much has happened since that night that young pastor cast his vision. "The population in the communities around the four churches has increased dramatically. In the midst of this growth, the churches, devoid of any sense of mission, have grown older and smaller. One church has closed; two of them have an attendance of fewer than ten on Sunday; and the other has fewer than twenty." How long before there will be three more funerals, one after another? "Yes, there will always be a special place in my heart for the small church," Bauserman writes, "but it hurts me deeply to see so many churches growing older and smaller."[14]

"Weep, Dear Lord, above Thy Bride Low Lying"

Some churches linger on long after they have enjoyed any sense of fulfillment or meaningful ministry. Their once-vibrant health slowly fades, and they painfully deteriorate and die of old age. This was true of Carl McIntire's Bible Presbyterian Church in Collingswood, New Jersey. The colonial brick building that once was home to hundreds of members almost swallowed up the few dozen elderly folks who hung on in later years. Finally, this dwindling group saw the writing on the wall and asked McIntire to retire after seventy-five years as their pastor. It was too much for the old man. He refused to quit. Forced out, he "defiantly began conducting services in the living room of his home" next door. A lead article in *Christianity Today* soon after his death at age ninety-five identified him as a "fundamentalist with flair" who "protested against nearly every major expression of 20th-century Christianity, and always with a flourish."[15]

How I, then in my early twenties, happened to take a bus filled with McIntire groupies to Washington DC to march around the Pentagon carrying a sign *supporting* the Vietnam War, with McIntire in the lead with his blow-horn, is a story that has no redeeming memories. My acquaintance with the man was distant at best. But I did know him and his reputation well enough to know that every denomination he ever touched he split. And who could calculate the pain he rendered to churches—some tiny to begin with—that split in the wake of his pompous and often poisonous preaching? Indeed, there are some churches that are better dead than alive.

14

New Life for the Left-Behind Church

What are the ten steps to revitalizing a left-behind church? If they are not found in PowerPoint seminars at Willow Creek or Saddleback or in the multiplicity of books, tapes, and journals, are there any surefire ways for a church to get out of the doldrums?

I put that question to my class when I was teaching MISS 812 Revitalization of the Local Church at Calvin Theological Seminary. There was an almost immediate class consensus. We all remembered the story told by an outside speaker some weeks earlier. As a "bishop" of sorts in charge of various revitalization efforts, he cited the one ingredient that was certain to turn around a church in decline. It was so obvious that it hardly seemed necessary to verbalize, though even he conceded this surefire factor of revitalization is often neglected and can sometimes backfire. Indeed, anything that points to change can potentially create tension.

What is the word that sums up this critical element? *Conversions*. Discipleship (some would say evangelism) was the key.

In the situation he told about, someone in the church simply behaved like a Christian ought to behave—by reaching out in love and service to a traumatized and hurting family in a nearby mobile-home subdivision. Other church families got involved with the family in what turned out to be a very large and extended network of kinfolk. Soon the church was invaded by strangers wearing blue jeans and T-shirts (some sporting tattoos and headbands and riding Harleys), paging through the Pentateuch looking for the book of Hebrews. These were the kind of people whose music tastes more likely ranged from Willie Nelson to the Dixie Chicks than from Brahms to J. S. Bach. They were *remedial* churchgoers, coming in with all their trash. Now when you combine the trash of religious *remedials* with the garbage of religious *redundants*, it can end up smelling worse than sewage spilling over the septic tank. But if that garbage is mixed all together and turned into rich compost, it nourishes the garden that was so recently grown over with weeds—one of the little gardens in God's kingdom we call *church*. In this case, the old standbys intermingled with the newcomers, and a left-behind church was revitalized and reborn.

Another way to keep the left-behind church alive is to specialize in ways that keep and attract families. Many churches are mega-wannabes. They live in the shadow of the mighty megachurches and seek to emulate them. What else can a church do, living in the shadow of Faith Reformed Church? That was the question facing Henry Reyenga, copastor of Community Life Church, near Lockport, Illinois. He is convinced that many moderate-size churches are unwittingly serving as "farm teams" for the megachurches. They are trying to replicate the worship services and the programs and giving their people a taste for professionally designed church, but they are unable to pull it off.

At Community Life there is a spirit of community that no megachurch could match—a community, in this case, centered largely around similar interests. Many of the members are young families who are involved in home schooling, and here church and schooling are brought together.

When we visited the church last year, we were surprised by all the well-behaved young children who were actively participating in the service. They knew Bible verses, and they sang hymns word for word. We had gotten a taste of this earlier in the morning when we attended a *home* church meeting with the Reyengas. Here were three generations of family, ranging from preschoolers to seventy-year-olds, all singing hymns and/or playing instruments, including saxophone and accordion. Bible memory appeared to be easier for the little ones than for the grandparents, but there was a spirit of fun-loving competition.

The same emphasis on Bible memory and hymn-singing and family togetherness was demonstrated in the afternoon church service. With this spirit multiplied in the church setting, there is no likelihood that this congregation is serving simply as a farm team for Faith Reformed. Indeed, there is no way that Faith Reformed can *do* church better for these folks than what Community Life is already doing, where growth in numbers is not a over-riding objective.

"Help Me, Jesus"

There are many ways a pastor can revitalize a left-behind church, but the first step involves self-revitalization. Without soul-searching and personal renewal, the pastor cannot lead the church into new life. Richard Lischer reflects on this kind of personal redemption that took place in his first little Lutheran parish in New Cana, Illinois. With his brand-new doctoral degree, he set out to impress the uneducated farmers with his brilliance: "Before I could talk about Jesus," he writes, "I apparently found it necessary to give my farmers a crash course in the angst-ridden plight of modern man. With the help of clichés from Joyce, Heidegger, Camus, and even Walker Percy, I first converted them to existential ennui so that later in the sermon I could rescue them with carefully crafted assurances of 'meaning' in a meaningless world."[1]

That such a sense of meaninglessness had never occurred to the people blankly starring out from the pews never occurred to Lischer. Thus, he laments, "My audience paid a heavy price for the gospel. The farmers had to swallow my sixties-style cocktail of existentialism and psychology before I served them anything remotely recognizable." His efforts in that little country church resulted in "homiletical gridlock." What this educated man needed was "a new education," but he was clueless.

> Why couldn't I see the revelation of God in our little church? In our community everyone pitched in and learned how to "pattern"

a little girl with cerebral palsy. We helped one another put up hay before the rains came. We grieved when a neighbor lost his farm, and we refused to buy his tools at the auction. As a people, we walked into the fields every April and blessed the seeds before planting them. Weren't these all signs of "church" that were worthy of mention in the Sunday homily? Whatever lay closest to the soul of the congregation I unfailingly omitted from my sermons. I didn't despise these practices. I simply didn't see them.[2]

Lischer's personal redemption and revitalization came not through preaching to his own people, whose attitude seemed to be, "We *dare* you to move us. Just try it." Rather, it came when he was preaching at Shiloh, a Black congregation some distance away. He was filling in for one of his colleagues who had agreed to preach there but became ill on the designated Sunday night. For Lischer, it did not entail extra preparation; he had a sermon ready to go: "When I launched into the reprise of my Sunday morning sermon," he writes, "it took the people of Shiloh about thirty seconds to recognize a preacher in trouble." His redemption began when "an old woman in the second row said softly, 'Help him, Jesus.'" At that moment he began to realize how much he needed help—and not just for this Black congregation. "Soon, others were saying, *Well? That's all right, Preach! Make it plain*, and *Come on up!*" *Make it plain* rang in his ears as he returned to his own congregation.[3]

The title of the chapter that recalls this story of Lischer's early preaching is "Help Me, Jesus." That cry should be the cry of any pastor who is given the opportunity to stand in the pulpit of a left-behind church. That acknowledgement of need is the first step in personal and congregational revitalization.

Raising the Bar

"After eighteen years of ministry, I've become convinced that the way to lead a dormant church into exuberant, committed discipleship is not by lowering the bar, but by raising it," writes Brian Metke. "Our members are required to participate in at least one specific ministry, attend a weekly Bible-study class, and tithe regularly. We call it 'intentional Christianity.'"[4]

Such high goals and demands look good on paper, but can they actually be enforced in a church? Other pastors had warned Metke when he came as the new pastor that Trinity Evangelical Lutheran Church in Pell Lake, Wisconsin, was a difficult place, probably worse than the rocky soil of Jesus's parable. Indeed, the landscape of this town of fifteen hundred, with "no inviting skyline, no manicured lawns," had the look of a rocky-soil parable. "Amid fields and farmland are narrow dirt roads, dilapidated homes, and a mudhole that, once upon a time, was considered a lake."[5]

Nor was the church—across the street from the local watering hole—a fountain of life. In fact, the church council gathered in that local bar for its monthly meetings. And in addition to all his other duties, the pastor was expected to do the janitorial work. Before he arrived at the church, fresh out of seminary, Metke had been told there were three hundred members and a good salary. "But I quickly discovered that most of the 300 members couldn't be found," he writes. "Sunday attendance was around 60, and if I wanted to receive my salary, it was pretty much up to me to raise funds."

The biggest problem, however, was that there were no leaders. When the previous pastor had left after three years of ministry, things had fallen apart. "I made a vow to myself that when I left, there would be biblically knowledgeable leaders in the congregation so that the ministry wouldn't cease when I left."[6]

Changes in Trinity Lutheran did not come overnight. For two years Metke viewed himself as a "one-man show." His first radical adjustment came when he enrolled the church in the Bethel Bible Series, which demanded a serious, two-year commitment from a minimum of ten participants. Two days after the deadline had passed, ten reluctant students had joined—agreeing to meet two and a half hours each week for intensive Bible and discipleship training.

> Slowly our congregation's attitude began to change. Every week, others enrolled. I learned an amazing lesson: people are more willing to make one long-term, intensive commitment to something like Bethel than they are to smaller, low-commitment programs. . . . I think [the] sense of excellence and challenge is part of the reason we've had over 100 students complete the Bethel Series in the past 16 years.[7]

191

The Bethel Bible Series was not the only idea that Metke introduced to the church. His was not an effort to reinvent the wheel. Rather he looked to effective programs that had stood the test of time. More than one hundred members over the years participated in the Cursillo retreat involving lay renewal weekends. The Stephen Ministry program served to train lay leaders for caregiving outreach. Celebrate Recovery (from alcohol and drug addiction) allowed the church to be an oasis in a community with high rates of family violence and substance abuse.

In the process of reaching out, the church has grown. There is a warm welcome to visitors—in part due to "undercover greeters" who commit themselves to introducing themselves each week to at least one person they do not know. "Today," writes Metke in the summer of 2000, "there are 200 baptized members at Trinity and some 285 weekly worshippers. . . . More people are moving to the community. Some are even building new homes. There's new life. And now the county is dredging and replenishing the lake."[8]

Servant Evangelism

Evangelism in my church upbringing was perceived to be more related to words than deeds. Not so, certainly, in the ministry of Jesus. Nor should deed ministry be considered "such a 1960s thing," as a denominational leader suggested, tongue in cheek, to me recently. In fact, there are some who would argue that the best way to attract the younger generation is through a service-oriented ministry. "This generation [is] . . . looking for new ways to serve others," writes Andrew Black.[9] Jim Kitchens agrees. In reflecting on the postmodern generation he writes: "For them, it is not enough to send money to support the mission of the denomination or to help finance the local soup kitchen or homeless shelter. Postmoderns want to send *themselves*, not just their dollars, into mission. They are looking for ways to become directly involved in working for justice, providing acts of hospitality and service, and offering healing to those in need."[10]

Efforts to revitalize a church can easily become numbers oriented, and such an orientation often sets the stage for falling into a vicious cycle. More people are needed so that collections will increase so that we can hire more staff and build bigger buildings so that more people will come to the church and collections will increase. And on and on we go in circles. But that is not the way of true discipleship. True discipleship is not self-focused. Yet this is how the world perceives the church—even a left-behind church. The church in the eyes of the outsider is a company, like a small business, that wants to grow and be successful like the big boys. The left-behind church would solve its problems if it had more capital, prime real estate, modern facilities, better technology, expanded markets. But such is not the way of the gospel. When people think of the church, they ought to think of generosity and love and kindness. This has been the philosophy of Steve Sjogren, the founding pastor of Vineyard Community Church in Cincinnati. Servant evangelism is his emphasis:

> This is all supported by what I think is the most profound verse in the book of Romans, ". . . the kindness of God leads [you] to repentance," (Rom. 2:4). I read that verse for years but didn't get it. I thought it was vertical kindness. That somehow God would come along and reveal his love to people and that somehow amounted to kindness—a nice interpretation but not very practical.
>   One day it hit me that God's kindness is more horizontal—that it happens from one person to another. God always uses people to do his bidding. That's the way he works throughout the ebb and flow of the Scriptures.[11]

There are many ways for a church to demonstrate such acts of kindness, and the youth should not be excluded from such opportunities. In one instance the church sponsored a free car wash in the parking lot of a well-known bar in Cincinnati, with signs reading, "Totally Free Car Wash," "No Kidding—Free Car Wash." When people offered to pay, they were turned down. They meant what the sign said.

As we were winding down, recalls Steve, "an expensive Lexus came driving into the lot with the driver yelling, 'Got time for one more?' " . . . As we washed his car this man asked lots of questions about the wash. He started by pulling out his checkbook and asking how to spell the name of our church. 'We aren't taking any donations,' I said. 'But what did the last person give?' he asked." Steve had to tell him repeatedly that there was no catch, the car wash was free. "Those who don't understand generosity think that the Church is all about two things—asking for money and parenting. When we connect with the not-yet-Christ-following public through acts of kindness, and don't ask for money or seek to parent them, we more or less blow their minds!" Through this little act of kindness, this man, a recently retired pitcher for the Chicago Cubs, "came to Christ right there in the parking lot of the biggest party place in Cincinnati."[12]

Us and Them Evangelism

There are two kinds of people in the world—the saved and the unsaved. This was the theme of "Spiritual Emphasis Week" one year while in undergraduate school in Texas. The morning chapel speaker asked all of us who were saved and knew we were going to heaven to stand up. Approximately half of us stood as he admonished us to have a greater concern for evangelism. He then told us to move to one side of the auditorium, and as we did, he told those who were seated to go to the other side of the auditorium. When we were all in place, facing each other, he told those of us who were saved to go over to the other side and witness to those who were unsaved. We had obediently followed instructions up to that point—both saved and unsaved—but within a matter of minutes most of us had walked out, both sides in apparent agreement that this speaker had overstepped the bounds of decency. Some who had been up to this point genuinely seeking a relationship with God were put off.

But should the speaker be faulted? Was I justified in being upset with the exercise? After all, dividing the world in two such categories had been part of my understanding since I was a child. Wasn't this simply putting the rubber to the road?

Today—at least in the Reformed circles I travel in—the lines of demarcation between the Christian and non-Christian are often expressed in more fuzzy terms. We emphasize that judgment belongs to God alone and are more hesitant to declare that our neighbor is going to hell. But we still unconsciously judge ourselves and our kind to be on the inside while everyone else is on the outside. By doing so, we often miss opportunities to invite our neighbors to join us in the ministry of the Kingdom.

Ron Crandall recounts an example of one such missed opportunity in his book *Turnaround Strategies for the Small Church*. The pastor found himself in the midst of controversy—not because the left-behind church he was serving in Pennsylvania was not growing. To the contrary, it had been "wonderfully revitalized"— in part because he was convinced that "even persons on their way to Christ but not yet Christians, have gifts to give and can serve." In one instance, an "unmarried couple who were living together began to attend the church. Before they had joined or publicly acknowledged their Christian faith they were allowed to use their gifts and serve by standing at the door as greeters." But there were strong objections, some demanding that this couple be immediately "removed from any and all positions of ministry." The matter was eventually decided by the church elders and counsel, who both affirmed the pastor's position that "this was their congregational philosophy of ministry. Jesus loved the outcasts, the sinners, and the tax collectors and let them serve Him."[13]

A Conspiracy of Kindness

Welcoming neighbors to join in serving side by side in kingdom ministry is a concept that ought not to exclude youth. But how do we involve neighborhood kids in such activities? It has been years since I have led a youth group, and youth ministry is not my specialty. But I propose an idea for a youth club that I have never heard offered before.

The idea came to me as I was viewing—with my students for a class on church revitalization—Robert Duvall's film, *The Apostle*. Duvall stars as the very flawed Pentecostal minister who is running from the law. Unlike most films that caricature such ministers with no redeeming qualities, "Sonny" is sincere and has an incredibly good heart. In one scene he is involved in opening a closed church by effectively reaching folks in the neighborhood. His big heart shines when, at his own expense, he buys groceries and with his sidekick, leaves boxes on porches. Many churches conduct such charitable programs. But Sonny's is different. He sneaks around under the cover of darkness and surreptitiously does his deeds. As I watched, I couldn't help thinking, *What*

195

fun! And, even to a greater extent, *What fun for a youth group!* But such an activity would pay far bigger dividends than what is classified as "fun." It has potential to change a community, a church, and individual lives.

What if a youth group were to do the very thing that Sonny is doing in the film with his sidekick? This is a perfect concept for a left-behind church that is relatively small in size and is close by or in the midst of a needy neighborhood. This is not mega-church material. It simply will not work, and it shouldn't even be attempted in such a setting. Most megachurches are suburban, and thus are not *neighborhood* churches. And the youth groups are far too large—especially when "conspiracy" is a requisite. Plus, megachurch youth are typically spoiled with too many ready-made programs. They go to Acapulco on spring break for mission trips—well, perhaps not—but they have a very different mind-set than do left-behind church youth groups. Left-behind youth are often just that. Like Sonny and his sidekick, they are not used to being spoiled. They are often left behind by their social status and environment: rural, small-town, or inner-city.

So I offer this idea and challenge to pastors and youth leaders. Here is the only ten-point program for church revitalization offered in this book—a skeleton concept that must be fleshed out in each individual setting:

1. Purchase Robert Duvall's film *The Apostle* and watch it for the purpose of developing a "conspiracy of kindness" with one or two trusted individuals.
2. Establish a code of secrecy. From the beginning, anyone who is in on this idea must be extremely tight-lipped. If this activity becomes merely another youth program with the church council and other adults involved, it loses its uniqueness and its appeal for youth.
3. Lay out a tentative plan of how a secret "conspiracy of kindness" youth club could be developed.
4. Set up a meeting (with no more than one other adult) with two or three leaders (officers) of the church youth group—or with one or two youth in the church if there is no youth group—to present the idea. Continued secrecy is critical.

5. If the youth leaders show interest, set up a regular youth group meeting (billed as a night featuring a movie and snacks) for the purpose of showing the film and introducing the idea. Make this an early meeting that can stretch into three hours or more, preferably at a non-church location.

6. Following the film, before the idea is discussed, the concept of the "club" should be presented. Explain that the "youth group" will continue as a regularly scheduled program of the church, but that there is a secret club that is being established for anyone who is interested. Explain that a commitment of secrecy must be agreed upon by each individual who wants to remain and hear about the club.

7. Once there is an assent to secrecy by each individual present, explain the essence of the club—that just like Sonny and his sidekick, club members will be secretly distributing food (and perhaps other goods) to the needy. Draw out ideas and input from the group and ask if there are any present who would like to join the club. Again, emphasize that this is top secret—that those who join must continue to pledge themselves to secrecy as the months and years go by.

8. With the conspiracy mentality in mind, challenge those who have committed themselves to the club to reach out to other youth—in the church, but especially outside the church. The only requisite for membership is a promise of secrecy—and along with that, honesty. Here is a situation where a "commitment to Christ" does not come into play. This is a program of church revitalization, and one way to revitalize a church is to reach out to those who do not attend church and those who do not profess faith. Hopefully, the club will have a majority "membership" of those outside the church. This is not a Bible study or prayer group. It is separate from the youth group. It is best done without religious trappings and in a locale that is not the church.

9. With the club defined, a plan to choose officers should be considered for a future meeting. Even if the group is very small, some form of leadership should be established within the group. Officer titles ought to be more creative than simply president, vice-president, secretary, treasurer, etc. Club rules will also be developed at a later meeting.

10. The purpose of the club should be plain—not just to have fun, but to serve others without praise and credit. The commitment relates not only to secrecy but also to sacrifice. Funds to purchase goods to be distributed must come from the members themselves. One or two members might give up a Saturday afternoon to rake leaves or shovel snow or a member might set aside ten percent of wages at a fast-food joint. Since this is a "private club," youth group project money and (God, forbid) church money should not be used. Goods (concentrating on non-perishables) should be purchased and distributed quickly, so as not to create an environment of temptation associated with money "laying around." To be successful, this club must be kept secret. The deeds of kindness must be carried out very creatively and surreptitiously. Any breech in security has great potential to damage the program.

So what is the point? If this youth club actually works, what will be the end result? Needy people will receive goods on their doorsteps, but how does this revitalize the church? Shouldn't needy people be given skills and job opportunities rather than handouts? Shouldn't the church get credit for its charity? There are many theoretical and practical flaws in any such plan. Some may argue that it does not have merit. Many youth ideas already in practice are short on merit. I simply challenge my readers to try this out—with your own variations—if it fits your situation. Stand back and let God work through it.

Social Activism as a Drawing Card

This same general concept—without the conspiracy element—can be developed for adults inside and outside a left-behind church. When a church develops a reputation for social activism, it becomes, often without knowing it, a drawing card for certain kinds of people who are unchurched. "Many disillusioned activists are now seeking ways to bring together social concerns with spiritual fulfillment," writes Ronald Sider and his colleagues in *Churches That Make a Difference*. "Baby boomers, especially, crave a sense of belonging to a meaningful effort to improve society.

Young generations are also showing an increasing attraction to activism."[14] Sometimes the social activism is heavy-duty work with the homeless and with women and children who are suffering amid domestic abuse. But in other instances it is light duty—as simple as giving a cup of cold water. For example, Media Presbyterian Church in a Philadelphia suburb sets up a booth at the summer street fair and hands out cups of cold water. This is just one little act of kindness that sometimes startles people. When they ask *Why?* they are handed a brochure with the gospel text of Jesus admonishing people to give a cup of cold water in his name. This is an instance of a very simple way to show the love of Christ—perhaps attracting others to come not to fill pews to increase church rolls but to become a disciple and reach out to others.[15]

Friendship Evangelism in Reverse

I grew up in the Christian and Missionary Alliance church, where *hard-sell* evangelism was taken very seriously: *If you died tonight, where would you spend eternity?* But in my college days the concept that was touted as the wave of the future was *friendship evangelism*. In the 1960s we were confronting an entirely different world. No more hard sell. We were instructed that we should no longer confront people head-on. No longer would we feel guilty because we did not treat the gospel like the cure for cancer. How often the guilt had welled up within me as I reflected on that often-repeated analogy, knowing that if I had the cure for cancer I would be shouting the news from the housetops. But I wasn't doing that with the gospel. Friendship evangelism was a welcome alternative—and it came with no guilt trips attached.

Now we could invite our unchurched ("unsaved" is what we called them) friends and neighbors to play golf or to go shopping or to come over for dinner. And best of all, we did not have to be confrontational and give the hard sell. We did not have to pretend that they were banging down our doors for a cure for cancer and we were keeping the news to ourselves.

This concept of friendship evangelism is still alive and well. In fact, it was featured on the front page of a Home Missions bulletin for the Christian Reformed Church. And it came with specific suggestions. *Babysit for neighbors. Take a spaghetti dinner to someone who is recuperating from surgery.* It might have included: *Invite a coworker for dinner and then the symphony afterwards.* What struck me was that there was not one word in the suggestion list about knocking at the door and giving the neighbor a tract or calling up that coworker and inviting him or her to an evangelistic crusade.

Friendship evangelism of this nature has no doubt brought many *unchurched* people into the circle of friendship of *churched* people, and I am sure there are countless stories of success—success meaning introducing people to the Lord and ultimately being a part of bringing them to faith in Christ. We should affirm this kind of outreach.

But there is another kind of so-called *friendship evangelism* that is more authentic and straightforward. Most people are more than a bit suspicious of someone who is befriending them for ulterior motives. *Why* that spaghetti dinner? *Why* the golf outing? I'm reminded of a suggestion list distributed by Mormons that tells its people to participate in church groundbreakings and bring a nice shrub to be planted. I'm suspicious. I'm thinking, *what are they really up to? What do you want from me in exchange for your shrub or your spaghetti?*

The kind of friendship evangelism that is most authentic and biblical is that which Jesus so prominently utilized. Simply, *Come, follow me.* Many congregations are already very involved in outreach ministries—often ones that minister to those who are far less fortunate materially than most church members. Such churches frequently participate in Habitat for Humanity building projects, in a Christmas store, in supplying backpacks for children, in Thanksgiving meals, and in many other helping ministries.

This is how we *behave* as congregations. As folks in left-behind churches, however, we realize that there is far more to do than what we can accomplish. We need help. We may have meals and symphony tickets to give away to our affluent coworkers and neighbors, but more than that, we need their help. We are followers of the Lord. God has called us. We have been *chosen*, as the late Bishop Lesslie Newbigin so aptly expressed, and this is "not special privilege but special responsibility." We are chosen "for service."[16] Jesus calls, *Come, follow me*. He needed help in his earthly ministry. And we need help from those we encounter in our workplace and neighborhood.

Instead of inviting a friend who works in the lab alongside me to play tennis with me a week from next Saturday, I will ask her if she can bring a hammer and pound some nails at the Habitat house, or I will ask if she can come join me in a church project to fill Valentine gift bags with toiletries for needy women and then the following week come along to distribute them at the place these women call home. In the process, I'll simply be acting like a follower of Jesus acts. We might have a devotional time at our group "bagging session," and I'll be asking the recipient of the gift bag if there are needs she has that I can remember in prayer before we leave.

This is friendship evangelism in reverse. I am reaching out in caring ministry as a follower of Jesus is called to do, and I am asking others to come along. I have nothing to give my colleagues and neighbors except the privilege of joining me in doing the things a follower of Jesus does. Along the way, I will leave the convicting and converting up to the Holy Spirit. My job is simply to faithfully represent and serve my Lord and Savior in word and deed.

Albert Schweitzer, who left behind fame and fortune as a theologian, medical doctor, and musician, followed Jesus to Africa to serve among those who most needed his healing touch. He writes of this discipleship in his controversial and less-than-orthodox book, *The Quest of the Historical Jesus*:

> He comes to us as One unknown, without a name, as of old by the lakeside, He came to those who knew Him not. He speaks to us the same word: "Follow thou me!" and sets us to the tasks which He has to fulfill for our time. He commands. And to those who obey Him, whether they be wise or simple, He will reveal Himself in the toils, the conflicts, the sufferings which they shall pass through in His fellowship, and, as an ineffable mystery, they shall learn in their own experience Who He is.[17]

The Christian church represented by one-of-a-kind congregations around the world can do nothing more simple or profound than to take seriously the words of Jesus, "Follow thou me."

Notes

Introduction: Left Behind with Purpose

1. Peter De Vries, *The Mackerel Plaza* (New York: Little, Brown and Company, 1958), 7.
2. Ibid., 7–8.
3. Thomas Reeves, *The Empty Church: The Suicide of Liberal Christianity* (New York: Free Press, 1996), 1–2.
4. Ibid., 11–13.
5. Wade Clark Roof, *Spiritual Marketplace: Baby Boomers and the Remaking of American Religion* (Princeton, NJ: Princeton University Press, 1999), 49.
6. Robert N. Bellah, William M. Sullivan, Steven M. Tipton, Richard Madsen, and Ann Swidler, *Habits of the Heart: Individualism and Commitment in American Life* (Berkeley: University of California Press, 1985).
7. Roof, *Spiritual Marketplace*, 146.
8. Jim Wallis, *Who Speaks for God?* (New York: Delacorte, 1996).
9. Reeves, *The Empty Church*, 35.
10. Frederick Buechner, *The Final Beast* (San Francisco: Harper & Row, 1965), 28.
11. Robertson Davies, *The Cunning Man* (New York: Viking, 1994), 17–18.
12. Chris Knape, "New Oil Tycoon Has Altruistic Plans," *Grand Rapids Press*, May 22, 2005, E3.
13. John Hogan, "New Urbanism," ibid., L1.

Chapter 1: Personal Reflections on Left-Behind Churches

1. Ruth A. Tucker, *Walking Away from Faith: Unraveling the Mystery of Belief and Unbelief* (Downers Grove, IL: InterVarsity, 2002).
2. Ruth A. Tucker, *Private Lives of Pastors' Wives* (Grand Rapids: Zondervan, 1988).

Chapter 2: The Wal-Mart Gospel Blues

1. Tom Kuntz, "War of the Words," *Grand Rapids Press*, January 4, 2004, D5.

2. Erica C. Barnett, "The Wal-Marts of Religion," *Austin Chronicle*, November 19, 1999, http://www.austinchronicle.com/issues/dispatch/1999-11-19/pols_fea ture3.html.

3. Tom Nebel, *Big Dreams in Small Places: Church Planting in Smaller Communities* (St. Charles, IL: ChurchSmart, 2002), 37.

4. Leith Anderson, *A Church for the 21st Century* (Minneapolis: Bethany House, 1992), 58–60.

5. Andy Crouch, "Stonewashed Worship," *Christianity Today*, February 2005, 82.

6. Ibid.

7. John Sweeney, "Wal-Mart's Model," *Detroit Free Press*, February 25, 2005, 11A.

8. Philip D. Kenneson, *Life on the Vine: Cultivating the Fruit of the Spirit in Christian Community* (Downers Grove, IL: InterVarsity), 16.

9. Kanzo Uchimura, "Can Americans Teach Japanese in Religion?" *Japan Christian Intelligencer* 1 (1926): 357–61, cited in Andrew Walls, "The American Dimension in the History of the Missionary movement," in Joel A. Carpenter and Wilbert R. Shenk, eds. *Earthen Vessels: American Evangelicals and Foreign Missions, 1880–1980* (Grand Rapids: Eerdmans, 1990), 1–2.

10. Ibid.

11. Steve R. Bierly, *How to Thrive as a Small-Church Pastor: A Guide to Spiritual and Emotional Well-Being* (Grand Rapids: Zondervan, 1998), 62.

12. Jane Newstead, "You're Moving Where?" in *Mustard-Seed Churches: Ministries in Small Churches*, ed. Robert B. Coote (Minneapolis: Fortress, 1990), 11, 13.

13. William H. Willimon and Robert L. Wilson, *Preaching and Worship in the Small Church* (Nashville: Abingdon, 1980), 14.

14. Matt Vande Vunte, "Weight of a Congregation," *Grand Rapids Press*, February 26, 2005, D1.

15. Willimon and Wilson, *Preaching and Worship,* 18.

16. Martin M. Marty, "Imagining Futures of the Rural Churches in America," Humanities Iowa Day '99, Rural Ministry Conference, Dubuque, Iowa, March 7–9, 1999, www.uiowa.edu/~humiowa/mmartyspeech.htm.

17. Ibid.

18. Mike Lupica, *Travel Team* (New York: Penguin, 2004).

Chapter 3: The Precipice-Driven Pastor

1. Cathy Booth-Thomas, "The 25 Most Influential Evangelicals in America," *Time*, February 7, 2005, 34–45.

2. Ibid., 45.

3. Samuel D. Rima, *Rethinking the Successful Church: Finding Serenity in God's Sovereignty* (Grand Rapids: Baker Books, 2002), 11–14.

4. Ibid.

5. Ibid.

6. Garrison Keillor, *Leaving Home* (New York: Penguin, 1987), 90.
7. Eugene Peterson, "The Jonah Syndrome," *Leadership*, Summer 1990, 42.
8. Ibid., 40.
9. Ibid., 42.
10. Lewis B. Smedes, *My God and I: A Spiritual Memoir* (Grand Rapids: Eerdmans, 2003), 103–4.
11. Bierly, *How to Thrive as a Small-Church Pastor*, 46.
12. Eugene Peterson, "Fyodor Dostoevsky: God and Passion," in *More Than Words: Contemporary Writers on the Works That Shaped Them*, ed. and comp. Philip Yancey and James Calvin Schaap (Grand Rapids: Baker, 2002), 174.
13. George MacDonald, *The Curate's Awakening* (Minneapolis: Bethany, 1985).
14. George R. Hunsberger, "Sizing Up the Shape of the Church," in *The Church Between Gospel and Culture*, ed. George R. Hunsberger and Craig Van Gelder (Grand Rapids: Eerdmans, 1996), 335.
15. George MacDonald, *The Prodigal Apprentice*, cited in Marva Dawn, *Reaching Out without Dumbing Down: A Theology of Worship for the Turn-of-the-Century Culture* (Grand Rapids: Eerdmans, 1995), 218.
16. Buechner, *The Final Beast*, 12–13.
17. Olov Hartman, *Holy Masquerade* (Grand Rapids: Eerdmans, 1963), 9–10.
18. Gordon MacDonald, "Stepping Off the Treadmill," *Leadership*, Fall 1999, 37.
19. Donald W. Morgan, *Share the Dream, Build the Team: Ten Keys for Revitalizing Your Church* (Grand Rapids: Baker Books, 2001), 13–16, 25.
20. Larry Gilbert, "Lead or Get Out of the Way," *Leadership*, Summer 1995, 126.
21. Bierly, *How to Thrive as a Small-Church Pastor*, 64.
22. Paul Harvey Jr., "The Church in the Wild Wood," foreword to Philip Gulley, *Front Porch Tales* (Sisters, OR: Multnomah, 1997), 7–8.
23. Gulley, *Front Porch Tales*, 166.

Chapter 4: A Left-Behind Theology

1. Michael Yaconelli, *Messy Spirituality: God's Annoying Love for Imperfect People* (Grand Rapids: Zondervan, 2002), 77–78.
2. Douglas J. Brouwer, "Called to Be a Loser?" *Leadership*, Summer 1999, 31.
3. Leonard L. Sweet, "The Nerve of Failure," *Theology Today*, July 1977, 145–46.
4. Barbara Brown Taylor, "Spectacular Failure," *Christian Century*, February 22, 2005, http://www.findarticles.com/p/articles/mi_m1058/is_4_122/ai_n13490407#continue.
5. Roland Allen, *Missionary Methods: St. Paul's or Ours?* (London: World Dominion, 1930), 3–4.
6. Michael Duncan, "The Other Side of Paul," *On Being*, June 1991, 23.
7. Donald A. Carson, *From Triumphalism to Maturity: An Exposition of 2 Corinthians 10–13* (Grand Rapids: Baker, 1984), 116.

8. Duncan, "The Other Side of Paul," 23.

9. Carson, *From Triumphalism to Maturity*, 117.

10. Duncan, "The Other Side of Paul," 23.

11. Martin Luther, cited in Mark Shaw, *10 Great Ideas from Church History* (Downers Grove, IL: InterVarsity, 1997), 35.

12. Frederick Buechner, *The Longing for Home* (San Francisco: HarperCollins, 1996), 128–29.

13. Stanley Hauerwas and William H. Willimon, *Resident Aliens* (Nashville: Abingdon, 1989), 15–16.

14. Brian McLaren, *A New Kind of Christian: A Tale of Two Friends on a Spiritual Journey* (San Francisco: Jossey-Bass, 2001), xiv.

15. Mark Galli, "The Virtue of Unoriginality," *Christianity Today*, April 1, 2002, 62.

16. Bierly, *How to Thrive as a Small-Church Pastor*, 49, 59.

Chapter 5: Burnout in the Parsonage and Parish

1. Richard Lischer, *Open Secrets: A Spiritual Journey through a Country Church* (New York: Doubleday, 2001), 107.

2. Denise Turner, *Home Sweet Fishbowl: Confessions of a Minister's Wife* (Nashville: Word, 1982), and Frances Nordland, *The Unprivate Life of a Pastor's Wife* (Chicago: Moody Press, 1972).

3. Tucker, *Private Lives of Pastors' Wives*, 13.

4. Jeff Berryman, *Leaving Ruin* (Orange, CA: New Leaf Books, 2002).

5. David T. Wayne, "The Life of a Small Church Pastor," Gollyblogger, August 5, 2003, jollyblogger.typepad.com/jollyblogger/2004/06/review_of_leavi.html.

6. Berryman, *Leaving Ruin*, 17.

7. Ibid., 20.

8. Ibid., 68.

9. Ibid., 110.

10. Georges Bernanos, *The Diary of a Country Priest*, trans. Pamela Morris (New York: Carrol & Graf, 1937), 8–11.

11. Ibid., 28, 40, 87.

12. Robert Moeller, "Pastor David or Pastor Solomon?" *Leadership*, Winter 1989, 104–5.

13. Ibid., 109.

14. William H. Willimon, *Pastor: The Theology and Practice of Ordained Ministry* (Nashville: Abingdon, 2002), 22.

15. Geoffrey Chaucer, *Canterbury Tales*, cited in Willimon, *Pastor*, 171.

16. The Vincent van Gogh Gallery, http://www.vangoghgallery.com/misc/archives/sermon.htm.

17. Ibid.

18. Vincent van Gogh, cited in Jan Hulsker, *Vincent and Theo van Gogh: A Dual Biography* (Ann Arbor, MI: Fuller Publications, 1985), 42.

19. Ibid.

20. Henri Nouwen, cited in Michael Ford, *Wounded Prophet: A Portrait of Henri J. M. Nouwen* (New York: Doubleday, 1999), xi.

Notes

21. Denny Gunderson, "The Plight of the Christian Artist," Last Days Ministries, www.lastdaysministries.org/articles/theplightofthechristianartist.html.
22. Brouwer, "Called to Be a Loser?" 31.
23. Karl Barth, cited in Eberhard Busch, *Karl Barth: His Life from Letters and Autobiographical Texts*, trans. John Bowden (Grand Rapids: Eerdmans, 1975), 60–61.
24. Ibid., 64.

Chapter 6: Megachurch Mania

1. Tom Raabe, *The Ultimate Church: An Irreverent Look at Church Growth, Megachurches & Ecclesiastical "Show Biz"* (Grand Rapids: Zondervan, 1991), 13–17.
2. Ibid., 18–19.
3. Os Guinness, *Dining with the Devil: The Megachurch Movement Flirts with Modernity* (Grand Rapids: Baker, 1993), 11–12.
4. Ibid., 12.
5. Ibid., 16.
6. Anderson, *A Church for the 21st Century*, 54.
7. Philip D. Kenneson and James L. Street, *Selling Out the Church: The Dangers of Church Marketing* (Nashville: Abingdon, 1997), 26.
8. Ibid., 34.
9. George Barna, *A Step-by-Step Guide to Church Marketing: Breaking Ground for the Harvest* (Ventura, CA: Regal, 1992), 26–27.
10. Donna Gehrke-White, "Titans of Worship: South Florida's Megachurches Draw Crowds with Popular Pastors, Self-Help Classes and a Nontraditional Atmosphere," *Miami Herald*, June 3, 2001; Michael Clancy, "Rise of the 'Megachurch' Valley Has 11 Non-Traditional Congregations of 2,000-Plus," *Arizona Republic*, March 27, 2003, cited in David R. Fletcher, "Acceleration of Change Induced by the Megachurch," XPastor, www.xpastor.org/drf/xp8acceleration_of_change.htm.
11. Rima, *Rethinking the Successful Church*, 13.
12. Dana Calvo, "Largest Church in the USA Moves into Stadium," *Houston Times*, July 6, 2004, http://www.skylineborneo.com/world%20news.htm #stadium.
13. Ibid.
14. Ibid.
15. "DAWN Fridayfax 2004 #36," Jesus Fellowship Church, 2004, http://www.jesus.org.uk/dawn/2004/dawn36.html.
16. Don Kroah, "Reach Africa Now," http://www.reachafricanow.org/wfkbio.html.
17. Rob Marus, cited in Barnett, "The Wal-Marts of Religion."
18. Ibid.
19. Kris Axtman, "The Rise of the American Megachurch," *Christian Science Monitor*, December 30, 2003, http://www.csmonitor.com/2003/1230/p01s04–ussc.html.
20. "MegaChurches: Large Congregations Spread across Black America," *Ebony*, December 2004, http://www.findarticles.com/p/articles/mi_m1077/is_2_60/ai_n7577968.

21. Ibid.
22. Rima, *Rethinking the Successful Church*, 73–74.
23. Gene Appel and Alan Nelson, *How to Change Your Church without Killing It* (Nashville: Word, 2000), 10.
24. Rima, *Rethinking the Successful Church*, 44–48.

Chapter 7: Literature, Seminars, and Theory of Church Growth

1. Richard Lischer, *The Preacher King: Martin Luther King, Jr. and the Word That Moved America* (New York: Oxford University Press, 1995), 23–24.
2. Ibid., 24.
3. Raabe, *The Ultimate Church*, 48–49.
4. E. Stanley Ott, *Twelve Dynamic Shifts for Transforming Your Church* (Grand Rapids: Eerdmans, 2002), ix.
5. George Barna, *Turn-Around Churches* (Ventura, CA: Regal, 1993), 14–15.
6. Ibid., 47.
7. David C. Kelsey, *Between Athens and Berlin* (Grand Rapids: Eerdmans, 1993), 46.
8. Peterson, "The Jonah Syndrome," 41.
9. MacDonald, "Stepping Off the Treadmill," 35–36.
10. H. B. London Jr., "Shepherd or Leader: Why Pastors Must Be Shepherds," *Leadership*, Fall 1996, 50.
11. Ibid.
12. Kevin E. Ruffcorn, "Rekindling an Old Flame," *Leadership*, Winter 1992, 75–76.
13. Rima, *Rethinking the Successful Church*, 31–32.
14. Neil Sims, "A Theology of Failure for a Ministry of Success," The Uniting Church in Queensland, September 2, 2004, www.journey.ucaqld.com.au/news/a_theology_of_f.html.
15. Ibid.
16. Anderson, *A Church for the 21ˢᵗ Century*, 183.
17. Ibid.
18. Ott, *Twelve Dynamic Shifts for Transforming Your Church*, 6.

Chapter 8: Left Behind with a Woman's Touch

1. Tucker, *Private Lives of Pastors' Wives*, 13.
2. Roland H. Bainton, *Women of the Reformation in Germany and Italy* (Minneapolis: Augsburg, 1971), 73.
3. Philip Schaff, *History of the Christian Church* (Grand Rapids: Eerdmans, 1979), 7:633.
4. Anne Wilson Schaef, *Women's Reality: An Emerging Female System in a White Male Society* (San Francisco: Harper & Row, 1985), 19.
5. Janell Paris, "Is 'A Generous Orthodoxy' Generous to Women?" December 20, 2004, http://jenellparis.blogspot.com/.
6. *Emerging Women Leaders*, December 17, 2004, http://www.emergingwomenleaders.org/.

7. Rebecca L. Harmon, *Susanna: Mother of the Wesleys* (Nashville: Abingdon, 1968), 47–49.

8. John Wesley, *The Works of John Wesley*, 13 vols. (Grand Rapids: Zondervan, 1958), vol. 1, 385.

9. Ibid., 386.

10. Edward C. Lehman Jr., "Women's Path into Ministry: Six Major Studies," *Pulpit and Pew: Research on Pastoral Leadership*, Fall 2002, 33, www.pulpitand pew.duke.edu/index.html.

11. Sara L. Anderson, "Dr. Rose," *Good News*, March/April, 1989, 16–17.

12. Barna, *Turn-Around Churches*, 67.

13. Anne Lamott, *Traveling Mercies: Some Thoughts on Faith* (New York: Pantheon, 1999), 51–55.

14. Ibid., 55.

15. Texas Women's University, Texas Women's Hall of Fame, August 18, 2004, www.twu.edu/twhf/tw-burgin.htm.

16. Mission Arlington Metroplex, "To Reach the World for Christ," 2005, www.missionarlington.org.

17. Ibid.

18. Samuel G. Freedman, *Upon This Rock: The Miracles of a Black Church* (New York: HarperCollins, 1993), 42.

19. Ibid., 42–43.

20. Ibid., 44.

21. Ibid., 58.

22. Lehman, "Women's Path into Ministry," 32.

23. Newstead, "You're Moving Where?" 15.

24. Rebecca Hazen, "Pastoral Care Comes to Eagle Creek," in *Mustard-Seed Churches*, ed. Coote, 145.

25. Ibid.

Chapter 9: Left Behind in Community

1. Gary Farley, "Missouri Rural Church Study: Some General Observations about Churches and Pastors," Missouri School of Religion, Center for Rural Ministry, www.msr-crm.org/GenOb.htm.

2. Lauren Winner, cited in Bill McGarvey, "Girl Meets God: A Conversation with Lauren Winner," Mars Hill Review, www.marshillreview.com/menus/in terviews.shtm.

3. Jan Karon, cited in Dale Brown, "Called to Write: An Interview with Jan Karon," *Radix Magazine*, 30, no. 4, www.radixmagazine.com/page4JanKaron .html.

4. Lauren F. Winner, "Inhabiting Love: Hannah Coulter: A Novel," *Image*, Spring 2005, 119.

5. Ibid.

6. Mark DeVries, *Family-Based Youth Ministry* (Downers Grove, IL: Inter-Varsity, 1994), 117.

7. Joani Schultz, "How Small Churches Minister to Youth," *Leadership*, Spring 1985, 80.

8. DeVries, *Family-Based Youth Ministry*, 68.

9. Kenneth E. Kovacs, "Welcoming the Child," Catonsville Presbyterian Church, September 21, 2003, http://www.catonsvillepresb.org/sermons/2003/20030921.html.

10. Ibid.

11. Busch, *Karl Barth*, 69–70.

12. Eugene Peterson, "Spirituality for All the Wrong Reasons," interviewed by Mark Galli, *Christianity Today*, March 2005, 45.

13. Ibid.

14. Tim Stafford, "The Church—Why Bother," *Christianity Today*, January 2005, 44.

15. Ibid., 45.

16. "The World Has Yet to See," *Christian History & Biography*, January 1, 1990, ctlibrary.com/.

17. Richard Lischer, "Preaching as the Church's Language," in *Listening to the World: Studies in Honor of Fred B. Craddock*, ed. Gail O'Day and Thomas Long (Nashville: Abingdon, 1993), 120.

18. Walter Brueggemann, *The Message of the Psalms: A Theological Commentary* (Minneapolis: Augsburg, 1984), 51.

19. Rick Warren, *The Purpose Driven Church: Growth without Compromising Your Message and Mission* (Grand Rapids: Zondervan, 1995), 287.

20. Dawn, *Reaching Out without Dumbing Down*, 92–93.

21. Rick Bragg, *All Over But the Shoutin'* (New York: Vintage Books, 1997), 3–5.

22. Ibid.

23. Philip Gulley, *Home to Harmony* (San Francisco: HarperCollins, 2002), 5, 8.

24. Ibid., 139–49.

25. Barna, *Turn-Around Churches*, 24.

26. Kathleen Norris, *Amazing Grace: A Vocabulary of Faith* (New York: Riverhead Books, 1998).

27. Peter J. Surrey, "Changes in the Small-Town Church," *Christian Century*, October 31, 1979, 1060.

Chapter 10: Left Behind with a Sense of Humor

1. Garrison Keillor, *Lake Wobegon: Summer of 1956* (New York: Viking, 2001), 20.

2. Robert Fulford, "Can Garrison Keillor Make Lutherans Funny?" *National Post*, February 5, 2002, http://www.robertfulford.com/GarrisonKeillor.html.

3. Keillor, *Lake Wobegon: Summer of 1956*, 86–87.

4. William Faulkner, "Shingles for the Lord," in *Collected Stories of William Faulkner* (New York: Random House, 1950), 27–43.

5. Steven L. McKinley, "Knowing Laughter," *The Lutheran*, March 8, 2005, http://www.thelutheran.org/0308/page6.html.

6. Beth Quinn, "Laughing in Church," Beliefnet, www.beliefnet.com/story/107/story_10774_1.html.

Chapter 11: The Messiness of the Left-Behind Church

1. Marilynne Robinson, *Housekeeping* (New York: Farrar, Straus & Giroux, 1981).

2. J. A. Gray, "Christ and Casserole," *First Things*, March 2005, 37–38.

3. Marilynne Robinson, *Gilead* (New York: Farrar, Straus & Giroux, 2004).

4. Gray, "Christ and Casserole," 40.

5. Buechner, *The Longing for Home*, 165.

6. Lischer, *Open Secrets*, 129.

7. Scott Hoezee, "A Patient Shining," sermon on Matthew 12:24–30, 36–43, Calvin Christian Reformed Church, http://www.calvincrc.org/sermons/2002/matt13Weeds.html.

8. Sietze Buning [Stanley Wiersma, pseud.], "Excommunication," *Purpaleanie and Other Permutations* (Orange City, IA: Middleburg, 1978), 55–57.

9. Ibid.

10. Philip Yancey, "A State of Ungrace," *Christianity Today*, February 3, 1997, 31, 35.

11. Lamott, *Traveling Mercies*, 46.

12. Book Browse, "An Interview with Anne Lamott," *Presbyterians Today*, www.bookbrowse.com/index.

13. Jeffrey Powers-Beck, "'Not Onely a Pastour, but a Lawyer also': George Herbert's Vision of Stuart Magistracy," *Early Modern Literary Studies* 1.2 (1995): 3.1–25, pp. 259–260, http://purl.oclc.org/emls/012/beckherb.html.

14. Ibid., 259.

15. Ibid., 265.

16. Ibid., 260.

17. Berryman, *Leaving Ruin*, 249.

18. Ibid., 150.

19. Peterson, "The Jonah Syndrome," 40.

20. Bierly, *How to Thrive as a Small-Church Pastor*, 42.

21. Nathaniel Hawthorne, *The Scarlet Letter* (Boston: Ticknor, Reed, and Fields, 1850; New York: Dodd, Mead & Company, 1948), 46–51, 113, 165, 178, 207. Citations are to the Dodd, Mead & Company edition.

22. Peter De Vries, *Slouching Towards Kalamazoo* (Boston: Little, Brown and Company, 1983), 74–81.

23. Norris, *Amazing Grace*, 269.

24. Hendrik Kraemer, *The Christian Message in a Non-Christian World* (New York: Harper, 1938), 24, 26.

Chapter 12: Spiritual Memories of the Church in the Valley

1. Jim Jones, "Modest Church Inspired an Elvis Hit," April 4, 1998, Knight Ridder Newspapers, www.texnews.com/1998/religion/chapel0404.html.

2. Artie Glenn, "Crying in the Chapel" (Knoxville, TN: Valley Publishers, 1953).

3. Norris, *Amazing Grace*, 6.

4. Ibid., 64.

5. Charles (Chuck) R. Swindoll, "Three Cheers for the Church," www.direct.ca/trinity/cheers.html.

6. Ibid.

7. Susan Fleenor, "A Place Called Home," in *Mustard-Seed Churches*, 173–74.

8. Stephen Dunn, "At the Smithville Methodist Church" in *New and Selected Poems, 1974–1994* (New York: W. W. Norton & Company, 1995), 183–84.

9. Gordon Atkinson, "The Preacher's Story," Real Line Preacher, July 2005, http://blogs.salon.com/0001772/stories/2002/12/26/thePreachersStoryIn4Parts.html.

10. Ibid.

11. Herbert Brokering, "Holy Places," Evangelical Luthern Church in America, December 12, 2004, http://www.elca.org/middleeast/advent/1212.html.

12. Ken Bradbury, "Standin' in the Need," Creative Ideas, Inc., 1995, www.creativeideas.com/store/merchant.mvc?Screen=PROD&Product_Code=106.

13. "There Is a Balm in Gilead."

14. Robinson, *Gilead*, 173, 235.

15. Ibid., 26.

16. Ibid., 70.

Chapter 13: The Church in the Valley of the Shadow of Death

1. Charles Kingsley, 1848, http://oldpoetry.com/poetry/45086/showline=1.

2. Barna, *Turn-Around Churches*, 24–25.

3. Ibid., 108.

4. Book review of *Upon This Rock: The Miracles of a Black Church*, by Samuel Freedman, in *New York Newsday* inside cover.

5. Freedman, *Upon This Rock*, 3.

6. "Church Gets New Life on Living History Farm," *Grand Rapids Press*, May 18, 2005, B8.

7. Ibid.

8. Newstead, "You're Moving Where?" 14.

9. Tim Stafford, "God's Missionary to Us," *Christianity Today*, December 9, 1996, 26.

10. Ibid.

11. Rose Sims, *The Dream Lives On* (Wilmore, KY: Bristol Books, 1989), 11.

12. Philip Yancey, *Soul Survivor: How My Faith Survived the Church* (New York: Doubleday, 2001), 1–5, 16.

13. Ralph E. Bauserman, "Developing a Discipleship Plan: Revisiting an Old Vision," General Board of Discipleship, United Methodist Church, June 19, 2003, www.gbod.org/evangelism/programs/offeringchrist/revisit-vision.html.

14. Ibid.

15. Randall Balmer, "Fundamentalist with Flair," *Christianity Today*, May 21, 2002, 56.

Chapter 14: New Life for the Left-Behind Church

1. Lischer, *Open Secrets*, 73–75.

2. Ibid., 74–75.

3. Ibid., 76.
4. Brian Metke, "Sharper Definition," *Leadership*, Summer 2000, 61.
5. Ibid.
6. Ibid.
7. Ibid., 62–63.
8. Ibid., 64.
9. Andrew Black, cited in Robert E. Webber, *Younger Evangelicals* (Grand Rapids: Baker Books, 2002), 49.
10. Jim Kitchens, *The Postmodern Parish* (Herdon, VA: Alban Institute, 2003), 72.
11. Steve Sjogren, "Going into All the World with Soap and Water," Church Central, November 5, 2004, http://www.churchcentral.com/nw/s/template/cht%2Ccht110904.html.
12. Ibid.
13. Ron Crandall, *Turnaround Strategies for the Small Church* (Nashville: Abingdon, 1995), 123–24.
14. Ronald J. Sider, Philip N. Olson, and Heidi Rolland Unruh, *Churches That Make a Difference: Reaching Your Community with Good News of Good Works* (Grand Rapids: Baker, 2002), 43.
15. Ibid., 29.
16. George R. Hunsberger, *Bearing the Witness of the Spirit: Lesslie Newbigin's Theology of Cultural Plurality* (Grand Rapids: Eerdmans, 1998), 88–89.
17. Albert Schweitzer, *The Quest of the Historical Jesus*, trans. W. Montgomery, (London: A. and C. Black, 1922), 401.

Bibliography

Anderson, Leith. *A Church for the 21ˢᵗ Century*. Minneapolis: Bethany House, 1992.

Appel, Gene and Nelson, Alan. *How to Change Your Church without Killing It*. Nashville: Word, 2000.

Bainton, Roland H. *Women of the Reformation in Germany and Italy*. Minneapolis: Augsburg, 1971.

Barna, George. *A Step-by-Step Guide to Church Marketing: Breaking Ground for the Harvest*. Ventura, CA: Regal, 1992.

———. *Turn-Around Churches*. Ventura, CA: Regal, 1993.

Bernanos, Georges. *The Diary of a Country Priest*. Translated by Pamela Morris, NY: Carrol & Graf, 1937.

Berryman, Jeff. *Leaving Ruin*. Orange, CA: New Leaf, 2002.

Bierly, Steve R. *How to Thrive as a Small-Church Pastor: A Guide to Spiritual and Emotional Well-Being*. Grand Rapids: Zondervan, 1998.

Bragg, Rick. *All Over But the Shoutin'*. New York: Vintage, 1997.

Buechner, Frederick. *The Final Beast*. San Francisco: Harper & Row, 1965.

———. *Longing for Home*. San Francisco: HarperCollins, 1996.

Busch, Eberhard. Karl Barth: *His Life from Letters and Autobiographical Texts*. Translated by John Bowden. Grand Rapids: Eerdmans, 1975.

Carson, Donald A. *From Triumphalism to Maturity: An Exposition of 2 Corinthians 10–1.* Grand Rapids: Baker, 1984.

Coote, Robert B., ed. *Mustard-Seed Churches: Ministries in Small Churches.* Minneapolis: Fortress, 1990.

Crandall, Ron. *Turnaround Strategies for the Small Church.* Nashville: Abingdon, 1995.

Davies, Robertson. *The Cunning Man.* New York: Viking, 1994.

Dawn, Marva. *Reaching Out without Dumbing Down: A Theology of Worship for This Urgent Time.* Grand Rapids: Eerdmans, 1995.

DeVries, Mark. *Family-Based Youth Ministry.* Downers Grove, IL: Intervarsity Press, 1994.

De Vries, Peter. *The Mackerel Plaza.* NewYork: Little, Brown and Company, 1958.

———. *Slouching Towards Kalamazoo.* Boston: Little, Brown and Company, 1983.

Faulkner, William. *Collected Stories of William Faulkner.* New York: Random House, 1950.

Ford, Michael. *Wounded Prophet: A Portrait of Henri J. M. Nouwen.* New York: Doubleday, 1999.

Freedman, Samuel G. *Upon This Rock: The Miracles of a Black Church.* New York: HarperCollins, 1993.

Guinness, Os. *Dining with the Devil: The Megachurch Movement Flirts with Modernity.* Grand Rapids: Baker, 1993.

Gulley, Philip. *Front Porch Tales.* Sisters, OR: Multnomah, 1997.

———. *Home to Harmony.* San Francisco: HarperCollins, 2002.

Hartman, Olov. *Holy Masquerade.* Grand Rapids: Eerdmans, 1963.

Hauerwas, Stanley and William H. Willimon. *Resident Aliens.* Nashville: Abingdon, 1989.

Hawthorne, Nathaniel. *The Scarlet Letter.* New York: Dodd, Mead & Company, 1948.

Karon, Jan. *At Home in Mitford.* New York: Penguin, 1996.

Kelsey, David C. *Between Athens and Berlin.* Grand Rapids: Eerdmans, 1993.

Kenneson, Philip D. *Life on the Vine: Cultivating the Fruit of the Spirit in Christian Community.* Downers Grove, IL: InterVarsity, 1999.

Kenneson, Philip D. and James L. Street. *Selling Out the Church: The Dangers of Church Marketing.* Nashville: Abingdon, 1997.

Keillor, Garrison. *Lake Wobegon Summer of 1956.* New York: Viking, 2001.

———. *Leaving Home.* New York: Penguin, 1987.

Kitchens, Jim. *The Postmodern Parish: New Ministry for a New Era.* Herndon, VA: Alban Institute, 2003.

Kraemer, Hendrik. *The Christian Message in a Non-Christian World.* New York: Harper, 1938.

Lamott, Anne. *Traveling Mercies: Some Thoughts on Faith.* New York: Pantheon, 1999.

Lischer, Richard. *Open Secret: A Spiritual Journey through a Country Church.* New York: Doubleday, 2001.

———. *The Preacher King: Martin Luther King, Jr. and the Word That Moved America.* New York: Oxford University Press, 1995.

McLaren, Brian. *A New Kind of Christian: A Tale of Two Friends on a Spiritual Journey.* San Francisco: Jossey-Bass, 2001.

Morgan, Donald W. *Share the Dream, Build the Team: Ten Keys for Revitalizing Your Church.* Grand Rapids: Baker Books, 2001.

Nebel, Thomas P. *Big Dream in Small Places: Church Planting in Smaller Communities.* ChurchSmart.com: ChurchSmart Resources, 2002.

Norris, Kathleen. *Amazing Grace: A Vocabulary of Faith.* New York: Penguin, 1998.

Ott, E. Stanley. *Twelve Dynamic Shifts for Transforming Your Church.* Grand Rapids: Eerdmans, 2002.

Raabe, Tom. *The Ultimate Church: An Irreverent Look at Church Growth, Megachurches and Ecclesiastical "Show Biz."* Grand Rapids: Zondervan, 1991.

Reeves, Thomas C. *The Empty Church: The Suicide of Liberal Christianity.* New York: Free Press, 1996

Rima, Samuel D. *Rethinking the Successful Church: Finding Serenity in God's Sovereignty.* Grand Rapids: Baker Books, 2002.

Robinson, Marilynne. *Gilead.* New York: Farrar, Straus and Giroux, 2004.

———. *Housekeeping.* New York: Farrar, Straus and Giroux, 1981.

Roof, Wade Clark. *Spiritual Marketplace: Baby Boomers and the Remaking of American Religion.* Princeton, NJ: Princeton University Press, 1999.

Schaef, Anne Wilson. *Women's Reality: An Emerging Female System in a White Male Society.* San Francisco: Harper & Row, 1985.

Schweitzer, Albert. *The Quest of the Historical Jesus.* Translated by W. Montgomery. London: A & C Black, 1922.

Sider, Ronald J., Philip N. Olson, and Heidi Rolland Unruh. *Churches That Make a Difference: Reaching Your Community with Good News of Good Works.* Grand Rapids: Baker, 2002.

Sims, Rose. *The Dream Lives On.* Wilmore, KY: Bristol, 1989.

Smedes, Lewis B. *My God and I: A Spiritual Memoir.* Grand Rapids: Eerdmans, 2003.

Tucker, Ruth A. *Private Lives of Pastors' Wives.* Grand Rapids: Zondervan, 1988.

Warren, Rick. *The Purpose Driven Church: Growth without Compromising Your Message and Mission.* Grand Rapids: Zondervan, 1995.

Wesley, John. *The Works of John Wesley.* 13 vols. Grand Rapids: Zondervan, 1958.

Willimon, William H. *Pastor: The Theology and Practice of Ordained Ministry.* Nashville: Abingdon, 2002.

Willimon, William H. and Robert L. Wilson. *Preaching and Worship in the Small Church.* Nashville: Abingdon, 1980.

Yaconelli, Michael. *Messy Spirituality: God's Annoying Love for Imperfect People.* Grand Rapids: Zondervan, 2002.

Yancey, Philip. *Soul Survivor: How My Faith Survived the Church.* New York: Doubleday, 2001.

Index

Index

Ruth A. Tucker holds a Ph.D. in history and is associate professor of missiology at Calvin Theological Seminary in Grand Rapids, Michigan. She has written seventeen books, including *From Jerusalem to Irian Jaya* and *Walking Away from Faith*.